7 Skills for Parenting Success

Laurie Berdahl Johnson, MD

Brian D. Johnson, PhD

Illustrated by Rev. Dr. Charles A. Berdahl

For our wonderful children,

Natalie and Luke—

who bring so much joy and love to our lives.

And for our parents—

whose care gave us our great beginnings.

Acknowledgements

Many friends and colleagues have helped us to complete this project over the last few years. We are immensely grateful for the work of our editor Cate Huisman. Her insight, advice and expertise have been invaluable to us. Many thanks are also due to Meg Spencer, a technical editor and good friend who gave us early advice and encouragement.

We were fortunate to have Charles Berdahl agree to share his talent in this work. His drawings are just what the doctors ordered to enhance and illuminate the text for our readers. Stacy Lane's fresh and eye-catching book cover design is also greatly appreciated.

Special thanks are owed to the following reviewers, all of whom are parents themselves, for their evaluations and recommendations, as well as their support:

Kyle Waugh, MD, Thomas Kenigsberg, MD, Orest Dubynsky, MD, Trisha Multer, RN, Kimberly Henkle Duhrsen, PhD, Debbie Brethauer, RN, CLC, CLE, CHPN, Terri Bradshaw, LCSW, Meshelle Kolanz, MD, Julie Rojas, RN, Jami Benson, RT(R), ARDMS, Kris Howard, RN, LCCE, CLC, Kathy Hagihara RN, FNP, Vicenta Rossing, RN and Lori Berdahl, OTR/L.

About the Authors

Laurie D. Berdahl, MD is a board certified obstetrician-gynecologist with a background in genetic research. Her interest in parenting education has followed naturally from caring for women during their pregnancies and over the years while their children are growing up. Dr. Berdahl's talent for simplifying and explaining large amounts of complex information for patients and their families, while anticipating questions and concerns, has been combined with her research skill and the expertise of her coauthor in this comprehensive guide for parents. Her private practice includes consulting on emotional health matters as well as parenting with her teenage and adult patients.

Brian D. Johnson, PhD is a licensed child psychologist and parenting expert. He is a full professor and Director of Training for the doctoral program in Counseling Psychology at the University of Northern Colorado. An editor and author of the *Encyclopedia of Counseling*, he has published in the areas of parenting and emotional and behavioral disorders in children, including attention-deficit/ hyperactivity disorder. Dr. Johnson has helped many parents with their children in his private practice, and gives seminars in parenting and play therapy to mental health professionals. He has also consulted with educators to help them assist students with psychological disorders. He and Laurie are happily married and raising their two teenage children together with great success.

7 SKILLS FOR PARENTING SUCCESS

Table of Contents

Introduction: How these skills work for all kinds of parents and kids | 1

Part I
THE 7 SKILLS

Chapter 1   Skill # 1   PREPARE YOURSELF: How to get ready for parenting success | 3

Chapter 2   Skill # 2   PAY ATTENTION: How to give your children attention in ways that work | 29

Chapter 3   Skill # 3   CALMLY TALK TO TEACH: How to lower your stress while teaching kids to listen, be respectful and build healthy self-esteem | 53

Chapter 4   Skill # 4   SEIZE CONTROL: How to set limits on what they do, choose your battles, and help them develop good character | 77

Chapter 5   Skill # 5   PLAN DISCIPLINE AND FOLLOW THROUGH: How to use consequences, teach responsibility, and be consistent | 101

Chapter 6   Skill # 6   BALANCE YOUR SUPPORT AND CONTROL: How to optimize your parenting style for good behavior, independence and resilience | 145

Chapter 7   Skill # 7   KEEP A CLOSE EYE ON THEM: How to monitor and manage outside influences to prevent problems | 181

Part II
EXPANDED USE OF THE 7 SKILLS

Chapter 8   START SUCCESS EARLY: How to give you and your

baby or toddler a great start | 213

Chapter 9   MORE ON SUCCESSFUL PARENTING OF TEENS: How to deal with the developing brain and other challenges | 235

Chapter 10   SIBLINGS: How to turn foes into friends | 264

Chapter 11   SUCCESSFUL PARENTING IN THE STORM: Pearls for handling divorce | 273

Chapter 12   GOING SOLO: Pearls for successful single parenting | 281

Chapter 13   HOW TO HANDLE COMMON PARENTING ISSUES: Attention Deficit Hyperactivity Disorder to Yelling | 286

Chapter 14   TEMPERAMENT SKILLS: How to manage the traits that children are born with (how active, adaptable, bold versus shy, distractible, intense, moody, persistent, regular, and sensitive they are) | 307

Appendix A   WHAT KIDS CAN DO BY AGE: Communication, self-care, social skills and chores | 323

Appendix B   FEELING WORDS TO TEACH YOUR CHILDREN: Words to use when they are happy, sad, scared, confused, or angry | 336

References and Resources for Parents | 340

Index | 355

Introduction

Greetings! In today's complex world, it takes more than love and natural instincts to raise happy, well-behaved kids. It takes some skill, too! After years of gathering and simplifying all the methods that work best, we are now pleased to provide you with complete instructions for successful parenting. These easy-to-read instructions aren't based just on theory or opinion, but on evidence from research showing the most important things that parents do to raise emotionally healthy and successful children. They're also founded on what professionals know to work best for all kinds of parents and kids over time. We think you'll find this to be the most helpful, complete parenting manual available.

These methods are organized into seven basic skills that any parent can learn. Unlike other parenting books, we'll not only tell you what to do, but also **how to do it**, why it's best, how to know if it's working, and what to try if it's not working.

The *7 Skills* are explained as plainly as possible, with lots of examples. You'll find down-to-earth phrases to make things easier to learn and use. Each skill has a symbol to help you remember it. **Things you can say to your kids** to help things work are given as quotes in italic letters. Key methods and topics are in boxes, making them easier to find again. At the end of each skill chapter is a summary box that you can cut out and put on your fridge, or carry with you for easy reference. This book is also unique in covering **what you can expect from children**, and giving you tools to check how well things are going. And since parenting isn't all serious business, we'll lighten it up for you.

Using these skills can help parents in all stages of parenthood. Maybe you're just preparing for children, or you are already in turbulent times with teens. Perhaps you are a parent who feels that things are going pretty well, but just have some questions. Or, maybe you're really struggling with challenging kids, and just want the stress to stop. If you feel you already know what is best for your kids, these skills can optimize what you're already doing. No matter what stage you're in or type of parent you are, using these instructions will help make life with your kids much easier and more satisfying.

Luckily, the basics of parenting success are the same for raising all kinds of children— even those with behavior or learning problems. These instructions cover all ages and stages of childhood. We give parents the keys to developing good behavior, character, responsibility, motivation, emotional intelligence, healthy self-esteem and independence, as well as resilience and happiness in their children. How to manage a child's temperament and the most common problems for which parents seek professional help are also covered. It's all here.

We begin with the most important part of successful parenting—the part that is often skipped over in other guides—a healthy relationship between you and your children. In the first three skills, we'll tell you how to develop it, repair it and keep it strong. You'll also find advice to help you lessen your stress. In the next three skills, you'll learn discipline methods that work, and how to modify your parenting style for best results. The seventh skill is the newest necessary parenting skill: monitoring and managing outside influences (from television to friends) that can mess up even the best parenting these days.

This book may look long, but you don't even have to read the whole thing to learn what you need! If all of your children are 4 years old and up, you could just read chapters one through seven, plus chapter nine if you have teenagers. For children 3 years old and under, we suggest reading chapters one, two, three, seven and eight for now. The rest of the book is your complete reference guide to use as needed. We include a handy advice list for specific issues, such as whining and toilet training, in chapter 13. Our instructions will be easiest to learn if you take your time reading, and try a few new things before going on. You may want to skim through the bold headings before you actually read the book.

 We think raising children is the most important job in the world, and we feel that parents deserve honor and praise—and help—to make it easier. Parenthood doesn't have to be an experiment in terror! Learning these skills will make you confident that you know what it takes to happily raise good kids. But first, try setting aside the thought that parents should just naturally know what to do. That will help you be open to new advice. Learning and trying new things can make life with your kids much simpler and better. Read on for success!

Skill #1

PREPARE YOURSELF: How to get ready for parenting success

"When he was little, he was my sweet little boy. I've always loved him, but he doesn't seem to care about me anymore. He even cusses at me. He's been staying out late, and I'm afraid he's getting into trouble. And now, no matter what I do, my other kids won't do what I say. I can't believe this is happening." This tearful mother's story is like so many told to us these days.

It's always nicer to hear something like what this parent recently told us, "My kids are great. I'm so proud of them and love being with them. Why do they have to grow up so fast? Well, even when they move out on their own, we'll always have each other."

What made the difference for these two parents? Is there really any control that parents have over how their kids turn out? The answer is YES! Both of these parents love their children, but today it takes certain skills to raise happy, well-behaved kids. Learning these methods when your kids are very young makes parenting the easiest, but it will make parenting easier with children of any age. In fact, we have a surprise for you—both statements came from the same parent, before and after she learned new parenting skills! She turned life around for herself and her children. The good news is, most anyone who wants to can learn the skills that successful parents use.

There is a huge amount of parenting information out there, and most people have opinions on how to raise kids. Parents often get conflicting or complicated advice. Your mother may tell you one thing, and your friend may tell you something different. It can get confusing, and it's hard to know whose advice to trust, including advice from professionals like us. When we started our family together, we joked with our friends that our poor kids would have no chance of being normal, since one of us is a child psychologist and professor, and the other is a physician. Well, we actually have two fantastic, happy teenagers! We are a husband-wife author team who use the *7 Skills* ourselves with great results.

These methods are based on what research and professional experience have shown to work best for raising kids. But before we get to all the practical how-to instructions to use with your children, this chapter is all about you! That's because **the main key to successful parenting is found in parents.** We'll tell you how you can prepare for success. Since it involves looking at yourself as a parent, our symbol for this skill is a mirror. Just as it pays to prepare before playing in the big game or taking a long trip, it pays to prepare for parenting, too. If you haven't already, please read the short introduction on pages 1 and 2, and let's get started.

Research clearly shows that one of the most important things that successful parents do is form strong relationships with their kids. So preparing means getting yourself ready for a good relationship by dealing with things that can get in the way. First, let's look at why having a strong connection is such a big deal.

Children are happier if you have good relationships with them

Plus, happy kids are easier to parent. It's that simple. What makes kids truly happy? Being raised in a supportive and safe place, by adults who love and treat them well makes children happy. Children who have strong connections with loving families usually grow up to be emotionally healthy adults. Also, if you're close to your kids when they're growing up, they'll want to stay a

part of your life. You know, you may need your kids when you're old (to change *your* diapers, get rid of those pesky facial hairs, or pick a nice nursing home for you)!

A good relationship is the best way to avoid behavior problems

One of the hardest jobs we parents have is to teach our kids how to act. When children feel close to us, it's easier to teach them, and their behavior is naturally better. In fact, when parents and children say they have a close relationship, serious behavior problems are rare. When your bond is strong, kids are more sensitive to what you want, and they want to please you. So you won't have to discipline as much, but when you do, it'll work much better and for longer. So, the time you spend on your relationship now will save you tons of time and energy in the future.

Get yourself the signs of a good relationship

The things listed here describe a strong bond between parent and child. See if you think they are true for you and each of your kids. If not, we'll help you get there.

- You talk often with your child and you both usually feel comfortable doing so.
- Both of you know that you'll be there for each other when needed.
- You both feel safe around one another.
- Your child feels sure that you'll do what is best for him or her.
- You remain calm when disciplining your child.
- Your child trusts that you'll do what you say you'll do.
- Both of you look forward to your future relationship as adults.
- You are both usually respectful of one another.
- Both of you care about what happens to each other.
- Your child knows that you'll respond and help with his or her fears and concerns.
- Both of you look forward to and enjoy spending time together.
- Both of you know about the other's likes, dislikes, fears, friends.
- You both want to do nice things for one another.
- Your child trusts you to judge his or her behavior fairly.
- You treat your child the same in public as you do in private.

Now let's go over the things about parents that can hurt relationships with children: expectations that aren't reasonable, hurtful emotional reactions, and common adult problems.

Unreasonable Expectations Can Harm Parenting

Have realistic expectations for your children

Well-mannered, respectful behavior should be expected from children. But when we expect good behavior most all of the time, we just get frustrated and our kids fail. It ain't gonna happen! Even good children in good families disobey. Children who are expected to be well behaved almost all the time can become angry teenagers who don't care what their parents think. Also, when parents expect kids to do things they aren't capable of doing yet (because their minds and bodies aren't old enough), it causes stress and anger that breaks down the relationship between them. That makes it harder for kids to keep behaving well.

Set realistic expectations by knowing about child development

This means knowing what children are developed enough to do at certain ages. For example, expecting a 4 year old to clean a kitchen or garage is just going to frustrate both of you. That's because mind and body aren't developed enough to do that at age 4. Use the table in Appendix A (on page 323) to find out what you can expect from your kids at various ages. It lists many of the things that parents ask kids to do. Here's a small piece of the table so we can show you how to use it.

	<1	1	2	3	4	5	6	7	8	9
									AGE	
Child can empty home trash cans and take trash to a garbage bin.									X	
Child follows daycare/school rules.								X		

Gray boxes are found below the ages that a child can start to do something. So don't expect them to do it when they are any younger than that. Let's look at taking out the trash on the first line. A child can learn to do that chore at age 5, 6 or 7 (those are the ages above the gray boxes), and some normal kids can't until age 7.

The age above the X is when they should be able to do this for sure. So an 8 year old should be able to take out the trash after you show him or her how to do it. If your 8 year old can't, work on it together. If your child still can't (or just *won't* even though you have tried using your seven skills for a while), get professional help. The second line shows that a child can follow school rules starting at age 5 or 6, and should be able to by age 7.

Use this table in Appendix A to help you know what to expect from your kids. Also, your child's temperament (or ways of reacting to things) can affect what you can expect from him or her. See chapter 14 to learn about this. Having realistic expectations of your children is a very important way to avoid unnecessary stress and anger in your family. It's a big key to parenting success.

Set realistic expectations for yourself: be a good enough parent

Setting realistic goals for yourself is important too. Being a parent is a demanding labor of love. Since we aren't perfect, we can't do what we think is best all of the time. Trying to be close to perfect leaves us feeling stressed and inadequate, because we *all* mess up sometimes. Fortunately, you don't need to be even near perfect to raise happy and well-behaved children. You don't have to be Dr. Spock, or "The Nanny"—all you have to be is good enough.

What do good enough parents do? Let's just say they love their kids and work to form close relationships with them. They use discipline methods that don't hurt, but help. They have fun with their children and don't physically or emotionally abuse or neglect them. Parents are good enough when they're willing to learn and try new things. They try to recognize and learn from mistakes. (Remember, what doesn't kill us makes us stronger.) They try to see how their own behavior affects their children's, and avoid letting their own problems interfere with their children's lives. Good enough parents take care of themselves, too.

Avoid the three reasons that good parenting advice fails

Sometimes when parents read advice, or get professional help, things still don't go well. Don't let this happen to you! The most common reason it happens is that **parents decide not to follow the advice.** For any of you, that may happen because you don't think you can do it, you don't understand it, you don't believe or trust it, or you just don't want to try it. You may not think you need to, since things "aren't that bad," even when others see problems. You may hope that your child will just outgrow the bad behavior. You may not feel comfortable because you weren't raised that way. Pride, fear or embarrassment may keep you from acting. Maybe you're just worn out and don't care what happens anymore. WARNING! That's often the case before the worst things happen.

Here's another reason that parents don't succeed with good advice: **they actually aren't doing what they think they are doing.** In other words, they don't recognize that they aren't following the advice. It's natural for parents not to clearly see what they are doing with their kids. Why? First of all, parents are really busy! There's so much to do and it can be a tiring, thankless job. There's also so much emotion involved in raising kids. All these things make it hard to remember or see clearly what is happening. If you want to check what you're doing, listen to others about how they see you work with your kids.

The third reason advice may not work is the **natural defenses found in every parent**. We naturally defend our kids. We worry that people will think less of them if we are working on a problem. We also naturally defend what we do with our kids. We want people to think we're doing a good job! But people in any job get raises and promotions when they can take feedback and turn it into better performance. People who only see what others say as criticism can't use it to benefit themselves. It's the same with parenting—good enough parents realize that someone else may know better sometimes, and there's always room for improvement. So, being able to look at oneself honestly and improve is a skill of successful people, including parents.

Next, let's look at how a parent's personality and behavior can make parenting easier and better. Don't sneak off now—it won't hurt a bit.

Common Adult Problems Can Harm Parenting

Stress is a part of parenting that makes it harder

Even though having children is a wonderful part of life for many, it sure can be stressful. And when we're stressed, it's harder to communicate with and hear our children. It's tougher to be patient, and children are less able to understand what we want from them. Stress can keep us from staying calm when kids misbehave. So why is it that kids seem to know when we're under pressure and seem to be at their worst then?! Well, with a strong  relationship, your kids will often try to help you out when you're stressed. Without a strong bond, they may actually try to push your buttons instead.

Decreasing stress is one of the most important ways to make your life as a parent easier. Using the *7 Skills* will help you learn and fit these stress busters into your busy life. Just try one or two of them at first.

1. Simplify your life by cutting down on activities you and your kids are involved in.
2. Get counseling for relationship or job problems you have.
3. Get help from friends and family often.
4. Exercise two or three times a week.
5. Meditate and/or pray.
6. Schedule "me-time" for yourself.
7. Laugh, and laugh some more.
8. Clean out clutter and organize your home (but relax on neatness).
9. Have regular family meetings.
10. Use routines for mornings, meals, bedtimes and others.

The discipline skills you'll learn in this book will also lower your stress by helping you cover up your buttons so your kids can't push them!

Denial ain't just a river in Egypt—don't deny real problems

Denial is one of the biggest reasons that parents and kids aren't successful. It makes it hard for people to see when a problem is real and needs to be dealt with. It's often why people don't get help when they need it. Parents often deny that their child has a problem because they don't know what to do, or don't want to deal with it. Or maybe they're embarrassed or afraid of what people will think. That may lead a mother to feel mad that all the "mean teachers" are picking on her son, when he actually has behavior problems that disrupt class.

One good way to know if you should be concerned about something is to look for a pattern by using the "**Rule of 3's**". This rule simply says if something happens three or more times, it's a pattern showing that the problem is probably real and needs to be dealt with. If you have a real problem with your child, ask yourself, "What is my part (and my child's part) in it?" For example, if your child has conflicts with three or more teachers, find out what you and your child can do differently.

Sometimes the Rule of 3's doesn't apply, such as with illegal things like drug possession, or theft. Here's where "one strike and you're out" applies. (One episode like this means your child needs help now.) A police official once told us that parents of kids who have repeat problems with the law tend to deny that their child's behavior is a real problem. They tend to blame others for it, like the police or society. So, when parents deny that their kids or the family needs to change, it keeps them from getting the help they need to make life better. Their denial keeps their children from success.

Substance abuse is one of the most common problems we deny

If a child is using substances like drugs or alcohol, some parents will deny it's a problem and do little. Parents can deny that they have a problem too. Almost one in five children comes from a home where a parent is abusing drugs or alcohol. These children are more likely to have problems like Attention-Deficit/Hyperactivity Disorder, learning disabilities, delinquency and depression. If you have a problem with drugs or alcohol, please get help now! Otherwise, being a successful parent will be very difficult.

A mother once brought her 9 year old son into my office. She said she was bringing him in because he didn't obey. "He steals my stuff" and "jumps on my bed while I am sleeping." When I spoke to the boy about this, I learned that he was "stealing" her vodka bottles and pouring the contents down the drain. He would jump on her bed to wake her up after she passed out. Now that mother was in denial!

Many parents struggle with depression, anger or anxiety

Many adults who have problems like these aren't aware of how their parenting is affected. But it's hard to form lasting, healthy relationships with your children when you don't get the help you need for dealing with these common adult issues.

You may be depressed if you feel sadness, hopelessness or helplessness that doesn't go away; have low energy, fatigue or frequent symptoms of illness such as pain; are sleeping and eating too much or too little; have trouble with memory, concentration and making decisions, or have lost interest in things you used to like. There is no shame in depression—it's just a common fact of life in today's world. If you have depression, you don't have to suffer. It can be treated. Denying depression can also hurt your children. Half of all children living with parents who have untreated depression are themselves depressed. Children with depressed parents do worse in school, and have fewer friends and more behavior problems.

Signs of an anger problem are feeling angry most days (or most of the time), feeling very mad over small things, yelling or physically lashing out when upset, anger causing trouble in relationships or work, feeling angry when you're not sure why, and losing sleep over things that make you mad. Excess anger hurts a person's health and happiness. If this could be you, things can be much better for you if you get help.

You may suffer from anxiety problems if feelings of worry and fear are overwhelming and persistent, and interfere with your life and normal activities, or if you have unpleasant physical symptoms of panic attacks. Anxiety is a very common treatable problem.

Listen to family, friends or coworkers if they say you may have one of these issues. Remember the Rule of 3's: if your anger, depression or anxiety has created problems for you three or more times in the past month, get professional help. Do it not only for your kids, but also for a happier, easier life for yourself. You deserve that.

Depression and anger-control problems are common in homes with **domestic violence**. Up to 20 percent of children in America come from homes where there is violence. Kids who see this violence are more aggressive, do worse in school and have trouble making friends. They are more likely to be abused and to abuse others. If violence is a problem in your home, please take steps to stop it now for you and your children's sake. Try our advice for dealing with anger (see page 53), and get treatment for substance abuse or emotional problems in family members that can lead to this problem. Stopping the violence needs to be your top priority. Get help from a mental health professional or local social service agency. Or contact the National Domestic Abuse Hotline at 1-800-799-SAFE (7233), or go online to www.ndvh.org.

Hurtful Emotional Reactions Can Harm Parenting

Good enough parents tend to stay calm

Relationships and discipline work best when parents can stay calm, even when kids are out of control. The more upset we get, the more kids act out. How do you know that you're being calm? Basically it means that you speak slowly and quietly, and your behavior and words are logical and unemotional. Discipline works best when we deal with misbehavior logically, instead of emotionally. Easier said than done when your kids spill on the new carpet or wreck  the car? Yes, but we'll show you one way to do this next. Other ways to express healthy anger and stay calm and cool are in chapter 3.

Negative emotional reactions hurt relationships

So start preparing for a good relationship by looking at how you feel about and act with your kids. If you are usually pleasant and relaxed around your kids, they'll probably act the same way and want to be with you. If you're often unhappy, they'll start to act the same, and pull away. That's because **kids imitate and learn from what they see parents do**. When children see Mom burn her hand on a hot stove, they don't need to touch the stove to know it's hot. People can learn all sorts of behaviors (even overcoming a fear of snakes) by watching other people first.

We all have our usual responses when we get really angry at our kids. Take a minute to think about what you do. Do you yell? Lecture? Swear? Spank? Give them a look? Cry? Not talk to them for a while? Now write down the three things you most often do when you're mad.

1. _____
2. _____
3. _____

How does it feel when you get to the point where you are this mad? What things don't you like about yourself then? Does it feel like you're in control?

Now, think about when you were young. What are three things your parents did when they were upset with you? Write them down here.

1. _____
2. _____
3. _____

Most parents find that when they're stressed, they respond in a way that is similar to how their own parents did (even when they don't like what their own parents did). How close are your two lists to being the same? If your lists aren't very similar, we suspect that you have tried to do things differently with your own children. Also, think about how you want your adult children to respond when they're mad at *your* grandchildren. Ways to raise kids don't have to run in families. Look again at the three things you do when you're angry. Focus on changing the ones that don't feel good, are stressful, or that don't seem right. We'll give you ideas for how to do this in this chapter and throughout the book.

Emotional reactions keep discipline from working

We naturally feel things like anger, embarrassment, and fear when our children misbehave. Parents can react by yelling, crying, lecturing, physically lashing out, or with silence. These are all stressful emotional reactions. Remember how kids learn from what they see? So, when the kids see Dad scream when upset, they learn to do it too.

Parents who react emotionally often discipline just because they're upset—and not for good, logical reasons. This makes for angry kids who act out more! Kids must feel that their behavior is judged fairly and logically in order to trust and respect us. Kids who respect their parents will behave better. If you let feelings like sadness, hopelessness or anger take over, you'll be less able to think logically and discipline well.

Also, when emotional reactions come before discipline, parents often lose control. Parents who physically abuse their children don't just wake up one day and say, "I'm going to abuse my child today." Usually, they get really mad at their kids first. Then, while still mad, they decide to discipline, causing physical or emotional harm. So when you're mad, don't discipline right away. Take five deep breaths. Call a friend. Sing a disco song! You can always go back and discipline later. We'll give you specific instructions for discipline in later chapters. For now, just remember that discipline needs to be done calmly to work well, even if you have to wait a short time to cool off.

How to avoid emotional reactions before you discipline

So, avoiding unnecessary emotional reactions is a big part of a good relationship and making discipline work. It also makes life a lot less stressful. A key to avoiding these reactions is the same as a key to managing marriage, family and workplace problems. This is a big secret that many parents don't know. But now, *you* will, and you can use it to your advantage. Yes, please try this at home!

The first part of the key to avoiding unnecessary emotional reactions is found in one simple fact: **we think things *before* we react.** Because thoughts come first, they strongly affect how we feel or what we do about something. But our thoughts aren't always true or healthy! We all make mistakes that can lead to trouble. Fortunately, we can learn to  check and change untrue thoughts before we react to our kids.

The second part of the key to avoiding unnecessary emotional reactions with kids is this: our thoughts, actions and feelings are all related, like in a triangle. So if we change one thing, the other two change automatically. Here's a visual for you.

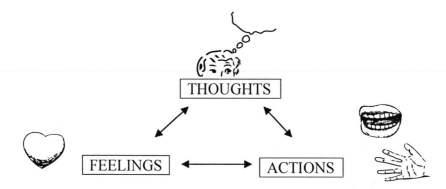

Here are examples of how this mega triangle works for parents. 1) Say your child behaves well at a school picnic while other kids are acting out. You may think, "I have a good kid" (**thought**), so you feel proud (**feeling**) and you tell him how awesome he is (**action**). That triangle doesn't need any changing! 2) Now let's say you feel depressed because your kids are hard to handle, and so you act depressed (withdraw from them) and have depressed thoughts ("things will never get better"). Remember, changing one part of the triangle can change the other two parts. So even if you feel depressed, you could decide to change how you act (focus on noticing when your kids do something right), which can make you start to feel less frustrated and begin thinking, "Maybe my kids aren't so bad." Choosing to change one part automatically changed the other two for the better!

Here's another handy tip. Knowing about the triangle can also help you deal with your child's **crankiness** (or someone else's, including your mate's). If you notice your child acts upset, and you don't know why, ask him what he was just thinking about. Maybe he's thinking something that isn't true, or just needs to talk something out.

Just saying what we're worried or upset about can help us feel better, and not be so dang moody. If your kids talk about what is going on, they won't act out as much. Using this triangle gives you great power, oh mighty mom or dad!

When kids misbehave, our thoughts can cause us to react

emotionally

Since our thoughts lead to feelings and actions, what we think about bad behavior leads to how we feel and what we do about it. But a feeling can come on so fast that we don't even realize we had a thought that caused it. In fact, most parents only notice how they *feel* about misbehavior, and act on their feelings alone. Or, they may recognize what they were thinking only *after* they react, in order to justify what they did. Maybe they yell at a child and then think, "Why did I do that?" The goal is to get to the point where you check your thoughts before you act, so you know why you want to discipline. Why? Because your thoughts may not be correct, and that can cause real trouble. We'll go over examples and show you how you can change this pattern in the next few pages.

What you think about your kids' behavior may be wrong

Since thoughts lead to feelings and actions, inaccurate thoughts can spoil relationships. Here's an example of our very own! Remember the triangle as you read. Once upon a time, I was hiking with my 7 year-old daughter in the Rocky Mountains on a lovely April day. Snow was still on the ground, and there were also large mud puddles. After the hike, I told her it was getting late and to get in the car. She walked to the car, stopped, turned around and ran to a pile of snow and began jumping on it. I saw her do this and immediately thought, "She is not listening to me and is still playing when I told her we need to go." So I became angry (feeling) and raised my voice, saying "Get into the car right now!" (action). My daughter started crying and said, "I was just trying to get the mud cleaned off my boots so the car won't get dirty." Then I felt horrible (feeling), and said to myself "I'm such an idiot," (thought), and apologized (action).

The thought I had about my daughter was wrong. I assumed incorrectly. She was not disobeying on purpose, but trying to save my car mats. If I had taken the time to challenge my thought and ask myself if she could be doing something other than disobeying, I may have noticed her wiping her boots and realized that she was trying to be good, not bad. If I had, my feeling would have been pride because she was being so considerate. I would have thanked her instead of yelling.

An added bonus of having a more accurate thought would have been a high chance that she'd wipe off her muddy boots again in the future! Because I scolded her when it wasn't called for, she would be less likely to do the right thing again. Kids who are yelled at or disciplined when it isn't called for will misbehave out of anger more often. It's almost like they decide, "If you think I'm a rotten kid, I'll show you just how rotten I can be." Good grief! This is especially true when parents don't notice that they have been out of line and when they don't apologize to their kids.

Changing Your Responses

Reasons why kids may not be misbehaving when we think they are

There may be another explanation for what a child did besides choosing to disobey. Here are some examples:

- She was trying to keep your car mats clean!
- He isn't developed enough to do what you want.
- She did her best, or what she thought was best.
- You didn't explain clearly what you wanted.

There may not really be any evidence that she disobeyed (maybe you're just upset about something else, or you just assumed she did something). Or, you may be wrong because you are thinking stinky thoughts! Say what?? Read on.

Relationships often suffer from untrue thoughts

To make the relationships with your kids as strong as possible, try not to have inaccurate thoughts about them. Try to judge their behavior fairly. If a child psychologist can be wrong, every parent can be! One of the easiest ways to tell when you have had an inaccurate thought is when you think you **really overreacted** to something. Yep—we all do it sometimes. Overreactions, or blowing things out of proportion, are usually caused by inaccurate thoughts. Doing this a lot can cause your kids to tune you out, and we don't want that! Overreactions are stressful, and can make kids lose trust, respect and affection for you.

Many untrue thoughts come from "stinking thinking"

Hey, we didn't name it! A famous psychologist named Albert Ellis came up with this great term for false thoughts that hurt relationships. It's his name for jumping to conclusions based on thoughts that aren't

true. It's tough to have close relationships with people who tend to have stinky thoughts, and kids naturally think stinkily a lot. So, your job will be easier if you teach your kids not to think this way. Not allowing stinking thinking in families helps avoid arguments, anger and bad feelings.

There are two common kinds of stinkin' thinkin'. The first is called **all-or-none thinking**. These thoughts include words like *must, should, always, all, every, any* or *never.* We bet you know someone who says these words a lot. Thinking this way leads to feeling that something's or someone's all good or all bad. But the world usually doesn't work in all or nothing ways, so these thoughts tend to be false. Examples are:

- "My Mom *always* says no" (not true since you say "yes" sometimes).
- "Children should *always* obey their parents" (normal children won't always obey their parents).
- "My son can *never* be trusted" (your son actually does do things you want sometimes).

If you tell your son that he can't be trusted enough, he'll start to believe you and act that way even more. Lumping your kids' actions into all-or-none or good or bad categories makes it hard to be fair and logical.

A second type of stinking thinking is called **awfulizing**. It's when we **exaggerate** the importance of things, or think of the most awful thing that could possibly happen. Awfulizing hurts parenting. It's hard for kids to trust parents (and parents to trust kids) who exaggerate a lot. It wears people out and pushes them away.

Besides, if we focus on only the worst possible thing that can happen, we begin to act as if that will happen for sure. In addition to thinking about the worst case scenario, it's also important to think of the *most likely* thing, or even a good thing, that could happen in a situation. If we awfulize and get bogged down in all the possible bad stuff that could happen, we won't have as much energy to fix something or make it better. It's tough to stay logical and fair if you awfulize.

If you find you or your kids are getting stuck in awfulizing thoughts, ask, *"What are the worst thing, the best thing, and the most likely thing that will happen?"* By answering these questions, most people begin to see that the world isn't ending. While they may be in for an unpleasant experience, they realize they can get through it.

For example, here are possible thoughts a parent could have after learning their son got a dreaded F in math.

- Worst Case scenario thought: this is terrible, he won't get into college or get a good job, and he will end up living with us forever!
- Best Case scenario thought: he'll take the class again and get an A, and will take school more seriously from now on.
- Most Likely scenario thought: he will have to work hard on math, perhaps go to summer school or get a tutor, but his future is not really affected.

Check what you think and then replace untrue thoughts

 If kids trust you to make correct judgments, they'll pay more attention to what you say, and show you more respect. Using this skill leads to logical parenting, instead of emotional parenting. It helps you feel in control and less stressed.

The big picture: think about their behavior first and then react

If your child seems to be misbehaving (or if you feel yourself getting upset), ask yourself, "What was I just thinking?" Then test that thought by asking yourself:

1) **"Is there another explanation for what my child did?"**
   (Did someone or something make it hard to obey? Did she do what she thought was best or the best a kid can do? Did I not explain clearly what I wanted?)

2) **"How do I know what I'm thinking is true**—what's the evidence?"
3) **"Was it a stinky thought** (all or none, awfulizing or exaggerating)?"

If your thought wasn't correct, replace it and then react to your kids. Now feel the control this gives you—mmm, that feels good!!

EXAMPLE ONE: You tell your 13 year old to hurry up and get dressed because you have to leave in 10 minutes. Ten minutes later, she isn't ready. (Does this sound familiar?) So what are you thinking? Let's say you thought, "She heard me and did this on purpose." Now test your thought: **"How do I know** that she heard me?" You ask if she heard you say you were leaving in ten minutes, and she says, "Yes," but makes an excuse. **"Is my thought stinking thinking?"** No, you didn't think she was trying to make your life miserable (awfulizing), and you didn't think she never listens (all-or-none). **"What is another explanation** for what she did?" You can't think of one, since she can't give you a good explanation. Your thought that she chose not to obey is correct. Your anger is justified, but you control it before disciplining and express it to her in a healthy way (stay tuned).

EXAMPLE TWO: You told your 4 year old son to watch your toddler while you take a shower. When you get back, the baby has knocked over a plant and is eating potting soil. Let's say your thought was, "He didn't help me like I asked." Test your thought: **"How do I know that's true?"** The baby has a mouth full of potting soil! **"Is my thought stinking thinking?"** No, you didn't think he did it because he doesn't care about the baby (awfulizing), or that he never helps you (all-or-none). **"What is another explanation?"** BINGO! A 4 year old is not capable of babysitting a toddler for the amount of time it takes to shower. *So replace your thought*—"I need to make sure I'm asking my son to do what he is capable of doing so I don't set him up to fail." Then you would feel frustrated at the situation, but not at your son.

Choose your own mood—don't let your kids do it

Another big thing that can hurt relationships and discipline is when parents let their kids have the power to "make them" feel a certain way. To be prepared for successful parenting, remember that nobody can make you feel mad or sad or whatever, unless you let them. In other words, the only person responsible for the way you feel is YOU.

Of course feelings come up when children misbehave, so it's easy to assume that they "made" us feel that way. But *we* are responsible for our reactions, because we actually choose our feelings. If you find yourself getting upset, think of being upset as your choice. That will give you the power to choose a different response, like calmly using discipline, or taking a break. With choice comes control and less stress. Also, your kids can learn to control their own moods by watching you do it.

Also, please don't tie your self-esteem to your kids. Some parents feel good about themselves only when their children are good or successful. Don't let your children's behavior determine your worth as a parent. Great parents have kids who get F's. Kind, loving parents have kids who throw temper tantrums in public. Being a parent is only one part of being you.

Find Out How Strong Your Relationships Are With Your Children

Now that you've learned how to prepare for a strong bond and parenting success, you can get an idea of how strong your relationships are. Just answer the survey questions below for each of your children.

> If the statement is true, usually or mostly true, circle "T"
> If the statement is false, usually or mostly false, circle "F"

For your children who are 1 to 4 years old, just answer the first 21 questions. For your children 5 to 12 years old, keep going so you answer the first 36 questions. If your child is 13 or older, answer all 42 questions.

Answer the questions according to the way things are today, *not* the way you would like them to be, or the way things were when your children were younger.

	Start here for children 1 year old and up	Child 1		Child 2	
1.	I sometimes worry that I'm not a good parent.	T	F	T	F
2.	When we're apart, I often find myself wanting to be with this child.	T	F	T	F
3.	This child usually seems happy to see me after we have been apart.	T	F	T	F
4.	I often have to sacrifice things I want to do for this child.	T	F	T	F
5.	I often smile or laugh when I am around this child.	T	F	T	F
6.	I usually talk about this child to other adults in a positive way.	T	F	T	F
7.	When I get upset with this child, he or she often acts afraid of me.	T	F	T	F
8.	This child usually likes being held, or hugged, or kissed by me.	T	F	T	F
9.	This child often makes me mad.	T	F	T	F
10.	I enjoy spending time alone with this child.	T	F	T	F
11.	My spouse/partner and I seldom disagree about parenting this child.	T	F	T	F
12.	Parenting this child often leaves me drained and exhausted.	T	F	T	F
13.	I like being with this child.	T	F	T	F
14.	When I think about this child, I realize how lucky I am.	T	F	T	F
15.	I worry that this child may have/has a behavior problem.	T	F	T	F
16.	When this child seems upset, I can usually figure out why.	T	F	T	F
17.	I am seldom embarrassed by how I have acted toward this child.	T	F	T	F
18.	This child often disappoints me.	T	F	T	F
19.	All things considered, I am thankful I am this child's parent.	T	F	T	F
20.	This child knows how to push my buttons.	T	F	T	F
21.	There are many times that I wish this child would just go away.	T	F	T	F

STOP here if your child is 4 years old or younger.

	Continue if your child is 5 years or older	Child 1		Child 2	
22.	Almost every day this child and I say, "I love you" to one another.	T	F	T	F
23.	This child freely shares his/her fears or	T	F	T	F

		Child 1		Child 2	
	concerns with me.				
24.	When this child wakes up in a bad mood, it will be a long day.	T	F	T	F
25.	This child usually treats me with respect.	T	F	T	F
26.	This child likes to be praised by me.	T	F	T	F
27.	Disciplining this child usually makes him/her mad and resentful.	T	F	T	F
28.	I can tell that this child wants to spend time with me.	T	F	T	F
29.	Other people give me compliments about this child.	T	F	T	F
30.	This child is usually kind to other kids.	T	F	T	F
31.	I know my child's friends and who their parents are.	T	F	T	F
32.	People who don't live with us tell me how to parent this child.	T	F	T	F
33.	This child usually tries to do his/her best.	T	F	T	F
34.	This child usually does what I tell him/her to do.	T	F	T	F
35.	I look forward to doing things with this child when he/she is an adult.	T	F	T	F
36.	I am proud of this child.	T	F	T	F

STOP here if your child is 5–12 years old

	Continue here if your child is 13 or older	**Child 1**		**Child 2**	
37.	When I get upset with this child, I sometimes worry that we will get into a physical fight.	T	F	T	F
38.	This child seems like he or she will be a good parent someday.	T	F	T	F
39.	I am afraid my child may be doing or is doing drugs, drinking or having sex.	T	F	T	F
40.	My child doesn't mind me being around the house when he/she is here with friends.	T	F	T	F
41.	My child likes to spend some time with the family, without friends along.	T	F	T	F
42.	My child confides in friends more than me.	T	F	T	F
	Total number of gray box "T" answers plus Total number of white box "F" answers **Equals your Total Score**	+		+	

Now add up your score. If the question was in a gray box, count the number of times you circled "T" for true and put it in the box above. If the question was in a white box, count the number of times you circled "F" for false. Add up those two numbers, and the total is your score. The higher your score, the stronger your relationship is. If you got the highest possible score, go back and make sure you understood the questions and answered them very honestly. Few parents will get a perfect score! Now see if your score is lower than average, average, or higher than average.

	Lower scores	Average scores	Higher scores
1–4 year olds	10 or less	11 to 17	18 or more
5–12 year olds	18 or less	19 to 29	30 or more
13 years old +	21 or less	22 to 35	36 or more

A lower score shows that you have the most room for improvement! Even if your relationship problems have been around for a while, things can still get better. Getting help is always better than ignoring problems and hoping they'll go away. First use the *7 Skills* for a few months. Chances are good that things will improve greatly. If not, see a mental health professional. Some parent-child relationships are so strained that they need professional help. As long as you continue to work on your relationship, you are not giving up. Congratulate yourself for making the effort. Your kids will be grateful too.

If you had an average score, you are doing some things well, but things can improve! This book will give you the skills you need to make things even better for yourself and your kids right now and to prevent problems in the future.

If you got a higher than average score, you appear to be doing many things well. As you read this book, look at how our suggestions can compliment what you're already doing. Also, since relationship problems can develop over time, use your *7 Skills* to prevent problems and help when things get more challenging.

Your score is really most useful as a guide to strengthening your relationship. Look for the gray box questions that you answered false, and the white boxes you answered true, and put a star by each. Keep these in mind when you read the book. You can take this survey again later to see how you are progressing. Try to improve your score over time, or keep it as high as possible. If your score gets lower, spend more relationship time with your child. Skills #2 and #3, described in the next two chapters, will help you do just that.

Another way to look at your results is to compare your answers for different children. Is there a difference of more than about five to seven points in your scores? If so, think about why your relationships are different.

So now you know what it takes to prepare yourself for success as a parent. This skill is as important as all the rest and can be the most difficult of the *7 Skills* for some. That's because it takes looking at yourself and your kids honestly, and not denying real problems that need work. Using this skill can mean finding the strength to get help with your own issues that hurt parenting. It involves learning one of the big keys to relationships and discipline (you know, how untrue thoughts can lead to unnecessary emotional reactions), and adjusting your expectations of yourself and your kids. Congratulate yourself for spending time and effort to make life as good as possible for your family, and your job as a parent easier.

And now, ladies and gentlemen, you're ready for prime time. The next two skill chapters will show you how to build strong relationships with your kids. Onward ho!

Skill #1 PREPARE YOURSELF: Get ready for parenting success

- **Work toward a good relationship** with each of your children. It's the single most important thing that prevents and treats behavior problems, and makes kids happy and successful.
- Use Appendix A to **check what you expect your kids to do.**
- Keep in mind that normal children disobey, so you can't expect anywhere near perfect behavior.
- There is no such thing as a perfect parent. **Be a good enough parent—** be open to looking at and changing what you do, and using new skills.
- What you are thinking about your kids leads to how you feel and act toward them.
  - ❖ **When your child is naughty, or you're upset, check your thoughts** to make sure you correctly judge behavior before you react.
  - ❖ Ask yourself, **"What was I just thinking about my child?"** Then test your thought by asking yourself: **1) "How do I know that my thought is true?" 2)** "Is it stinking thinking like all-or-none (always, never) or awfulizing (worst case scenario or exaggerating?)" **3) "What is another explanation besides disobeying for what my child did?"**
  - ❖ **Replace your thought** if you find a more accurate one before reacting to stay calm, logical and less stressed with your kids.
- **Don't give your kids the power to change your mood.** Choose your own mood.
- Remember the reasons for still having problems after getting advice: choosing not to follow it, not recognizing when you aren't following it, and letting natural defenses block your success.
- **Decrease your stress**:
  1) Simplify your life—cut down on activities you and your kids are in 2) Deal with relationship or job problems 3) Get counseling 4) Get help from friends and family often 5) Exercise 6) Pray and/or meditate 7) Schedule time for yourself 8) Laugh! 9) Avoid drugs and alcohol 10) Organize your home 11) Have realistic expectations 12) Learn and use discipline skills so your kids don't stress you out by pushing your buttons 13) Have regular family meetings 14) Use routines
- **Don't let denial keep you from dealing with problems** like substance or alcohol abuse, depression, anxiety, anger management or domestic violence. Don't deny real issues in your kids or yourself.
- **Check the strength of your relationship** with each child over time. Use your skills to make your relationship better and stronger than it already is.

Skill #2

PAY ATTENTION: How to give your children attention in ways that work

Homes with children can be like grand central station, and parents can lead hectic lives on the edge. We sure do! At times, it may seem like there isn't enough time to eat and sleep, much less pay attention to your kids. But, making your relationship better by paying attention doesn't need to take much time, and it saves you heartache and tons of time on discipline. Doing it doesn't need to be expensive. It  just needs to be a commitment. The symbol for this skill is a bell. It is ringing to get your attention and remind you how important attention is to your kids.

When you give hugs and say *"I love you,"* it helps jump start a positive relationship. But giving other kinds of attention makes the relationship stronger. How much and what kinds of attention do kids need, you ask? Plus, how do you know if it's good for them or just spoiling them rotten? Well, if we can have *your* kind attention, we'll explain. In this chapter, we will teach you skills and activities that will build your relationship and make your kids pay more attention to what you say. We bet that last part perked up your ears!

Children need time with you *and* certain kinds of attention

 Most parents spend daily time with their kids, tending to housework, homework, and other family routines. But studies show that most of this time together doesn't improve the relationships between parent and child. Children need certain types of attention, which we call "good attention," to nurture them and to strengthen their bond with us. Good attention is the kind that helps children learn good behavior, and feel special and loved. Good attention is the kind that builds children's respect and affection for their parents. It makes

parenting much easier. This chapter is all about giving good attention.

Nourish your child with good attention and not things

When adults are asked about their fondest childhood memories, they mostly remember things they *did* with their parents, and not what their parents bought them. So be careful not to think that good attention equals buying things for your kids. If you do, they may start to think that getting gifts or money means being loved. Many busy parents give presents to try to substitute for the time they can't, or don't want to, spend with their kids. When those kids grow up and know the difference, they realize they would rather have gotten good attention.

Think of your relationship as being a savings account

When you give your child good attention, you make a deposit into your **Relationship Savings Account**. Cha-ching! When you overreact, or harshly punish, you make a withdrawal. Make a strong relationship by making as many deposits and as few withdrawals as possible. Like any savings plan, the earlier you get started, the better. You'll really benefit from having a high account balance when your kids reach puberty! Thinking of good attention as putting money in the bank really isn't as far off as you may think. Having to send a troubled youth off to a residential treatment facility can easily cost over $100,000 a year, and insurance pays for little or none of it! The good attention you give your children today can literally save you thousands of dollars in the future.

How to know if you are spoiling your kids

Starting at about age 4, children may be spoiled if they're used to getting what they want and having things their own way. Spoiled kids think their needs and wants are much more important than others' needs and wants, and they complain, throw fits and otherwise manipulate parents into giving them what they want. They are demanding and hard to be around, and have trouble following rules. Makes you want one, huh?

Many parents find it hard to determine whether they are spoiling their children. Importantly, there are two ways to spoil: with attention and with things. Children are more likely to get spoiled when you buy them too many things (or give them too much money) than when you give them too much of your attention. So try for a nice balance between giving and not giving them things they want. The more they complain about not getting things they want but don't need, the more spoiled your children may be getting. Never give in to tantrums, threats, or guilt when they want something.

The other way you can spoil kids is with too much attention. This isn't very possible in the first couple years of life, but is later. **Your children may be getting *too much* of your attention if:**

1. You often plan activities to fill your child's whole day, or take your child to a special activity almost every day. Children need free time where they can just play or hang out at home, and so do you.
2. You often allow your child to interrupt you when you're talking to someone else, or your child hardly ever has to wait for your attention.
3. You don't get a few minutes alone each day because you're always with your children. Or, you act like your needs aren't important. Everyone needs alone time. Parents of small children can get this during naps, playpen time, or when someone else is babysitting.
4. You are usually directing how your kids should do things. They may tell you that it's embarrassing when you're involved in their activities.
5. You're doing almost everything for kids 3 years old and up, so that they aren't learning how to do anything for themselves. Children need to have some frustrations that they deal with themselves— don't always rescue them and fix things.
6. You are praising them too much. (We'll cover that later.)

Teach your kids what it means to be spoiled

Showing them how to recognize spoiled behavior can be pretty fun, and it opens the door to discussing how being spoiled is bad for kids. Veruca Salt in the movie *Willy Wonka and the Chocolate Factory* is a great example of an obnoxious, spoiled youngster. If both you and your child see another child acting spoiled (for example, fussing when he/she couldn't buy a treat), discuss it later. You could say, *"Most kids act spoiled sometimes, but that girl was a sight! I wonder if she gets what she wants too much."*

When your kids whine about not getting the latest toy or the best pair of shoes, **tell them that not getting everything they want is best for them.** Say, *"You're not going to get everything you want in life, so it isn't good for you to grow up thinking that you can."* Point out that spoiled kids often grow up to be sad and angry adults when they learn they can't get everything they want (like friends, jobs, awards, boyfriends or girlfriends, good health or talents). They'll have a tough time accepting that life isn't always fair. You can talk about how people don't like to be around spoiled kids, who act like their needs and desires are more important than everyone else's. The bottom line is that in order to avoid spoiling children, sometimes they need to hear the answer, *"No"*, and know that you mean it.

How to know if your kids are getting too little attention

Some children act like they don't want attention when they desperately need it. Some parents won't realize they're neglecting their kids by not paying enough attention. **Your children *may not be getting enough* attention if:**

1. They are over scheduled with activities so that you don't have to be with them as much. (It is possible to plan activities, *and* give them too little attention.)
2. They are having behavior problems at school or at home.
3. Talking to them is hard or uncomfortable because of conflicts between you and your children or because you feel no connection to them.
4. You usually don't know what to say to them.
5. You don't know their likes, dislikes, friends, fears, activities and interests.
6. They are spending much more free time with friends or media (TV, games, computer, etc.) than they are with you.
7. Your kids don't seem to confide in you or tell you things any more.

How to give good attention: have relationship building times

We're now going to explain three parent-child activities that work well. The most important feature of these activities is that they give your children chances to have good times with you. They are times set aside from your daily routines to connect with your kids. The second most important aspect of these activities is that you'll be using some child raising skills while you're doing them. Give yourself a few weeks to learn and use them regularly. As time goes on, we hope you'll look forward to doing them.

The three activities are special time, talk time and parent playtime. You think the names are goofy? Well fine! Once you learn them, name them whatever you want. Just use the same name consistently with younger kids, so they know what to expect. The table below lists what age range is best for each activity, how often to do them, and how long they take.

Activity	How often	How long	Ages
Special time (Hang time, You and me time)	Once a week to once a month	About an hour or so	3 and older
Talk time (Chat time, Let's talk, What's up)	Every day	About 10 minutes	About 8 and up
Parent playtime (Playtime)	Every day	About 10 minutes	1 and up

For children 3 years old and up, we suggest that each parent do two of the three activities with each child on a regular basis. Special time works well for most families, and we recommend that it be one of your choices.

Your choice of the second activity depends upon your kids' ages. For older kids, talk time may be best. Parent playtime works well for younger children, but can be adapted for teens as well. Doing these with each child alone works best. For example, in a one child–two parent family, each parent spends 10 minutes doing an activity with the child every day. This gives the child 20 minutes of good attention every day. Each parent would then have at least one monthly special time (so the child would have at least two a month). If both parents can't do an activity daily, at least one parent should try to, so the child has at least one activity with one parent every day.

For talk time and playtime, about 10 minutes is best. Five minutes is OK, less than five minutes isn't enough, and more than 10 minutes may be too hard to do regularly. This small amount of time will feel much longer to your child, and the effects on your relationship can last a lifetime.

As you read about the activities, you'll learn important child-raising skills, such as how to talk to kids. These methods not only help relationships, but also support children's emotional health and make parenting simpler. You may naturally have some of these skills, or already be doing similar activities. If not, at first you might feel overwhelmed by all the information. Read it in little bits. It'll take time to learn all the skills, but it's worth every minute.

Don't expect to be able to learn these skills all at once! First try things that seem familiar. Then try the things that seem more foreign. We hope that once you learn these methods, you'll also use them outside of these activities, like when you're running errands, helping with homework or anytime. Let's start with the activity we hope all children get to have with their parents—special time.

It's Special Time!
(for children 3 years old and up)

This is time set aside to do something fun with one child alone. It is doing something your child enjoys and something you don't often get to do together. Your child should notice this time is different from your usual family activities. While special time doesn't need to be fancy, it does need to be kind of fun for your kids. Running errands will never become special time! Do things that *they* like. What you do together will often become less important than the fun, relaxed time they spend with you.

Guidelines for special time

It's most special for a child when it's with one parent at a time. (Occasionally it can be with both parents.) It only needs to last about an hour. In general, have it *at least* once a month, but it's best to have it every one to two weeks for kids age 12 or less. Teenagers may be too busy to have it this often. For parents new to special time, or who are

 struggling with their kids, we recommend having it at least once a week. Special time isn't for every day, otherwise it isn't so special!

The busier you are, the more important special time is. Even if you're a stay-at-home domestic engineer, it doesn't always mean your kids are getting the fun, undivided attention they need. Homemakers are very busy, not only with housework and childcare, but also with their own projects or interests. No matter what you do for a living, put the brakes on your usual busy, stressed life, and have special time on a regular basis.

How to set up special time

Tell your children ahead of time so they can look forward to it. You can also surprise them if they have no other plans. For younger children, don't tell them until the day it will happen, and be specific about *when* they'll have it, so they won't bug you all day asking about it. Instead of saying, "We're going to have special time sometime today," say *"We're going to have special time right after lunch."*

For teens, you may have to sneak it in, since they'll often say they're too busy, or resist spending time with you. (Sad, but true!) You could say, *"Done with homework? Good, let's go see a movie, just you and me."* Don't take, "Ah, mom" or other comments personally—just do it anyway.

You can give your child a couple of activities to choose from, or just surprise them with one you think they'll like. They should choose what to do sometimes. Importantly, if you say you'll have special time, be sure you do. If you aren't sure you can, don't tell them in advance—just surprise them. If you have more than one child, be careful to alternate special times between them so it seems fair. Dad may have it with one child while mom has it with another.

Ideas for Special Time

Go to the library or bookstore
Play a game and eat snacks
Attend a local carnival
Go swimming (not to a lesson)
Go on a bike ride
Take a long walk or hike
Visit a new park
Listen to your child's music while giving her or him a back rub
Do a craft or small project
Surf the internet (about music, stars, activities, history, places they would like to go)
Drive to a new interesting place
Go to the zoo
Play arcade games
Cook something yummy
Make forts out of blankets/chairs
Pick them up early from school for ice cream
Go to a pet store

Meet them at school for lunch or take them to lunch
Make homemade ice cream
Go to a craft show or community theater
Fly a kite or shoot off a rocket
Go to the mall and pick out clothes they like
Watch a movie
Shoot hoops or play catch
Go roller skating or ice skating
Go bowling
Take them fishing
Play goofy golf
Explore a museum
Go to a sporting event
Watch their favorite TV show with popcorn
Plan a trip over dessert
Go out and look at the stars
Make a snow man
Pick out a new CD

What NOT to do during special time

Whatever it takes, don't criticize, tease, argue or try to solve problems during this time. Don't work on something, like how well your child catches a ball. There should be no pressure. Try to pick an activity that won't embarrass your child. (Showing up at an teenager's school for lunch may not be cool, for instance.) Don't talk about what you did with your other kids during special time. That way they can't complain that a sibling's time was better than theirs. Minimize TV and video games for special time, since kids tend to do these too much already.

It's best if special time isn't very time consuming or expensive, since it'll be easier to have it regularly that way. Don't feel you need to out-do what you did before. If you did something really exciting last time (rode go-carts), do something less exciting this time (go to the park).

Save the really big things like amusement parks or overnight trips for family outings.

Special time **should never be taken away as punishment**. Also, don't tell your children that it will happen only if they do something. For example, don't say, "If you're good today at school, we'll have special time before we go home." Then if your child doesn't behave well, you're put in the position of taking away special time for bad behavior. That's a big no-no because it will hurt your relationship instead of build it. Instead of promising special time *if* your child is good, surprise her with special time *when* she's good.

Things to try when having special time doesn't seem so special

Sometimes parents feel that no matter what they suggest, their child doesn't want to do anything, or only wants to watch TV or play video games. If this happens, try scheduling surprise activities. (Just pick them up and take them somewhere.) If your child continues to complain about what you do, or doesn't want to do anything, try to pick something together, or let your child pick. Also increase talk time and parent playtime so your child feels more comfortable being alone with you. Be sure that you're doing things your child enjoys and can do without much help. If your child still doesn't want to go, he or she may have something else going on that needs professional help.

Some parents say that their kids act out so much, or are so silly during special time, that they have to stop it early. Acting out is pretty common for kids when parents do something new. The kids may not be used to getting so much one-on-one good attention from you. Even though it's special time, don't allow your child to be disrespectful or disobedient. Use the discipline skills in this book if needed. If your child acts out more than usual, try activities that are structured (like a movie or bowling). Have special time *more* often, but for shorter amounts of time. Also, have talk time more often.

Talk Time
(for children age 8 and older)

This is when you have a one-on-one talk with each of your children. It may not be possible every single day, but hopefully you'll have it almost every day. Children younger than 8 often like playing more than talking, so we recommend parent playtime for them instead (see the next section). It's best to be alone with each child whenever possible. With two or more children there, it's hard to follow different conversations, and they may start competing for your attention.

Talk times don't have to be long (about 10 minutes is usually enough), but sometimes they'll blossom into longer conversations, and that's great. It's hard to believe that such a short time can make a difference, but it's the way you spend the time that makes the huge impact on your relationship.

Treat your children as young friends during talk time. It lets them know that you're there for them and interested in their lives. There should be no distractions, like TV, telephones, I-pods, work, or other children. Focus on the child in front of you. Talk time is time to talk about your child's life. Talk about what he or she wants to talk about. Avoid topics that might upset either of you, or require big decisions or problem solving. You can end up solving problems that they bring up, but don't start by bringing up a problem yourself.

For teenagers, you may not want to call this activity by a certain name, but just sneak it into the day. If you say, "It's talk time," teens may think, "It's time for my parents to interrogate and bug me." Instead, say something like, *"Just checking in"* or *"What's up?"* Or just start a conversation with a relaxed general thought or question. Sometimes they just won't feel like talking—don't force it. Hang out anyway—brush your teen's hair, rub his back, or bring him a glass of water—a conversation may start any time. Just be there ready to talk, and even more, to listen.

When and where to have talk time

If you can, do it about the same time of day, so it becomes a habit.

Good times include right before bed, driving to and from somewhere, snack time, while you're walking the dog, or during a meal. Telephone talk time also works if you can't see your child that day, but doesn't work quite as well as face-to-face talk time.

Talk time instructions

1. **Get things started.** You can start by asking your child a question, like, *"How was school?" "What is something fun you did today?" "What do you want to talk about?" "How's Sally doing lately?"* or *"How did you*  *like playing with Tommy?"* Or start with a pleasant comment: *"I saw the funniest thing today..."* Then let your child take over talking. You can start by talking about your day, or current events, but you want your children to start talking. Once your child starts talking, listen and just go on from what your child says, so he or she leads the conversation.

2. **Don't ask too many questions.** About 70 percent of everything that adults say to kids is a question. Using some questions to get the conversation started is fine, but too many questions can feel like a police interrogation! You know, "Where were you the night of..." Child therapists know that if you want to make a child talk less, just ask a bunch of questions! If you want to know about something, say, *"I was wondering if...," "it seems like...,"* or *"I noticed..."* instead.

3. **Keep the discussion on your child's topic and don't interrupt.** Try to keep talking about what your child is interested in. This isn't a time to talk about you or your problems.

4. **Occasionally repeat back what you heard.** Listen carefully and occasionally repeat back a short summary of what your child has been saying. For example, you might say, *"Wow, it sounds like you had a very busy day. You gave a speech, took two tests and had a fire drill!"* This shows you're listening and it keeps the conversation going. Also, say little things like *"Oh yeah? Really- uh-huh- hmm"* while listening.

5. **Leave pauses, and wait for your child to start talking or to answer your question.** Kids often need more time to respond than adults. Look in their eyes when you can.

6. **Don't argue, criticize or make other negative comments about**

your child. Avoid teasing also, even if you're just playing, since it can feel like criticism. If what your child says concerns you, and you want to challenge unhealthy thinking, gently say what *you* think about something, as an adult. But if it makes your child upset, move on and address it later (not during talk time).

7. **Talk time isn't meant for play or lots of silliness.** Say, *"I'd really like to relax and talk, so let's try not to be so silly right now."*

8. **Talk time should *never* be taken away as punishment.** When your children are at their worst, they need talk time the most. Even if you had a rough day together, make the last part of the day positive, so you both don't fall asleep feeling bad. Kids need good attention every day, no matter how they behaved. This teaches your children that you love them no matter what they do. If they are disrespectful (see page 86), you may need to end talk time early.

9. **Listen for the feelings behind the words they say.** Ah, we gotta talk about feelings with our kids? For sure—like, totally! Before we discuss why, here's how to do it. Every once in a while, say what it may have felt like to have the experience they told you about. Ask yourself what you would be feeling if it happened to you, and guess what they were feeling. So, if he tells you about how much the teacher liked his report, you might say, *"You sound proud. I would be."*

Talking about people's feelings makes us smarter

There are two common kinds of intelligence—emotional and intellectual. They are both important to success. Part of **emotional intelligence** is being able to recognize, express and manage emotions. When people can do this, they don't need to misbehave or hurt people when they're feeling bad. People who have this kind of smarts have better relationships and higher school grades than people without it, and they are happier and can solve problems and influence people more (including at work). Talking about feelings helps your kids develop this type of intelligence.

Sometimes parents have a hard time thinking of a word to describe a feeling. That's why we made Appendix B for you. If you use the feeling words found there, your kids will learn to use them instead of withdrawing or misbehaving when upset.

Another part of emotional intelligence is being able to show **empathy** (understanding and being sensitive to other people's feelings). Showing your children empathy teaches them how to show it to others. Saying, *"I understand why you'd feel that way"* when they are feeling sad (instead of "quit whining") helps them develop empathy. If you find it hard to see why they feel or think something, ask them, *"Is that how you feel (or what you think)? Why is that? Can you give me an example?"* Learning empathy helps kids think about others, and not just themselves. And that's good for all of us.

Let your children show all emotions to you. Yes, even the nasty, negative ones! When kids aren't allowed to be mad or upset, they have more social problems. But kids' emotions may not make sense to us adults. There will be times that they seem silly ("the rain makes me nervous") or are negative toward you ("you really make me mad"). If your child tells you that her best friend  ignored her today, you might say, *"I bet you felt really sad."* Then she may say, "No, I was really pissed off!" Don't argue or correct your child's feeling, even if it doesn't make sense to you. You could say, *"Oh, of course, tell me more."* If your daughter says, "You make me mad", you could say, *"I'm sorry you feel that way. How is being mad working for you?"* (or *"What can I do to help?"*) This works better than telling her she's rude. Just listen and keep the conversation going.

How to talk about happiness

There are some really awesome things that research on happiness has shown. First of all, it appears that anybody can choose to be happy. That's because people are happier when they choose to do certain things. You can gradually teach your kids what these choices are. Here are things that happy people choose to do:

- They figure out what they like to do and then do it often.
- They don't live like victims, blaming others when bad things happen.
- They appreciate good things every day.

- They talk nicely to themselves and don't cut themselves down.
- They surround themselves with people that support them.
- They're open to new things and friends.
- They are optimistic.
- They give to others.
- They have religious faith or spirituality.
- They work for a purpose they believe in.
- They work to find a job they enjoy.
- They are able to forgive others.
- They express and deal with emotions.

Happy people stay away from addictions and do what it takes to have broad career choices. What's more, people seem happiest when they're satisfied with having what they need for today (instead of living for the future). Happy people tend *not* to say, "I'll be happy when… (I get my next promotion, I get straight A's, I'm rich, I have a girlfriend/boyfriend, etc)." Tell your kids another truth about happiness—happy people aren't *always* happy, and that's OK.

By talking about it, even kids can gradually understand how happiness is their choice. That means happiness isn't all tied to good looks, money, fame, how well they perform something, or one particular friend. Those things can make people happy in the short term, but don't lead to lasting happiness and can even lead to great unhappiness. A lot of rich movie stars spend years being unhappy! It looks like as long as one has enough money to live an average lifestyle, happiness isn't greater with more money (in fact, great wealth often leads to misery). When your kids bring up people who are famous, rich, or have a lot of things, ask, *"Do you think that makes them happy for a long time?"* *"Would you rather have the newest game, or good friends and family?"*

Talk time topics

- Whatever your child wants to talk about!
- A time this week when your child felt scared (or sad, excited, mad, frustrated, happy, proud).
- If your child brought two friends on a trip, who would he or she bring and why?
- Happiness—how you both can choose it.
- Both of your dreams for the future (mostly your child's).
- Something new that your child learned today.
- Favorite books, movies, cartoon characters.
- Spirituality or faith, and how it affects your daily lives.
- Hobbies, family trips, school, sports and friends.
- Things your child is worried about (if he or she brings it up).
- Cousins and other family members.
- How to spend holidays.

Parent Playtime
(ages 1 and up)

We love to play! Don't you? Play is vital for everybody's health and happiness. All work and no play make Jack and Jill dull kids—and that goes for parents too. Children who don't get to play enough are less creative, less able to solve problems, and have poorer social skills than children who play more. For younger kids, play is an important way to learn how things work, how to get along, and how to express themselves.

Regular playing that children make up and do by themselves or with friends is important. Parent playtime, when you play with your kids on purpose, can be even more important. Mental health professionals have been teaching play skills to parents since the 1960s, because they are good for the family. Playing together using some play therapy skills strengthens your relationship with and promotes healthy development in children.

Guidelines for parent playtime

Playtime doesn't have to take long. Only about 10 minutes per child is really necessary. Play alone with your child, with no distractions. It won't always be possible for both parents to have a separate playtime with each child every day, but try to as often as possible. For young children, try to have it at about the same time of the day, in the same play area. If you have it different times each day, young children may bug you all day long about when they can have their playtimes. It works best after naps or after dinner. Having it at night before bed can be good as long as it doesn't interrupt a relaxing bedtime routine.

Sometimes parent playtime may blossom into a longer activity. Let's say on the weekend you have more free time and decide you can play an hour on Saturday and Sunday. Then Monday hits and you're back to the grind. You barely have time to play for 10 minutes. But you do, and your child's mad because he wants more time like he had yesterday. To avoid this, when you have more time to play, do it! Just don't call the extra time *playtime*. Have your regular 10 minute playtime. Then say, *"That was fun. I want to spend more time with you, and I have some extra time today, so what should we do?"*

Never take away playtime as punishment. Your children need playtime whether they've been wonderful or awful. Take away something else for bad behavior. By always having playtime, you're showing your children that you will always love them, no matter what. This will prevent bad behavior and help you form a close bond.

Toys to use for parent playtime		
Don't use electronic, battery powered things that move themselves. Use toys that let your children use their imaginations or create things, like the things listed below.		
building blocks Legos Duplos Tinker Toys	art supplies clay that doesn't dry out crayons and paper	dolls or puppets Mr. Potato Head Playmobil toys super-hero

erector sets	colored chalk and	characters
toy tools	board	Lincoln Logs
puzzles	toy kitchens	(remember those?)
masks	dress up costumes	stuffed animals
dollhouse	toy swords or lasers	toy farm
Avoid rough toys like boxing gloves or punching bags; messy ones like finger paint, scissors, glue, or glitter; fragile toys or toys that could be choked on; and toys that involve competition, or where there is a clear winner, like most video games, board games, and races.		

How to play with kids

Act like an older kid—be a goofball! Make funny faces, voices and noises; put on a mask or costume; and for goodness sake, laugh! If you look and act bored, your child will notice and won't have as much fun. Let your child decide what to play and how to play it. Avoid telling your child what to do (unless he or she is hurting something or somebody). For younger kids, start by saying, *"During our playtime you can do almost anything you want. If you're doing something that you shouldn't do, I will tell you. Let's play!"*

During playtime, your child will often get bossy. Let her! Your child may pretend to be a police officer, teacher or even a parent. If your child wants to be a parent, pay close attention to what he or she does. This might tell you how your child sees you. Scary!

Sometimes kids want parents to act things out, like in a play. Ask her what you should do. For example, she may want to be queen while you are her servant. She may say, "OK, servant. Go get me my supper. Do it at once!" You could whisper back a question like, "What should I prepare for the Queen's supper?" But avoid asking too many questions, since they take the lead away from kids. Adults tend to overuse questions or talk about what they are playing, rather than actually just playing.

Near the end, say, *"Our playtime is almost over for today."* Young children need this warning a couple minutes before the actual time to stop. Afterwards, say, *"Our playtime is over. I'm going to start picking up the toys. You can help me if you want."* If your child doesn't want to help, just pick them up yourself. Remember the point is for your child to have fun with you. You could also just let you child continue playing without you.

What to do if your child is naughty during play time

If he or she does something bad, like breaking or throwing toys, spitting, swearing, hitting or biting, give a warning: *"Remember when I said that there were some things that you can't do during playtime? (The naughty behavior) is one of them. If you keep doing it, I will either have to put the toy away or stop playtime early."*

If your child keeps throwing something, quietly take the object away. If he continues to misbehave, stop playtime early and say why. If your child is spitting, hitting or swearing, there really isn't anything you can take away. If the naughty behavior continues after a warning, stop playtime early. If you warned your child, be sure to follow through.

What if your child doesn't want playtime to end?

This is common, because kids love the special attention they get. Some may even act out when playtime is over. Don't let this keep you from having playtime again. When playtime's over, just say, *"Our playtime is over for today. I have to go and do something else. You can keep playing if you want."* Then leave! You can empathize by saying, *"Yea, I didn't want playtime to stop either. But it has to for today. I can't wait until tomorrow when we can have it again."*

Playtime for older kids

First of all, don't call it parent playtime—that's way too lame! You might use crafts, hobbies, games or sports instead of toys. You can build stuff like models, cook, or collect something together. Anything that is fun for your child and that doesn't involve competition between you is OK. You can do the same thing over and over if your child really likes it. It isn't what you do that matters, but the fun that you have together. If your child doesn't want to play, try changing the activity. Ask what he or she wants to do. Or try not planning it, but just sneaking it in. *"Hey, let's shoot some hoops."*

And that's how it's done! Congratulations—you've learned some great parenting skills in these three activities. They will work for most parents and kids. If you are struggling with activities like these (maybe your children are very challenging), it's time to see a professional.

Other Great Ways to Give Your Kids Good Attention

Be silly around your kids

Normal children act goofy or silly sometimes. Let them see you act that way, too. Occasionally act *their* age. When you do something unexpected, or something that makes them laugh, they see you as being more human and more like them. Just be careful that what you think is funny doesn't embarrass them. Topics that kids think are funny or gross are good. We're talking armpit farts, belching contests, singing made-up songs in weird voices, and snorting like pigs. Let loose! Your friends don't have to know.

There are times when you'll need to stop the silliness, like when things are getting out of hand or someone is getting hurt. Watching how you shift from silly to serious helps your kids learn how to do it. But it takes children much longer to make that shift. If they're getting too wild and need to settle down, say, *"It's time to be more serious and calm now."* Since it's harder for kids to switch modes, it helps to warn them. Just say, *"OK, we're going to have to settle down pretty soon."*

Make having fun together a top priority

When you and your kids don't have much fun together, being with friends can become much more important. Teenagers often have problems with adult authority figures who don't seem to understand kids. (We're sure some of you remember feeling that way.) If your kids see you as all up tight or critical, they'll start to see you as someone they can't relate to, or don't have much in common with. They may begin to identify with people who are more accepting of them (like peers, other adults, boy/girlfriends, and even gangs). During the teen years, relationships with friends are very important. But they can become most important if good attention is missing at home. Let go and goof off with your kids regularly. Successful parenting isn't all serious business!

Make bedtime a comforting time

The National Institute of Health recommends that bedtime include quiet time for children. Make it a nice, calm time to talk or read with your kids. Bedtime is a great time for talk time. Younger children usually love to be rocked while you are singing or reading to them. For older kids, give them a little back rub while talking about their day or reading. Tucking in your kids can be much more than covering them up. It can be a treasured time for both parents and kids (even for teenagers).

As we know from personal experience, it's hard to have a quiet, comfy bedtime when you're rushing around trying to get things done for tomorrow. So do chores and homework as early as possible in the day. When it's time for the kids to go to bed, try to put off things *you* need to get done so you can focus on bedtime. Avoid problem solving, confrontation or criticism also. Try to use a regular bedtime so they'll get enough sleep (and so you'll have time to yourself before your bedtime). By the way, television is the biggest obstacle to this. OK, note to self...turn it off!

Getting enough sleep is vital to a child's success and good mood. The table below shows the recommended number of hours of sleep for children of different ages. If your child's sleep is very different from this, ask your doctor or check out suggestions at www.sleepfoundation.org.

Age	Total sleep hours	Nighttime sleep hours	Comments
0 to 2 months	16 to 20	Any	Irregular sleep hours of course!
2 to 12 months	13 to 15	9-12 total (not all at once)	Gradually sleep longer at night, 3/4 of all babies sleep through the night at 9 months

1 to 3 years	12 to 14	11 to 12	At ~1½ years, most children nap once a day for 1-3 hours
3 to 5 years	12 to 14	11 to 13	Most don't nap after age 5
6 to 12 years	10 to 11	10 to 11	Most kids 10 and under have trouble sleeping sometimes
13 to 18 years	8.5 to 9.5	8.5 to 9.5	Tend to stay up late and sleep in—try to keep a regular schedule on the weekends

Have family meetings

This is a great way to reduce parenting stress. Once or twice a month, sit down with your kids to discuss what needs attention in your home and family. Don't always make it about solving problems, but it can be a great time to do so. You can establish what your family values, or plan fun events. Let your kids bring up things they want to talk about. Meetings should be distraction-free, and should be somewhat formal with a chairperson (that's you, Madam or Mr. Chairman), making sure everyone gets a turn to talk. Allow everyone to express his or her opinion. Don't allow anyone to be teased or criticized. Try to include a little of what everyone wants in decisions. Possible topics include:

- Chore schedules—everyone should have a job(s) in the house
- What to do for fun on the weekend, or planning a trip.
- Ways to help the kids do well in school.
- Someone's birthday or holiday coming up.
- What to do at bedtimes and mornings to make it easier.
- Volunteer activities or religious events.
- House rules—rules everyone is expected to follow without needing to be asked (see skill #4).

Eat meals together

Simply sitting down to eat at the same table helps keep families together. That's because it's a natural time to talk and relax together. Do it as often as you can. Don't use it as a time to solve problems, unless your kids want to. Turning off the TV helps you talk to your kids more.

The power of safe touch

All people need to be touched in safe, comfortable ways. Touch shows caring, and nurtures children. Studies with orphans and premature babies show that a lack of touch can lead to huge developmental and emotional problems, or even death. Touch your children daily: reach out and touch their arm as you say something, put your arm around them, rub their back, stroke their hair, or hold their hand. As they grow older, they may not be comfortable with this in public, so do as they wish. Touching children in sexual areas causes them great suffering and many long lasting problems, and is just simply wrong.

Teach your children how to ask for attention

Children often misbehave just to get our attention without realizing it. About 70 percent of misbehavior happens for this reason! After our son was born and we brought him home from the hospital, our three year old daughter was delighted to have her new brother. But not for long! Within a couple weeks, she was doing naughty things like poking her brother and breaking toys.

One day, when we noticed this, we asked her, *"Do you need a little attention?"* She began to cry and said, "I need attention." She came to us, we held her for just a minute, told her we loved her, and she was on her way playing again—nicely this time. After that, we taught her to ask for the same attention whenever she seemed frustrated or jealous. Within a week, those new naughty behaviors stopped! So even young children can learn to get the attention they need by simply asking, instead of misbehaving. Teach your children to say, *"I need a little attention,"* or *"I need to talk"* when frustrated or upset.

This is also a good way to stop a bad behavior situation. If your child is working up into a tantrum, asking if he or she needs attention gives your child a way out (something else to do besides screaming). Of course just because your child asks for attention and gets it doesn't mean she gets out of a consequence for bad behavior.

Now, let's move on to the skill of talking to your kids so they'll listen and learn.

Skill #2 PAY ATTENTION: Give your children attention in ways that work

- **Do things with your children**—they'll remember what you do together more than the things you give them.
- Teach what it means to be spoiled—unhappiness, trouble getting along.
- Kids may be getting **too much attention if**:
  They hardly ever need to wait for your attention, are over-scheduled with activities, are embarrassed by your involvement in their activities, or aren't learning to do things themselves; or if *you* don't have alone time each day, act like your needs aren't important, or use too much praise.
- Kids may be getting **too little attention if**:
  They're having behavior problems, you don't know what to say to them, you don't know their likes/dislikes/friends etc., they spend much more time with friends or media, or they don't seem to confide in you.
- **Special time, talk time and parent playtime** are three ways to give good attention. **Do two of these with each child on a regular basis. Don't cancel these activities as punishment.** But you may need to end them early for very disrespectful or bad behavior that continues.
  Don't ask too many questions, criticize, tease or make fun of your children. Let your child lead (talk about or do what is interesting or fun to him or her).
  For teens, sneak activities in if they resist. (Don't tell them ahead of time; just do it when they aren't busy.)
- **Special time**: age 3 and up, up to an hour, one to four times a month.
- **Talk time**: age 8 and up, about 10 minutes, every day possible.
  Start with a relaxed comment or question.
  Don't criticize or tease.
  Listen for feelings.
  Leave pauses (give them lots of time to respond).
  Repeat back what they say occasionally but don't interrupt.
  Don't ask too many questions.
  Talk about them and what they want to talk about.
  Occasionally talk about how people choose to be happy.
- **Parent playtime**: age 1 and up, about 10 minutes, every day possible.
- **Make having fun with your kids a top priority.**
- **Other important ways to give your children good attention:**
  be goofy, silly, and laugh with them; have relaxing bedtime routines and family meetings; touch them in nurturing ways; teach your kids to ask for attention when they need it so they don't have to act out to get it.

Skill #3

CALMLY TALK TO TEACH: How to lower your stress while teaching kids to listen, be respectful and build healthy self-esteem

It's every parent's dream to say, "When I talk, my kids listen." But not all dreams come true, even when you wish upon a star! Children hear many famous lines from parents, like "You're not listening again," "Why can't you listen?" and "Are you listening to me?" Well, apparently a child's brain translates these lines into, "Blah, blah-blah, blah-blah!" Kids don't listen any better after we say them. Many parents grumble that asking a child to do something over and over still doesn't get it done.

When you tell kids to do something, what you want is action! Well, how you talk to your kids makes all the difference. Here we'll give you proven ways to stay calm, and talk to your kids so that they will listen, understand and obey you more. We'll also give you ways to promote 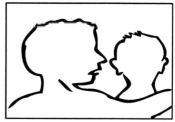 polite, respectful behavior while keeping a close relationship. How you talk to your kids also affects how they feel about you and themselves. We'll explain how self-esteem in children is often misunderstood, and how to make it healthy. This skill of calmly talking to teach helps you get what you want: a happy kid who wants to be good. Our symbol for this is a relaxed parent talking into a child's ear. First, let's start with a common stress in parenting...anger.

Controlling anger makes parenting easier and less stressful

Everyone gets mad, including the best parents. But anger can turn ugly for the family if parents are often angry, or if anger is expressed in unhealthy ways. **Unhealthy ways of expressing anger include** being aggressive, making fun of or putting people down, being sarcastic, or physically threatening others. Also, anytime you think, "Wow, I really over reacted" is probably a time when your anger was unhealthy. By **aggressive,** we mean dominating a child, as if he or she is the enemy. It means using hostile, shaming or threatening words, attacking a child's worth, throwing things, screaming at or hitting a child (or an object), shaking fists or snarling. Aggression and other unhealthy anger make parents lose their kids' respect and affection.

Unhealthy anger is a common cause of stress in parents. It's also linked to road rage, heart disease and physical abuse. It's one of the most common reasons that parenting gets harder over time. That's because, when it's expressed in the ways described in the last paragraph, it creates discipline problems. Please be aware that parents are more likely to express unhealthy anger when they've been drinking or getting high.

On the flip side, some parents deny their anger or bottle it up so no one else sees it. Not expressing anger enough can create other problems—depression, substance abuse and unpredictable outbursts that get you into trouble. Tears can be a healthy way to express anger, but get help if you find yourself crying often.

While it's natural to be angry, learning to express it in healthy ways does NOT come naturally—but we can learn it. Your kids will learn how to do it just by watching you. You know **you're expressing anger in a healthy way if** you can tell your kids why you're upset, and what they need to do about it, while staying calm and in control. This is a way to **be assertive** with your kids and stick up for yourself.

If you're very angry, count to ten before you say, *"I'm feeling very angry right now..."* Then talk it out. Say, *"I think..."* or *"I feel..."* instead of "You did..." Everyone needs an outlet for anger sometimes. Just be careful that your children don't become that outlet, just because they're around. Take a walk, run around the block, or hit a mattress, pillow or boxing bag instead of taking it out on your kids. Exercising, writing down your thoughts, prayer and meditation can also help you cool down.

Healthy anger can be a good motivator to change things that need to be changed. If you're angry with your child most days, it's a sign that you need to work on your relationship. Think about how much more energy it takes to get along with someone you're mad at (like an annoying co-worker, or a relative who drives you nuts). It may also be a sign that you need to work on discipline with your child. But all the discipline in the world won't force your child to behave well if either of you is so angry that you don't care about each other.

If you're not sure that your level of anger towards your children is controlled, try this fun little activity called, "**Mirror, mirror on the wall.**" Stand in front of a mirror. Close your eyes and try to imagine—no, not the evil queen from Sleeping Beauty—but a time when you were really upset at your kids. (Or do it while you're mad.) Now open your eyes and start speaking to the mirror as if you were talking to your child. So how do you look? Would you mind if friends or co-workers saw you look this way? It's a way to find out what your children see.

You already learned a way to stay calm by avoiding inaccurate thoughts and staying logical with skill #1. (Remember the thoughts-feelings-actions triangle? And stinking thinking?) Here are other ways to control your anger, and decrease stress.

Ways to stay cool with your kids

1. **Imagine that you are being videotaped**. How would you look on TV when you're dealing with the kids? (And we don't mean  your hairstyle.) How would you like your family, friends, and co-workers to see you act toward your children? How do you feel when you see other parents losing it with their kids? How embarrassing would it be to have a friend see you lose your cool? To help you act calmly, imagine that there's a news crew filming you.

2. **Pretend to be a robot.** Or, dance "the robot"! Pretending to be cool and unemotional like a robot can actually make you act that way. Talk like a robot or a computer voice if it helps. Or pretend to be your favorite vegetable! Saying, *"I'm as cool as a cucumber,"* can really make

you look like you are in charge in the face of disaster! Think to yourself, "A tiny kid is not going to make me lose my cool." Act it and believe it. Remaining calm, even if you are pretending, is good for you because it decreases stress. Remaining calm helps your children stay calm and behave better. Studies have clearly shown that when parents get worked up, their children get more worked up.

3. **Laugh to yourself!** Laughter and silliness are a big part of the best parent-child relationships. Sometimes nothing works better to keep a situation from spiraling out of control. Just be careful  that your child doesn't think you are laughing at him or her. If your child says, "Don't laugh at me," say *"I'm not laughing at you, but at what you're doing (or at the situation)."* Laughter is good medicine for stress too! Of course, if your children deserve a punishment, they shouldn't get out of it by amusing you. **You could also get their attention and lighten things up by talking with an accent**. Talk like a southern bell, a rapper, or an Irishman, *"Now lads and lassies, we have a wee bit of a problem..."* Then the kids might laugh and settle down!

4. **Whisper.** When your kids are acting out, whisper! Your children may quiet down just to hear what you're saying. Whisper in their ear for special effect. They may even whisper back.

5. **Take a parents' time out.** If you're having trouble staying calm, leave the room, or grab a towel and put your head under the faucet, or stand on your head, or go to the bathroom. OK, think of *something* to do that removes you from the situation for a couple minutes. Then go back when you're feeling calmer. Kids may not like it when you leave and may follow you. It's best to let another adult take over for a while. If this isn't possible, put your child in a safe place where he or she won't be scared, and lock yourself in a different room for a few minutes.

6. **Be upset with your child's *behavior* and not with your child.** Try to separate your frustration about how your child is acting from how you feel about him or her. If you remember that it's what your child is *doing* that is upsetting you, it can help keep you from over-reacting. You can love your child, but not really like his or her behavior right now!

7. **Keep it in perspective.** Lighten up! Your children's behavior isn't like dealing with terminal cancer, or losing everything you own in a hurricane. So don't let the kids' behavior affect you that much. Try not to take their behavior personally. It doesn't mean you're a bad parent.

8. **When you want to yell, sing!** When you've just about had it and feel like yelling, try singing instead. Instead of screaming, "You kids better get down here right now," try belting it out in your best opera singer voice. It can really get their attention, and make you feel better.

9. **Express anger in a healthy way.** Go back and read what healthy and unhealthy anger is like on page 54.

10. **Ask yourself, "Who am I really upset with?"** Maybe you're upset at someone else, like a spouse, boss, or the checkout clerk. Sometimes we take it out on our children. We act *as if* it were our kids we're upset with. When this happens, tell your kids, *"I'm in a bad mood because of something that happened today, and I'm a little cranky, but it isn't your fault."* Kids as young as 4 can understand this, and they might behave to try to help.

11. **Ask yourself, "What else am I feeling?"** When you're mad about something, there's often another feeling that is underneath the anger. People may act mad when they're really feeling unappreciated, scared, embarrassed, ashamed, sick or uncomfortable.

Talk to Your Kids in Ways That Teach Them:
The Talk to Teach Guidelines

So now that we've covered the "calmly" part of this skill, we'll explain the "talk to teach" part. Do you ever wonder why you have to tell kids things over and over? Well, do we have good news for you! There are ways to talk to your kids that help them understand and obey the first time. These talk to teach guidelines are based on what therapists and research have shown to work best. They have been used by professionals and taught to parents for many years. Using them helps kids *want* to behave and builds their self-esteem.

Some readers may believe that no matter how they say things, their kids better just obey, or else! But that approach doesn't get good, long lasting results. In fact, it prevents a close relationship with kids who want to do what is right, often without being asked.

Here are the "talk to teach" guidelines to use with your kids. You may already be using many of these. Start with the two or three that make the most sense to you, or are most similar to what you're doing now. As you feel comfortable with those, pick out a few more to try. We hope you'll use these so often that they become habit and feel natural to you. The more natural they feel, the more often you'll use them when you're stressed out or upset.

It would be very tough to use all these skills all the time, so it's a good thing you don't need to! Just use them as often as you can. Each guideline has a name, a reason or explanation, and examples of using it. **The first ones explain how to tell your kids to do something.** The rest help you build their self-esteem and encourage respectful behavior.

Be direct and specific about what you want.	When it's important that your child do something, don't *ask* him to do it; *tell* him to do it, and be specific about what it is he needs to do.	Say *"Josh, please take out the trash"* instead of "Would you take out the trash for me?"

There are two ways to tell your kids do something.

Direct commands work best. They make it very clear that you want your child to do something for you. *"Please hang up your coat," "Sit down in your chair,"* and *"Tess, please tell Sammy to come home for lunch,"* are all examples. Each one is very clear about what needs to be done and by whom. Adding *"please"* and your child's name make your requests work even better.

Roundabout requests, on the other hand make it seem like your child has a choice to do it or not. These beat-around-the-bush requests are often in the form of a question. Examples are "Would you like to sit down so we can eat?" "I need someone to call Sammy home for lunch," and "Would you hang up your coat?" These suggest that your child has permission to say "no." or to just not do it. If you need kids to do something, don't give them a choice to obey, and don't beat around the bush.

Besides being direct, **tell your child specifically what you want.** If you had a dime for every time you heard these fuzzy commands from parents, you'd be rich: "Watch it," "Knock it off," "Quit it," "You're asking for it," and the famous, "Don't make me come back there!" While these may make complete sense to us, kids may not have a clue what they mean. When you say, "Stop it," they may think, "Stop *what?*" When you say, "Act your age," they may think "How do I act my age?" As many as one third of naughty behaviors can be avoided if we just make ourselves clearer about what we want. So be specific!

Tell them what to do, instead of what NOT to do.	Say what you want them to do instead of what to *stop* doing. This teaches good behavior faster.	Instead of, "Stop screaming and running," say *"Use your inside voice and walk."* Instead of, "Don't be home late again", say *"I expect you home by ten o'clock."*

This teaches children what to do instead of misbehaving. Parents usually tell their children what *not* to do or what to *stop* doing, rather than what to do. For example, let's say you can't hear the car radio because your kids are being loud. You're trying to hear a breaking news story and tell the kids to "stop talking" (what to stop doing). The kids are quiet for a few moments and then start to play with a beeping toy. They didn't talk, but thought that playing was OK. Well, you still can't hear the radio! If you had said what to do instead, *"I need to hear this news so please be quiet for a few minutes,"* you would have been up on world events.

At first, it's easier to know what you want the kids to stop doing, and harder to think of what they can do instead. **Try telling your kids to do something that they can't do at the same time that they're behaving badly.** For example, if she's banging toys on a table, instead of saying, "Stop banging the toys," say *"Please be gentle with the toys."* If your child is popping wheelies on her bike, instead of saying "Stop popping wheelies," say *"Please keep your front tire on the ground."* If your son is insulting your younger daughter, instead of saying, "Stop insulting your sister," say *"Apologize to your sister right now. Please talk respectfully to her."*

Keep it simple.	Break down jobs into a series of smaller ones.	Instead of, "Clean up the family room," say *"Put the books on the shelf and then vacuum the floor."*

Even good kids will act out if they are told to do things they don't think they can do. When a job seems too big, people get anxious. To avoid this, break tasks down into parts. For example, **children 5 and under** may need to be given one task at a time when cleaning their rooms. First say, *"Pick up your books and put them on the shelf."* After that's done, say *"Put your dolls away."* Then say, *"Find your shoes."*

Six year olds can usually complete two instructions at a time. For example, *"Please put your books away and pick up your toys."* **Children 11 and older** can usually follow three different instructions at once. But with a big job, like cleaning a room, they may need directions. *("Please clean your room—and that includes your closet, under your bed and vacuuming.")*

Use polite words.	Say words like *please, excuse me,* and *thank you* to your kids so they'll do the same to you and others.	*"Please pick up your colors and put them away."*

Many parents naturally do this, so we might be preachin' to the choir on this one. When you use good manners, it teaches kids to do the same, since they learn from watching you. Do it even if they are misbehaving. Studies show that asking kids politely actually improves how often they obey. That means "please" really is a magic word!

Expect kids to be polite to you, other adults, and yes, even siblings. No, they won't be polite all the time. But take notice of opportunities to be polite that they've missed, and mention it to them. For younger children, be very specific. For example, say, *"When you want me to get you some juice, you need to say, 'May I have juice please?' Now go ahead and say that for me."* Older children may need reminders. *("If you want me to wash your uniform before school tomorrow, how do you ask politely?")*

Have practice sessions to teach social skills. Make it a little game by calling your children on the phone or coming to your own door, so they can practice answering the call or greeting you at the door. Tell them being polite makes them appear confident and nice. It will help them get places. People who use polite words during an interview are much more likely to get the job! Here are the ages by which you can expect children to learn these social skills:

- **By age 5:** Saying "please," "sorry," "I love you," "excuse me," "good night," "thank you," and "good bye."
- **By age 12:** When being introduced to an adult, 12 year olds should be able to say, "Hi, it's nice to meet you" while making eye contact and shaking hands. They should sometimes compliment others. ("You drew a nice picture," or "You look pretty, Mom," or "That was nice of you, Dad.") Telephone manners should include, "No he isn't home. Can I take a message?" and "I need to get off the phone right now. Can I call you back?"
- **By age 16:** Teens this age should be able to carry on a conversation with someone about something that person is interested in. ("How was your day?" or "How are your piano lessons going?") They also should be able to recognize when others need help and offer it. ("What can I do to help?" or "What can I do next?")

Use a calm voice.	Say what to do using a calm voice so your child will be more likely to stay calm and listen.	Quietly say, *"You are arguing with me. I need you to do what I said."*

This helps you and your children stay in control. Some children, especially those with spirited temperaments, are more likely to get worked up when *you* get worked up. And some kids like to see how mad they can get mom or dad. Don't let them get your goat!

Give a reason.	Say why they need to do something *before* you tell them what to do. This decreases arguing and increases obeying.	*"We have to leave for school, so please put on your shoes and coat."*

Kids are much more likely to do what you want when they know *why* they're doing it. Just like adults, they like to feel they aren't being ordered around just for the heck of it. Providing a reason also gives you a chance to check that there really *is* a good reason for telling your kids to do something. It also makes your kids more likely to do something again without being asked (because they know why they should).

Telling children the reason first, *before* saying what to do, works best. *"We need to leave for church soon—please turn off the TV,"* works better than "Please turn off the TV—we need to leave for church." That's because the last thing they hear is what they need to do.

Keep the reason short and sweet. If it's too long, your kids will stop listening, or you'll give them more information to argue with. We don't need that! Here are examples of phrases to use:

- *I don't want you to get hurt, so please…*
- *We need to be on time, please…*
- *I don't want you to ever get lost, so please…*
- *I don't want you to get sick, so …*
- *It makes the housework easier if …*
- *You need to help the family too, so…*
- *I've worked hard, am tired and need you to…*
- *It will give us more time to play if …*
- *I don't have time, so please help…*
- *We both have chores today, so…*
- *Because I want to teach you how…*
- *Because it isn't good for the family…*
- and the famous, *You could put an eye out with that!*

(Just kidding on the last one.)

Giving a reason won't totally stop your kids from **arguing**, but it helps. When they argue, just repeat the command in a calm but firm tone. Look them in the eye, and lay a hand on a shoulder. If you can't or forget to give a reason first, or if your kids look confused or continue to argue, say *"I'll explain why after you're done."* They may do it just to find out the reason. Never fear—we'll have more tips for dealing with arguing later.

You may be thinking, "Why should I have to explain? They should just do it because I said so." While that may be true, there is usually a very good reason why you need your kids to do what you say. Actually, although it is commonly said, one of the worst reasons you can give a child is, "Because I said so." This puts your child down and sets up future power struggles with you—no thanks! No matter how frustrated you are, try not to say this often. Instead, say, *"Because I need you to."* Even *"I feel upset with you right now, so I'll tell you why you're doing this later"* is better.

Whenever possible, give your kids real choices.	Choices increase obedience, help develop decision-making skills and responsibility.	*"Do you want to set the table or clear it off?"* or *"We need to do chores today. Which do you want to do first, clean your room or mow the lawn?"*

Everyone likes to have choices. Choices are a key ingredient of happiness, and happier kids behave better. Some people agonize over a choice, or wait until someone else makes it for them. So making choices is an important skill to learn. Giving kids choices helps them practice.

Giving **a real choice is** when you let your kids decide between two things that they would want about the same. Saying, "You can either go to the arcade or clean the house" isn't a real choice (since nobody in their right mind would pick cleaning). *"You can go to the arcade or the movie"* and *"You can help me clean the kitchen or the garage"* are offers of real choices.

You may be thinking, wait a minute—a previous guideline said to be direct; don't give them a choice as to whether or not to obey! Hey, you were paying attention—you rock! It *is* best not to give a choice when you are telling them to do one specific thing. But here we are talking about giving them a choice of a couple things you want done. The choice you are giving is, either do one or the other, but do one of them.

A common complaint of parents is that their children don't take **responsibility**. Giving kids real choices helps them develop responsibility. That's because when kids make a choice, they learn that what happens is a result of their decision. Since it's their decision, they are responsible for what happens next. Letting kids choose what to do and letting them do it themselves shows them that they are competent at doing that thing. It's very important that kids feel they can accomplish things. If you ask them to do something new, teach them how to do it first. Then avoid criticizing how well they did it, even if you could have done it better. This helps build their self-confidence, and with confidence they'll take on more responsibility.

Give them specific praise.	Saying why you are pleased at what they did encourages kids to do it again.	*"Thanks for getting ready so fast. Now I won't be late."*

When your children do what you want, praise them almost every time. Praise early and often. There are two kinds of praise. **General praise** is saying things like *"That's great,"* *"I'm proud of you,"* or *"Nice job."* **Specific praise** is when you make it very clear **why** you are pleased, emphasizing what your child did. *"You did a great job cleaning the kitchen! You even did the floor without being asked. Thank you."* Or *"Thank you for emptying the dishwasher and not forgetting."*

Praise helps kids feel better about themselves and about you. It shows that you bothered to recognize good work, and that your kids *can* do something right. General praise says that you care about and appreciate them. Specific praise encourages them to do good things again. Saying things like, *"You're such a big girl, you got ready for bed all by yourself,"* or *"Thanks for filling the car up with gas after you used it. That really helps when I'm rushing to work in the morning"* is worth the price of gold. Praise is a big deposit into your relationship savings account. Cha-ching!

Specific praise is really important for older kids. If you tell your teen, "You're a great kid" she might think, "Yah, right" or "Why?" If you say, *"You're a great kid. I can count on you to take care of your younger sister and keep her safe,"* then she knows why you think she's great and will believe you.

And while it's best to pour on the praise when kids are little, you'll want to **back off some when they're teens**. Teens will get annoyed with constant attention to what they're doing and need to learn to be self-motivated. Help motivate them by asking little questions when they succeed. *"Great job—how did you ever get an A on that?"* *"Wow, that's awesome how you could put that together. How did you figure it out?"* *"I hope you feel proud of yourself."*

Praise their effort more than the result. Success and good outcomes come from great effort. This is also a key to **motivation.** Some kids are naturally able to do something well without trying hard. If those kids are praised only for things that come easily to them, they may not be motivated to work on things that are harder for them. Also, if kids are praised only when they do well, they'll be afraid to try new things. Praising the effort may mean praising them for how hard you saw them study, even if they didn't get an A. Or it may mean praising them for practicing, not for winning the competition.

So, let your children know that it's how hard they try that is really important. Instead of saying "Fantastic job, you got an A in algebra," say, *"Fantastic job, doing homework and studying hard really paid off. You got an A!"* Instead of saying, "Way to go—you won!" say, *"Way to go, you worked hard, played good defense, and scored two goals."* Saying, *"I like how hard you tried. I bet you can do other things you want if you try"* motivates better than, *"Wow you did great. I bet you'll win again."* This doesn't mean you can't celebrate successes or wins—that's just plain fun.

Kids need your support when they lose or can't accomplish things even after trying hard. Tell them if they keep learning and trying, things will most likely get better. This encourages them and doesn't minimize their pain. Telling them to "just try harder" is like rubbing salt on the wound when they feel they did their best and failed anyway. If they don't seem motivated even with praise for their efforts, sometimes giving rewards can help.

Caution: Praise can go overboard without a lifeboat (see skill #5).

Catch them being good.	Notice good behavior and reward it to make it happen more often.	Your son is helping his sister, even though you didn't ask. Say, *"Wow, thanks for helping. What a great brother."*

⭐ **Any behavior that you pay a lot of attention to (whether naughty or nice) will happen more often.** It's natural to focus on all the bad stuff kids do, and forget to pay attention to what they do right. Plus, some kids don't like to obey unless they get something good out of it—like praise. Try to catch any little good thing they do, and reward them with praise, or something else.

You aren't going to get everything you want from your kids at first, (OK—or ever), so praise them for the part they *did* do, and leave out criticism for the part they *didn't* do right. Clap for young children, and give high fives, pats on the back and hugs for all kids. You can say things like, *"I like how you did that," "That was so cool,"* or *"You're such a good kid—you did the right thing."*

Some of you may be thinking that your children do nothing right and wonder how you can possibly catch them being good. Using words like *nothing, never,* or *always* are clear signs of stinkin' thinkin'. (And we don't like to stink!) All kids do *some things* right, even if they are just little things surrounded by bad things. Sometimes we have to start off by praising the little good things before the bigger good things start happening. Thank your teenager for turning off his radio at night, your 8 year old for taking a shower without being asked, or your 4 year old for helping you to unbuckle his car seat. You could praise kids for getting along, learning in school, or helping with something. In general, kids *do* want to please their parents. Let them know that they please you every chance you get, especially if you're having trouble.

Please note: If your child is used to getting attention by acting naughty, expect his or her behavior to get worse before it gets better when using praise. Some kids are so used to being criticized that they actually feel uncomfortable with praise at first. Don't let this keep you from praising—it'll get better.

Compliment your kids.	This help kids feel better and behave better.	*"You're really fun to be around."*

While praise is given right after a child has done something good, compliments tell your kids that you approve of who they are any old time. Compliments make a child feel loved and special.

Private compliments—Compliment your children in private almost every day. You don't need a special moment—anytime will do. Look them in the eye or touch their shoulder when you compliment them. When they believe you are sincere, their faces will shine. You will know that it's working when they start complimenting you! Examples are:

- *I really missed you today.*
- *I'm so lucky to have you for my child.*
- *I'm proud of what a nice kid you are.*
- *I love you so much.*
- *I am so glad we're together today.*
- *You're a nice person.*
- *You're so funny.*
- *Thank you for being so wonderful.*
- *You are very caring to your brother.*

Public compliments—Your children will know that your praise is real when they hear you tell other people. When they do something good like creating a great school project, helping someone, or peeing in the toilet for the first time, tell somebody! Let your kids hear you brag about them when you call a relative or friend to share the news.

Adolescents may act confused when you praise them in public—shocking news, we know! They may say something like, "I don't know what all the fuss is about." Don't let that stop you from sharing their accomplishments—they still need the positive attention. If your child isn't there to hear you when you tell others, tell him about it later (*"I saw Jordan's mom in the store and told her about the birthday card you made for me. She thought that was so neat."*) However, if your child says that sharing her good qualities or accomplishments with others will be embarrassing, don't do it.

Be respectful.	Be sensitive to your children's needs, and listen to their opinions without putting them down.	*"That is an interesting way to think about that."*

Just like Aretha Franklin when she sings, "All I'm askin' is for a little respect," parents need respect from kids. Well, parents have respectful children if those children are shown respect. Being respectful means talking politely to them, admiring their accomplishments or efforts, appreciating them, and being sensitive to their needs. It means listening to their concerns, and not putting them down. If you don't agree with what they are saying, say so and give a reason. But don't criticize, tease or belittle them for their opinions, no matter how ridiculous they may be. Kids can do and say really silly things when they're upset. Sometimes it's hard not to laugh at what they think. But having their opinions laughed at feels like criticism and disrespect to kids, so avoid doing it.

Say **"I feel…"** and **"I think…"**	This helps kids understand how you feel and what you need. It can prevent misbehavior and develop emotional intelligence.	*"I feel upset when you call me that,"* or, *"I think it's time we start acting more serious,"* instead of, "Cut it out, you're acting too wild."

Ladies and gentlemen, your attention please! Learning this part can save you and your kids a lot of trouble. Saying *"I feel …"* or *"I think …"* clearly tells others your feelings or opinions. Doing this **can prevent arguments** and **make your kids less defensive**. That's because it's hard to argue with someone's feelings or thoughts, since they are part of that person. Telling your child, *"I feel upset when you say I'm clueless"* is less likely to turn into an argument than saying, "You make me mad when you say I'm clueless." (Your child can't argue with you and say, "No, you don't feel upset.") Saying, *"I feel very upset with you right now, and I need time before I can talk to you,"* also gives you time to chill and think about things. Telling your son, *"I think it's time to go to bed"* will make him less defensive than saying, "Boy, are you tired and cranky!"

"*I can see why you'd think that, but I THINK …*"

In addition, saying *"I think…"* gives you **a way to challenge unhealthy thoughts in your child**. While it doesn't help to argue with feelings or thoughts, you can help your child by gently challenging those that can get him into trouble. Sometimes kids confuse feelings with thoughts. For instance, people may not "feel" that it's right to shoot someone to prove a point, but they can incorrectly "think" it is.

To challenge unhealthy thoughts, simply say, *"Well, I think..."* and tell them *your* thoughts. Avoid putting them down, and just say what you think as an adult (or as a parent). Hint that they may change their mind later. *"I think you'll find... as you get older."*

When you say, *"I feel...,"* you **teach your child to use words instead of misbehaving.** It shows kids a good way to handle being mad. It was much better to have our 4 year old son say, "I feel very upset—very, very, very upset! I'll be upset all day and all night!" than to have him throw something. When you describe bad behaviors with feeling words, kids can learn to say those words instead of acting out. For example, when your daughter yells because she can't have something, try saying, *"You feel upset because you can't have the squirt gun, don't you?"* After a while, she may say, "I'm so mad," instead of screaming.

Teaching kids to say "I feel" **helps them start to solve a problem** by recognizing their feelings. Teach your kids some words in Appendix B for how people feel. Then when your child seems to have a problem, say, *"I think you are feeling___"* or *"It seems like you are feeling___"* (fill in the blanks). The child may not agree with your word, and that's okay. It just gives you a starting point to talk about what is upsetting him or her, and to show you care. This is part of boosting emotional intelligence.

It's good for kids to learn that what they do can hurt other people's feelings, just like their own feelings can get hurt. **You can share hurt feelings with your children** by saying *"I feel...,"* but just don't make it extreme. Be as specific as possible about what they did that hurt your feelings, and try to use a calm voice. You can ask for an apology if they don't offer one. Avoid overreactions like those that come from stinky thoughts, which can make your children fail to understand how you feel. After you discuss hurt feelings, let it go. If you keep bringing it up, your children will tune you out. Pick and choose when to share hurt feelings, so you aren't doing it too often.

Say you're sorry sometimes.	This shows that you're not perfect either and that you care. It teaches your kids to apologize, and helps them learn responsibility.	*"I'm sorry I over-reacted. I need to work on that." "I'm sorry you're sick and will miss the dance."*

Saying *"sorry"* lets your kids know that it's alright to take responsibility for mistakes. Then you can expect your kids to say they're sorry to you and others. Show your child how by saying what you're sorry about and what you'll do to try to avoid making the same mistake again. *"I'm sorry I yelled at you. I should have listened instead. Do you want to talk now?"* or *"I'm really sorry I missed your concert—I got tied up in traffic. I'll try to leave work earlier next time."*

When people say "I'm sorry" after a mistake, others are more forgiving and less angry. Just like adults, kids are more willing to work things out if they feel like they're not the only ones who have done something wrong. Saying *"I'm sorry"* when they're disappointed shows that you care, and opens the door to talking.

Correct them instead of criticizing.	Criticism hurts self-esteem and relationships. Corrections help kids listen and learn what to do better.	*"Pretty good job on the test. You can do even better next time if you recheck answers before handing it in."*

Nobody likes to be "dissed," or criticized. Adults do better when they don't feel criticized, and so do kids. Limiting criticism helps build self-esteem and helps kids listen and obey.

So how do you tell them that they're doing things wrong without criticizing? The difference between correcting and criticizing is in how the message is delivered. **Criticism** is often given out of frustration or anger. It's often meant to embarrass or shame a child into doing something differently. Sarcasm, threats, put downs, whining and yelling are all ways to criticize. **Correcting** is done in a patient, concerned way. It's given to teach a child how to do something differently. The words in a criticism and correction may be similar, but it's how they are said that matters.

How to correct instead of criticize

Balance every negative point with a positive point:
"One thing I liked about what you did is _____ (positive point);
one thing I would like for you to work on is _____ (negative point)."

Positive Point	Negative Point
It was great that you came home before your curfew—thank you.	But you weren't supposed to leave the house until after your homework was done. It isn't.
Your backstroke is looking good. Your arms were really smooth in the water. I'm so glad you like to swim.	One thing you can work on next week is your flip turn. Practice trying to get more push off the wall.
Thank you for doing such a great job on your room. You picked up, and even cleaned under your bed!	Now let's see if you can keep your room this clean for a few days.
What a big boy going pee all by yourself!	I bet next time you'll work real hard to get your pee in the toilet!

Carefully pick corrections and give just one at a time. Even though Lord knows there may be plenty to pick from, try to limit yourself to only the most important ONE thing to correct at a time. Try to say just one positive and one negative thing. Then your kids won't see you as overly picky or too critical. Kids who think their parents are very critical stop listening and caring.

When you correct older children, approach it as if you are solving a problem. For example, your daughter failed her math test because she thought it would be easier. You could correct by saying, *"I'm really glad that you told me about this bad grade—thank you (positive point). Now you need to study harder for the next one or I'll take the internet away (negative)."*

Or you could use the correction to help her find ways to do better. *"I'm really glad that you told me about this bad grade—thank you. Now what are you going to do differently to make sure this doesn't happen again?"* Just correct one thing at a time (that is, forget the sloppy penmanship or anything else that needs correction; just focus on what will get a better grade on the next test).

Self-esteem in Children

This can be a confusing topic for parents. Simply put, self-esteem is feeling worthy and loved as a person. It means feeling good about oneself. Children who feel valued and loved by their parents, no matter what they can or can't accomplish, have good, healthy self-esteem. In other words, no matter what their grades, personalities, talents, and sports abilities, these kids feel loved and valued. Kids with healthy self-esteem also feel capable of doing many different things, but don't think they have to be the best at something to feel good about themselves.

On the other hand, good self-esteem is NOT being arrogant, or feeling superior (which is unhealthy). Healthy self-esteem doesn't lead people to expect special treatment in life, or to believe that they are above correction, learning, working, helping others and following rules.

What does self-esteem do for children?

It is linked with being happy and successful. It gives kids a sense of belonging to the family and to society, which helps them resist unhealthy and dangerous influences. Kids with good self-esteem are more involved in extracurricular activities and do better in relationships and in school. They are better able to take care of themselves as adults.

But, keep in mind that some children compensate for poor self-esteem by being overly involved in activities, trying to be popular and pushing themselves for the highest possible grades. These kids may strive to feel better about themselves through high performance, and may feel badly about themselves when they fail at something (which we all do).

How does a child get good self-esteem?

Self-esteem has to come from within a person, but parents can help their children gain healthy levels by doing certain things. Here are recommended do's and don'ts.

1. **Help your kids find success in a few activities and in school**, but not by doing things for them that they should be doing themselves. Just give them opportunities, assistance and encouragement.
2. Help them **set realistic expectations** for how well they perform, and challenge stinkin' thinkin' (such as saying, "I'm no good"). Recognize their efforts more than how well they perform (say good things when they seem to be trying hard, even when they don't win or get an "A"). Avoid pressuring them to do something better when

they really aren't able to. Allow them to experience disappointment and support them through it. Talk about the value of enjoying and sharing a talent or activity, even though others are better at it.

3. **Help them recognize their strengths, abilities and talents** (even little things), but don't pretend they're good at everything. This gives kids a chance to excel at things they are good at, and feel successful. *"That was nice of you to talk to that kid. You're good at making people feel comfortable.""You figured out how that goes together! You're good at that sort of thing."*

4. **Expect and help them to learn life skills**, such as how to behave, solve problems and get along with others. Children who learn these things feel better about themselves.

5. **Show interest** in your children's lives and activities.

6. **Show them that you care** about and love them using pleasant words and nurturing touch every day, no matter how they behave or perform. Show them that you value them just because they are yours. Be glad to see them every morning and evening with hugs and greetings *("Good morning, how'd you sleep?" "I'm so glad you're my son/daughter")*. What's corny to adults isn't to kids!

7. Get kids involved in **supervised activities** to give them a sense of accomplishment and acceptance in desirable peer groups.

8. **Use praise wisely**— notice when your child accomplishes something (even little things) and tell them specifically what they did well, or what you liked. *"You make me laugh. You're fun to be around.""How'd you remember that? I didn't. Good job."* But don't be insincere or make stuff up that they won't believe.

9. **Don't make fun of, tease, criticize or put your kids down about their behavior or their tastes**, or not being able to do things as well as you can. But do go ahead and correct bad behaviors and unhealthy thoughts using your *7 Skills*. Show concern and correct them rather than criticize them.

10. Caution! Being permissive and giving children most all things and privileges they want doesn't support healthy self-esteem, but just spoils them. On the other hand, being very controlling without affection also tears down a child's self-esteem.

Now that you're a regular guru of relationship building, we're ready to start the discipline skills!

Skill #3 CALMLY TALK TO TEACH: Lower your stress while teaching kids to listen, be respectful and build self-esteem

Keep anger under control for best parenting results:

- **Be assertive**—calmly tell your kids that you are feeling angry, and what they need to do about it.
- Imagine that **you're on TV**.
- **Pretend to be a robot** or your favorite vegetable.
- **Laugh!**   **Whisper** to your kids.   **Take a parent's time out**.
- **Ask yourself,** "Who am I really upset with?" "What else am I feeling?"
- Get some **perspective**—probably nobody's dying.
- **Be upset with your child's** *behavior* and not with your child.
- When you want to yell, **sing!**
- Take a walk; hit a mattress, pillow or boxing bag.
- Exercise, pray and/ or meditate, write your feelings down.
- Check your thoughts about your kids to avoid over-reactions.

Use the Talk to Teach Guidelines:

- **Be direct and specific** when you tell them to do something. Don't ask if they'd like to, or use roundabout requests (somebody needs to…).
- **Tell them what to do, instead of what NOT to do.**
- **Keep it simple**—break jobs down into parts.
- **Be polite** and **use a calm, neutral voice** even if you have to fake it.
- **Give your kids real choices**—let them decide between two things that they would want to do about equally.
- **Give a reason why** you want it done **first**—keep it short and sweet.
- **Give specific praise** often—make it clear why you like what they did.
- **Praise the effort** they give more than the result.
- **Catch them being good** and reward it.

Build their self-esteem and respectful behavior:

- **Compliment your kids** in public and private.
- **Say,** *"I feel…"* **and** *"I think…"* to avoid arguments. Teach your kids to tell you their thoughts and feelings instead of acting out.
- **Say you're sorry** when you mess up or if they are hurting.
- **Correct instead of criticize** in a concerned way to teach how to do something differently. Give one positive with one negative point. *"One thing I liked about what you did is __; one thing I'd like for you to work on is __."* Pick and choose corrections and give one at a time.
- **Show their worth** every day with positive words and affection.
- **Help them do well in school.**
- **Don't expect them to do things as well as you can**.
- **Be respectful**–don't tease or put them down.

Skill #4

SEIZE CONTROL: How to set limits on what they do, choose your battles, and help them develop good character

The biggest struggle for parents can be getting kids to obey and behave. Different challenges come up as they grow from little tykes to teenyboppers. Why is it that some kids seem to know right from wrong, while others get into trouble? And why do some parents seem to let their kids do anything, and others almost constantly order their kids around? This all has to do with how parents set limits.

The skill of limit setting will help you seize control of how your kids behave. Think of it as reaching for and holding your child's hand—which is this skill's symbol. Here we'll spell out how you can seize control of your children's behavior in ways that develop their own self-control and character.

A limit is basically how you want your child to behave

It's anything that you want your child to do ("brush your teeth every night"), or not do ("no hitting"). **It's a rule** that you set. Children need limits just about as much as they need food and clothing. Oh really? Well, proper clothing and food are essential for physical health, and limits on their behavior are essential for their psychological health— and yours!

Setting limits is the first step in fixing and preventing behavior problems. It's also the way parents develop a child's character. The methods in this chapter are recommended only for children 3 years and older. For infants and toddlers, please see chapter eight instead.

Setting limits helps parents raise good, happy kids

Children who aren't given proper limits miss out on an important part of childhood. That's because limits help make a child's world safe, structured and predictable. The more predictable their lives, the less stressed they are. Kids who are less stressed behave better and are happier. To feel secure and happy, children also need to feel that their parents have control.

One of the cruel facts of parenting is that while all children need, and often *want* limits, they will usually resist them. We'll give you ways to set limits to help your kids accept them. We'll help you deal with arguing and debating, and show you how to choose your battles to decrease your stress.

How to Decide What Behavior Limits to Set

Many parents wonder if they're setting the right limits for their children. What should they allow and not allow their kids to do? What should they insist that their kids do? We'll give you a tool to help you decide what you think is right. But first, let's see what happens when you set limits that are too hard, too soft, or just right. Yes— it's just like when Goldilocks tries all the bears' chairs to find the best fit.

What happens when you set limits that are too hard?

If children think limits are too hard to follow, or if there are just **too many**, they may feel like they can't do anything right. They may think that parents care more about orderliness and control than about them. Then they may act out more and rebel.

Limits that are **too hard to meet** can lead to trouble making choices, or anxiety about not succeeding. Too many limits (or **very rigid ones**) can also result in power struggles and irresponsibility as children get older. Parents who have a knee-jerk reaction to just say "no" to their kids will find that their children stop asking and start doing whatever they want.

What about limits that are too soft or not enforced?

It's also possible for parents to be too lax with their limits. Children who don't get enough limits feel like no one really cares about them (and they may be right). If taken too far, parents who don't set enough limits are guilty of neglect. Kids with **too few** limits have trouble behaving and becoming responsible adults. Parents can also be too soft by telling children to do something and not finding out if they actually did it. That's not limit setting…it's wasting time or lecturing. If you set a limit, you need to make sure your children follow it.

It's common for two parents to disagree about limits or change their limits because they hit roadblocks. If your limits become moving targets that change often, you are making the **most common mistake of parenting: inconsistency.** We're all inconsistent sometimes, but successful parents minimize it. Don't fret—we'll help you do that in skill # 5.

How to know if your limits aren't too hard or too soft, but just right

Setting good behavior limits consistently is easier if you just remember this: **P.S. I'M HELPING.** This is your handy-dandy limit tester we created just for you! The letters help you remember the five good reasons to set limits. If you know why a limit should be set, you'll set it and enforce it more consistently. P.S. I'M HELPING also reflects the attitude that limit setting should have. It says that you aren't setting limits to be mean, but to teach, protect and support your kids. If a behavior isn't found in P.S. I'M HELPING, then it probably doesn't need to be limited, and you can let it go without having to deal with it.

P.S. I'M HELPING -
the five good reasons to set a limit on a behavior:

1. **Personal Safety**: This behavior could affect the health or well being of your child or others.
2. **Important Morals and Manners**: This behavior violates your moral values, good manners, community laws or rights of others, or interferes with family functioning.
3. **How Emotional**: This behavior brings out an emotional reaction from you—you get very angry, frustrated, or sad, for example.
4. **Long-term Problem**: This behavior might still be affecting your lives one year from now.
5. **I'm Not Going there**: You avoid trying to deal with this behavior because your kids get really upset when you do.

If any of these are true about something your kids did or might do, chances are that you need to set a limit on that behavior.

Personal Safety in P.S. I'M HELPING

If a behavior will negatively affect the health, safety and well-being of your child or someone else, you need to set a limit on it. Well-being includes your child's physical development, emotional health and self-esteem. Examples would be to limit aggression, driving, video games, television, drugs, alcohol, and unsupervised time with other kids.

Normal kids will disagree with parents about whether something is safe. You, as their parent, are better able to make that decision—so go ahead and do so. Remember to consider the most likely outcome (not just the worst-case scenario) when deciding if something is safe. If your 17 year old wants to drive her little brother a few blocks to get ice cream, they'll probably be alright. But, you'd say no to riding in the back of a moving truck, since even a minor accident could be deadly.

Important Morals and Manners in P.S. I'M HELPING

Limit behaviors that violate your moral values, good manners, the rights of others, laws, or family functioning. When you think of morals and manners, think of how you want your kids to act with other people, and of the things you expect them to do for others, including the **family**.

As far as **morals** go, you can avoid problems by regularly discussing your family's moral beliefs with your children. Family meetings are good times to do this. That works better than to spring your beliefs on your children when they want to do something that you don't agree with. Some of your children's friends will have parents that allow their kids to do things that you don't think are alright. And for kids (especially teens), normal is whatever their peers are doing. So not letting your children do what most of their peers are doing can cause conflict. Still try to decide what *you* think is best, and compromise when you safely can.

Manners include showing respect to parents and other adults, being helpful and not acting rudely. Taking someone else's possession (such as a sister's toy) without permission is not showing good manners. Interrupting adults, including parents, when they're talking is not showing good manners. Bad manners can be fixed by setting a limit.

Teaching good moral behavior and manners at home can help your children act similarly outside your home. A child who helps the family (by doing chores, or giving up a night out to take care of a sick family member), will be more likely to help others in the community as an adult.

<u>H</u>ow <u>E</u>motional in P.S. I'M HELPING

How upset do you get when your kids do certain things? If something sets you off, it needs to be limited. These are behaviors that are hurtful or disrespectful, or that simply **push your buttons**. For example, your son keeps telling you, "Just chill out" when you ask him about school lately. It's starting to really annoy you and you find yourself not wanting to talk to him or exploding with anger when he says it. Setting a limit on it helps you stay calm, decreases your stress and keeps you talking to your son.

On the other hand, if stinking thinking or other inaccurate thoughts are giving you emotional reactions, your children's behaviors may not be the problem. Also, don't waste energy taking your children's behaviors or opinions personally. If you forgot how to know if stinking thinking is creating the badness, review page 18.

<u>L</u>ong-term <u>P</u>roblem in P.S. I'M HELPING

Behaviors that could still be affecting your child's life or the family one year from now need to be limited. These include things that draw her away from the family, drop her grades or could cause other long-term problems. Here are examples.

What are the chances that a 5 year old wanting to wear striped pants with a clashing plaid shirt to a birthday party is really going to have a long-term impact? Zip. Zero. Then, as long as this behavior isn't found in other P.S. I'M HELPING reasons to set a limit, you can allow it and not have to deal with it.

Now what if your 16 year old wants a tattoo or tries smoking? The effects of these behaviors may be big one year from now, and could include regret or tobacco addiction. Sometimes it isn't easy to know if a behavior will have a strong impact one year from now. Just think of what is probably best for your child.

When there is the possibility of a long-term impact from what your child is doing, a limit needs to be set right now. **Grades** are important to your child's career opportunities. If your child has trouble studying, or things interfere with it, set limits on activities and use routines to bring grades up. The use of **tobacco, drugs and other substances** should be limited both because of their potential to cause long-term problems and for personal safety reasons.

I'm Not Going there in P.S. I'M HELPING

If you avoid dealing with a behavior because of how your kids react when you do, you need to set a limit on the behavior. In other words, behaviors in this category are things you avoid dealing with by saying to yourself, "I'm not going there." Do you feel like you are walking on eggshells with your child? If you do, then it's time to start setting more limits...NOW.

Many parents don't set limits (rules) because they don't want their child to blow up or have a temper tantrum. If you find that you are avoiding setting a limit so you won't have to hear your kids complain, then it's time to set that limit! Otherwise, your kids will learn to fuss to get what they want. For instance, maybe the only reason you let your child wear striped pants with a plaid shirt to a party was to avoid a tantrum. If that's the case, it's time to say "No, you can't wear that." Be prepared with discipline skills for enforcing the limit, and forge ahead! Never fear— you'll learn all you need to enforce your limits in the next chapter.

Other ways to decide whether to set a limit

If you're still not sure if you should limit something your child does, ask yourself, "If a close friend or relative had a child acting this way, what would I think? What would I say if she asked me for advice?" A lot of times we can clearly see what needs to be done with other people's kids, even when we can't figure out what to do with our own. It's weird how we can think other people should stop something their child is doing, but somehow we don't take action with our own.

If you're still unsure, remember this: While love may be blind, your friends, neighbors and children's teachers are not. Talk to one of them that you trust. Be careful that the people you confide in aren't just telling you what they think you want to hear. You want, and need, honest feedback. Teachers work with kids all the time, so they have a good idea of what is typical behavior for children of a particular age. If you're still not sure, get professional advice.

Put it all together—how to know if limits are unreasonable or too hard

One way limits can be too hard is by having too many. **You may be setting too many limits if**:

1. You feel like a drill sergeant, giving orders all day.
2. You are often mad at your kids because they're not doing what you say well enough.
3. Having your children obey you seems more important than your relationship with them.
4. Your child is unhappy, anxious or afraid of not pleasing you.
5. Your child has no outside activities or friends.
6. Your child is rebelling against you.

If any of these describe you or your children, then your limit setting may have gone too far. When kids get a lot of limits that they don't see reasons for, they think their parent's just want to control them. Then *they* struggle for control.

Limits can also be too hard when you try to use them to change the **temperaments** that your children were born with. How active, intense, shy (or bold), moody, distractible, persistent, sensitive, adaptable and regular in habits your kids are comes from their natural way of reacting. You can't successfully discipline these traits, and trying to do so will not only frustrate you, but in the long run will make things worse. The good news is that these natural traits can be managed to work well enough for you and your child (see chapter 14 for tips).

Another way a limit is too hard is if it isn't found in P.S. I'M HELPING. If a behavior is not a threat to the life and well-being of your children or others—if it doesn't interfere with family functioning and it's not illegal, amoral, bad mannered, anger producing, possibly a long term problem, or something you avoid dealing with because of the reaction you'll get, then let the behavior go. This is part of an awesome strategy called "**choosing your battles.**" It reduces stress and power struggles with your kids.

Chose your battles by allowing personal choices

Parents may think a behavior should be limited, and a child may see that behavior as a personal choice that he or she should have. Wow, this can be an unpleasant conflict! Well, sometimes parents set unnecessary limits just because they don't like something personally. For example, a child's jean style is a personal choice that really doesn't have to be limited. You may only be creating a power struggle if you try to limit that or, let's say, a hairstyle. You could force your daughter to comb her hair when she leaves for school, only to have her mess it up when she gets to school. (She also may also feel bad about you all day.)

Put it all together—how to know if limits are too soft or too few

You are too soft on limits, or not setting enough, if your child doesn't seem to be developing maturity or seems irresponsible. You are too lax if you're not setting limits to help them stay safe. You're probably being too soft if you're not setting limits found in P.S. I'M HELPING and enforcing them. You are probably setting too few limits, or not enforcing them, if your child has behavior problems. Not enforcing a limit can be worse than not setting that limit at all. That's because your kids won't believe what you say, and will learn that they don't need to obey. You'll learn all about how to enforce limits in the next chapter.

Set Limits That Develop Good Character

Parents often ask, "How do I know if my kids are growing up alright?" They want guidelines for what kids do in order to grow into successful adults. In other words, parents want to know which behaviors are most important to a child's character and future. There is no one right list that everyone will agree on. But we believe if you work on the following things, your kids will be well on their way to becoming responsible adults with good character. Think of them as good limits to set as part of **I**mportant **M**orals and Manners in P.S. I'M HELPING.

Insist that your kids show kindness and concern for others

For example, do they ask, "Are you OK?" if someone falls, instead of laughing? Do they say, "What's wrong?" when someone appears upset? Kindness and empathy are keys to good relationships. Limit setting can help teach children these things. For example, you can tell your child to apologize and hug her sister after she hurts her, even if she hurt her accidentally. If your child seldom shows kindness, is cruel, harms pets or has a preoccupation with fire, seek professional help. And of course, if a child is not treated kindly, he or she won't know how to be kind.

Stop any bullying behaviors in your child.

Bullying is threatening to hurt or actually hurting someone physically or emotionally (by trying to humiliate someone). If your child often makes fun of others for the way they look, talk, or act, or just because they are different, this is a red flag that he or she isn't doing well. Limit setting can help. Make your child apologize and do nice things for the people they bullied.

Kids who are bullies often (but not always) are abused or neglected and have poor self-esteem. Children who bully often need extra good attention to feel better about themselves and their home life. Bullying should be taken seriously and strongly addressed in even young children. That's partly because kids who are aggressive in kindergarten are much more likely than other children to be aggressive in high school (if they don't drop out first).

Teach your children to share

Young children don't naturally share much, but they'll learn as you teach them. It's natural for kids to protect their stuff, but they should be able to let other kids use it sometimes. It's a good sign when you occasionally see them give things to others without being asked, especially if they seem happy to do it.

For younger kids, fighting over who gets to play with a toy is normal. Limit setting can help. *"You need to give your brother a turn or I will put the toy away."* If that doesn't work, take the toy away. And praise a child who lets someone else have something first. Or you can decide who gets the toy first, and you can give it to the other later, showing how to take turns. Other ways to teach sharing include taking your children to buy food and donating it together to a food bank. Talk about how lucky you are to have things, and how good it feels to share.

Expect them to show respect to adults

If you ask parents what showing respect is, you may get different answers. **Disrespect** is what most agree on. It is when kids swear, throw things, yell, threaten, or call their parents names. These behaviors are not acceptable. If your child exhibits one of these behaviors, say *"Stop right there! When you call me a name and yell at me, that is disrespectful. I don't deserve to be talked to that way. Give me an apology now please."*

About the yelling part—if you yell at your kids, they will likely yell at you when they're upset. All kids talk back (**argue or debate**) to their parents sometimes, so it's normal. When it happens, follow our suggestions later in this chapter for ending debates.

Older kids should usually tell the truth

Tell them that you'll usually figure out when they lie. Say they'll get into a lot more trouble if they lie than if they just admit they did something. Be softer on discipline when your kids admit doing something wrong—it usually encourages honesty. If being honest gets them into just as much trouble as they would have gotten into if they lied, then they'll lie to get out of it more often. Of course, don't let your children think they can do anything and not get into trouble as long as they fess up! But use a lighter punishment then. Also, explain that if they lie, you won't be able to believe them when they really didn't do something, no matter what they say.

Kids should be doing work around the house

When parents do most of the housework, and children act like they're allergic to helping, that's a problem. Kids aren't going to learn how to take care of themselves or a family if parents do everything for them. Adults work hard, and it's only fair that children help with housework. This develops responsibility and prepares them to hold jobs.

Chores are the first jobs your kids should have. Even a 4 year old can help pick up or do small tasks. The key is to let your kids help in ways they can't do harm, and make them feel good about being able to do things. It works best to say, *"I need your help."* This may motivate them to help, and show them how much work it takes to run a household.

Check Appendix A to see if kids are capable of doing what you ask. Use a lot of praise so they'll feel good about helping and want to help again. If you criticize your kids' work or do their jobs over again, they'll learn that they can't do it right and will eventually stop trying to help. So, even if they don't do a great job at first, if they tried, that's good enough. Cheerfully say, *"Thanks for helping—I like it when you help"* for young kids, and *"Man, that makes my day easier, thanks,"* for older kids. If they missed part of the job, say *"Thanks! Looks like you forgot ...—just do that and you're done."*

Try to make work around the house fun by singing silly songs, talking, and planning something fun after the work is done. Small rewards like allowance can help, but should only be given *after* they help. In general, it's best for kids to get work done before playing.

Expect them to say "I'm sorry" sometimes

This is one of those basic skills that successful people have. Tell your children that it's really OK to be wrong, because everyone makes mistakes. Build their confidence by saying that mistakes are not a problem if they admit them and fix things when possible. *"Saying sorry helps fix big mistakes and tells people you care when something bad happens."* Limit setting can encourage kids to apologize. *"You need to say sorry to your buddy or you will go to time-out."* *"I need an apology for lying to me."* It helps kids learn if they get apologies themselves.

They should not be using drugs, alcohol, or cigarettes

Have a zero tolerance policy. No ifs, ands, or butts (hey, that's a pun)! After they leave the house, you have a smaller say in what they do, so insist on not using substances while you can. If they don't start using as teens, they're less likely to get addicted and use substances later. Have frequent honest talks so they'll know good reasons to avoid them.

If you smoke, use drugs or get drunk, you're in a real bind. It'll be hard to convince your kids not to, but it can be done. Be honest with them about how it has affected your life. Say you want better things for them, and seek help for yourself.

Say that you expect them to wait until adulthood for sex

Studies show that just saying this helps kids abstain. Sex is associated with increased risks of pregnancy and disease in teenagers. Teens are often NOT able to make healthy decisions about this activity anyway.

Teach them why you disapprove of illegal and dangerous activities

Stealing, gambling, cheating, tagging, weapons, and gangs are all examples. For instance, tell them that stealing is wrong because they wouldn't like it done to them. Kids who respect their parents care about what their parents think. Gambling is becoming a big problem for people in this country, even teens. Talk about the dangers of gambling starting in grade school.

How to Set Limits for Your Kids

So far, we've covered how to decide what to allow kids to do and which limits help develop good character. If you think you've got a grip on what limits to set for your kids, strong work! Now you're ready for the next round—learning how to set those beautiful limits.

Use your Talk to Teach Guidelines for giving commands

We covered these in skill #3. Use these to tell your children their limits (what they should and shouldn't do).

Guideline	Reason	Set a limit
Be direct and specific.	Make it clear what you want, and don't give a choice not to do it.	*"Please take out the trash"* instead of, "I need someone to…" or "Would you…?"
Say what to do, not what to stop doing.	This teaches them what you want more quickly.	Instead of, "Stop yelling and running" say, *"Use inside voices and walk."*
Keep it simple for small children.	Break jobs down into a series of smaller ones to help them obey.	*"Put the books on the shelf… Now put the pillows up,"* instead of "Clean your room."
Be polite, respectful and calm.	Say *"please"* and *"thank you."* Use a calm, neutral voice. Don't criticize or tease.	*"Please pick up your toys and put them away,"* instead of, "You're so messy."
Give a choice of two about equal jobs.	Choices help kids obey, learn to make decisions and be responsible.	*"Please pick up your room. Would you like to put away your train or your books first?"*
Give a reason to do it first.	Saying why first helps decrease arguing and gets better results.	*"I will be in a hurry when I pick you up, so please be ready by the front door."*
Use specific praise when they obey.	Say what they did and why you're pleased.	*"Thank you for getting your shoes on so fast. Now we won't be late for school."*

Setting short-term limits

A short-term limit is when you want your child to do something right now, or just during a certain time or situation. ("Go to bed early tonight.")

Setting long-term limits: house rules

These are limits that will be in place for a long time, or apply to everyone (not just the kids). They are rules that your children know well, and expect to apply at any time or place. These can be called **house rules**, or **family rules**. Examples are: *brush your teeth every* *morning and night, put your dirty dishes in the dishwasher, no smoking in the house, and no swearing.*

Your house rules can include whatever you think are the most important things for your family. Just don't try to set too many, since that makes it hard to remember them all, or they may make the house feel like boot camp. If you ever say, "They should have known better" or "What were they thinking?" it should mean that your children broke a house rule that they knew well.

Family meetings

This is when everyone in the family sits down together and talks about events or situations. Review instructions in skill #2. A family meeting is a great time to set or remind each other about house rules, and what should happen if they're broken. Family meetings are also a good way to set up **family routines**—agreeing to do things in a certain order or within a certain time frame to make things easier. These can include chore, bedtime and morning schedules.

Family meetings work especially well with teenagers. When teens have input into what is expected of them, or what the consequence should be if they break a rule, they are more likely to follow the rule. And when they break the rule, they are less likely to argue about it!

How to set house rules at a family meeting

1. Start by setting only about three house rules.
2. Let all family members help decide what the rules should be and what the consequences should be if they're broken. If you can't agree, try to find a compromise. Make sure your children understand these are things they need to do without being asked. They apply any time and any place.
3. House rules should be for all family members, including parents. So if a family rule is *no swearing* and mom and dad cuss, then they can get busted and get a consequence also. The consequence can be something as simple as saying *"I'm sorry,"* or it can be something like paying a fine for every swear word (could be fun for the kids).
4. Write the rules on a piece of paper and put them somewhere everyone sees often (on the refrigerator, in the bathroom).

5. Make your house rules specific enough that everyone will know what the rules mean, but general enough to avoid loopholes. Confused? Say you have a house rule of "no hitting." What if your daughter decides to kick her brother instead? She did not hit. Do you make another house rule, "no kicking"? Do you need to make rules for biting, pulling hair and scratching too? If your rule was more general, such as *no hurting*, you would have all of the above behaviors covered! Here are other examples.

Instead of …	Say this instead …
"No biting," "No hitting" or "No calling each other stupid"	*"No hurting"*
"No breaking your sister's toys," "No taking her crayons" or "No eating all of her candy"	*"Respect each other's things"* (older kids) or *"Be nice to each other's things"* (younger kids)
"No swearing," "No teasing," or "No threatening"	*"Treat one another with respect"*
"No back talk" or "No arguing"	*"Say yes when I ask for help"*
"No stealing," or "No lying"	*"Be honest"*
"No bike riding without a helmet," or "No talking to strangers"	*"Be safe"*
"Do homework before watching TV" or "Do your chores"	*"Do chores and homework before playing or watching TV"*

How well do they need to follow limits (do what you say)?

It's good to give children "wiggle room" to obey. In other words, giving them flexibility actually helps kids obey better. Here are things you can compromise on, followed by examples.

1. The **order** in which kids need to do things (they can empty the dishwasher and then set the table OR set the table and then empty the dishwasher). Unless something will work only if done in a certain order, let them choose. They'll learn that sometimes doing things in a certain order is important. Having to mow a wet lawn once teaches that it's best to mow grass before it gets wet.
2. The **length of time** they have to get it done (*"I need it done in the*

next 10 OR 15 minutes"). Keep in mind that kids are going to take longer than adults to do things in general.

3. The **attitude** they have while doing it. Who cares how happy or crabby they are, as long as they obey! But disrespect does need to be limited.

4. **How well** or thoroughly they do it. We adults can do things better than kids, because we're older and have had more practice. Now here are examples of how to set limits with compromise built in.

No compromise limits	Compromising limits
Parent: "Tyrone, please set the table." Tyrone: "Can I finish watching this show first? It's almost over." Parent: "Set the table right now or you'll lose TV for a week!"	Parent: "Tyrone, please set the table" Tyrone: "Can I finish watching this show first? It's almost over." Parent: *"Yes, but if you forget, you can't watch TV tomorrow."*
Parent: "Dee, time to come in." Dee: "Oh Dad, we're having fun and it's my turn to be 'it'. Can't I play just a little longer?" Parent: "Dee, come in right now, or you can't play all day tomorrow."	Parent: "Dee, time to come in." Dee: "Oh Dad, we're having fun and it's my turn to be it. Can't I play just a little longer?" Parent: *"Just 15 more minutes. But then if you don't come in, you won't be able to play tomorrow."*

How to be flexible but still consistent in setting limits

Parents are **inconsistent** when they don't follow through on what they say without having a good, clear reason for changing their minds. **Being flexible** means having a clear, good reason for doing something different, that kids can understand. In the right hand column above, the parents weren't being inconsistent but were compromising. Both Tyrone and Dee were still expected to do what they were told. They were just given a little wiggle room in how or when they got it done. The parents compromised because it didn't make a difference and they knew their kids would appreciate it.

Kids appreciate compromise, and will obey more if they see you compromise sometimes. So, good enough parents compromise when they can, but still firmly set the limits they feel are best for their kids.

This is being flexible in a good way. If your kids see you as being flexible while watching out for them, they'll accept your limits better. But if you're changing your mind because you're afraid of what your kids will do, or you're sick of them complaining or arguing, that is a reason to go ahead and keep the limit you set. That's the ING—"I'm not going there" reason to set a limit in P.S. I'M HELPING.

Another dangerous thing to compromise on is teenagers wanting to be together without adult supervision (see Chapter 9, which has more instructions for parenting teens).

Ways to Avoid Arguing or Debating

Normal children will resist and argue over limits. But good enough parents still set and enforce limits because they want the best for their kids. Here are great ways you can decrease arguing.

The first and most important is to **consistently set the limits you think are best**. If your children learn that you often change your limits, they'll learn to argue to make you change your mind.

The second way to avoid debating over limits is to **have the respect of your kids**. But as the old saying goes, respect isn't given—it is earned. You can earn the respect of children by being fair and caring toward them. Using P.S. I'M HELPING helps them learn to trust that you have good reasons for rules and limits. Explain your reasons for a limit and why it is best for them, instead of putting them down or being sarcastic. Showing kids respect this way helps them respect adults.

You also earn your kids' respect by being consistent or predictable. There is that consistency thing again! So, say what you'll do, and do what you say. Even if your kids don't agree, at least they'll know where you're coming from and respect you for doing what you think is right for their sake.

Disrespectful limit setting	Respectful limit setting
"Since you don't have the common sense to bring your bike home, get out there now and get	*"I'm disappointed that you didn't take better care of your bike. Go outside and get it now*

it. It can get stolen. You idiot! Next time, you'll get in trouble."	*so it doesn't get stolen. You need to bring it in every night.* "

A third way to decrease arguing is to **point out other kids who argue a lot** to your children. Most of us know of at least one child who pretty much gets to do whatever he or she wants. This child's parents have loose or no limits, or give in to debates and temper tantrums. Kids like this are heading for real trouble. They're probably not well-liked and other children may think they are spoiled, mean or a troublemakers. Explain that kids like this will struggle with relationships and jobs. You don't want this to happen to them. Tell them that is why you set limits—because you care about them growing up happy and successful.

Use "open communication" to compromise and resolve arguments and conflicts

Open communication is the best method for solving disagreements and having difficult talks with your children. It's also a good way to come up with compromises on limits with your kids—and that's a big part of good relationships and discipline that works. Using open communication with teens has even been shown to decrease early sexual activity and drug use!

Instructions for open communication
Use it to resolve arguments on limits or anything else.

1. First, **let your child tell you his or her thoughts and feelings** about a limit, or any other topic. Have them say *"I think..."* and *"I feel..."* Use feeling words to help you both express how you feel (doing this doesn't mean you agree with each other).
2. Don't interrupt, and **repeat back what your child said** so he knows you heard. If your child takes too long to tell you his side, say, *"You have one more minute and then I'll say what I think."*
3. **Don't allow your children to get off the subject** with personal jabs or unrelated things that might sway you.
4. **If your child gets overly emotional or yells,** tell her that she needs to calm down to continue the conversation. Likewise, **if your child is disrespectful** (calling you names, cussing or using threats), say that the conversation is over unless she stops being disrespectful. Sit quietly and don't talk until she is calm.

---

5. If you have done something related to the argument that you regret, apologize, but don't let your children guilt you into giving in. By apologizing, you help your children own up to their part of the problem.

6. **If you agree with your child's point of view**, you can change your mind, but only after you have given your good reason for compromising. It's good to compromise sometimes! A common reason for changing your mind may be that a limit wasn't in P.S. I'M HELPING, making it a safe, personal choice for your child. You can also compromise by allowing something unexpected just this once.

7. **If you don't agree with your child**, explain your reasons and calmly set the limit. Say, *"I'm deciding based on what I think is best for you, because I care."* Say that decisions for parents are very hard sometimes, and maybe you make mistakes, but it's your job to do what you think is right. Don't expect them to understand or agree with you. BEWARE—for many kids, if you don't say what they want to hear, they will argue to try to change your mind. Your kids may also push your buttons to get you more emotional and less logical. Stay calm and talk quietly.

8. At this point, unless they have anything new to say, it doesn't do any good to discuss it anymore. Tell your children the talk is over. Suggest they spend time and energy doing something else. If they continue to state their case, that is now **debating** or **arguing**, and that needs to be stopped!

To debate or not to debate: JUST SAY NO!

After using open communication, if they continue to state their case—they are now **debating** or **arguing**! A common trap that many parents fall into is debating with their children whether or not they need to obey. *BEWARE—DON'T GO THERE !* (A rhyme for your reading pleasure.) Don't let your children drag you down the path of debating whether they have to obey. Sometimes debating becomes so much fun for kids that they will debate you on every little thing. If you stop allowing debate, the debating will stop.

First, **name their behavior,** so they know they crossed the line. Say,

"That is arguing," or *"That is debating."* Repeat your request with a firm voice, looking steadily into their eyes. If that doesn't work, simply say, *"We can talk more about this after you have done what I asked."* Or you can try changing the subject. Now here are some top kid debates and ways to handle them.

The "it's not fair" debate		
Your request	Child's debate	What you can say
"Please stop your game now and do your chores."	"My friends don't have to do chores, and they get to play games more."	*"I'll do what I think is best for you. Just because other parents do something doesn't make it good for kids."*

This could also affectionately be called the "poor me" debate. Give us a break! Most kids in America today don't have to work as hard as kids in the past, and it's up to us to promote good work habits. Many kids today are also used to getting what they want. This is a great chance to check reality with your kids. *"Kids must learn to work or they'll have trouble supporting themselves. I won't let you grow up that way."* *"Other kids in this world work and can't go to school. You're lucky. You don't have to work much, so don't give us the 'poor me' business."*

The "it's not my turn" debate		
Your request	Child's debate	What you can say
"Keisha, please do the dishes."	"But it's not my turn. It's Jerome's turn."	*"Jerome's gone. I need your help. If it's his turn, he'll do one of your chores later. Please do it now."*

This is a cute little variation on the "it's not fair" debate. The father in this example stayed strong—he's the man! He just pointed out that while it may be unfair now, he would make it up to her. The last thing he said was the original request, *"Please do it now."* If Keisha continued to debate, dad could have said, *"I'm done discussing this for now. I'll talk about it after you do the dishes."* Giving kids a chance to debate after the job's been done, usually leads to a very short debate!

The "it's not my fault" debate		
Your request	Child's debate	What you can say
"Please wipe	"But I didn't	*"Even if you didn't, I asked you to*

| up the spilt milk." | do it. I never drank milk." | *wipe it up. Do it or you can clean the whole kitchen. It's up to you.* |

Here's another lovely version of the "it's not fair" debate. The child again appeals to the parent's sense of fairness. But whether or not the child drank milk is not the point. The child was told to do something that can be done easily. This mother still set the limit. You go girl!

The "just one minute" debate		
Your request	Child's debate	What you can say
"Sam, dinner is getting cold. Please come now."	"Just a sec'. I am almost done with this game level."	*"Sam, please come to the table now, or you'll lose games for a day."*

Ah, we all fall for this one sometimes. But we shouldn't, because it's exhausting and stressful! It's an attempt to delay doing what we ask, so we need to ask again. Kids may learn that if they stall long enough, their parents forget, so they get out of obeying. Here the parent told Sam what would happen if he didn't obey (a consequence). If the game is keeping Sam from coming to the table, then Sam will be kept away from the game.

The "everybody else is doing it" debate		
Your request	Child's debate	What you can say
"Carlos, you need to come home right after the movie."	"But all my friends are going out afterward— to a pizza place."	*"While some of your friends can go out afterward, you can't. Your curfew is 10:00 p.m. You can come home after the movie or just stay here and miss the movie."*

Kids often try to guilt us into giving in by showing us what a rough life they have. Yeah, right! This parent did a nice job by pointing out a family rule. While Carlos may not agree with it, as long as he knew the rule in advance, he has no grounds for arguing.

The "I can make all my own decisions" debate		
Your request	Child's debate	What you can say
"You can't	"I'm old enough	*"Actually, you're a big kid who*

go out tonight. You have some homework."	to decide what I do. You don't know how it works."	*still needs help to grow up right. I care enough to help you make good decisions."*

You might hear things like this a lot from your teenagers. They have to be kidding. They are flat out wrong on this one! It's your job to help your kids learn to make good decisions. More exciting details are in the teen chapter (Chapter 9).

The "but Dad (or Mom) said..." debate		
Your request	Child's debate	What you can say
"Please wash the cars."	"Dad said I didn't need to."	*"I told you to do it, so you need to do it. I'll ask your father later."*

This is a clever way kids try to get what they want by **pitting parents against each other**. For instance, if Dad says yes to what the kids want much more often than Mom, kids may ask him for something after Mom said no. If your child does this often, when she asks to do something, ask her what her other parent said. Then check her story to see if she told the truth. Have frequent talks with your partner about what limits should be. Agree to be consistent with each other and back up each other's decisions. Try not to make one parent into the bad guy who says "no" more often.

If your kids continue to argue or debate you, this is an attempt to wear you down. Just leave the area calmly, without showing you are upset. Say, *"I can't talk about that anymore because you are arguing with me. We can talk more about it tomorrow if you want."* Then don't talk anymore about the issue that day! DON'T TALK—JUST WALK. This shows that you are staying in control of the situation—*not* that you are losing the argument, or giving in. The same rules apply if you talk about it tomorrow.

If you still can't get your child to obey, the final step is to use an action limit. You'll learn about this and other ways to enforce your limits in the next skill!

Skill #4 SEIZE CONTROL: Set limits on their behavior, choose your battles and help them develop good character

- Limits are like rules- what your children can or can't, should or shouldn't do.
- **Set limits on your children's behavior** to help them be good, happy kids and make your life less stressful.
- Use **P.S. I'M HELPING** to see whether to limit a behavior or activity.
  - ❖ **P**ersonal **S**afety- does it threaten the health or well being of my child or others? (Driving, internet, television, games, friends, aggression, substance use.) Curfews are limits that help kids.
  - ❖ **I**mportant **M**orals and Manners- does it violate my morals, values, good manners, right of others, laws or interfere with family?
  - ❖ **H**ow **E**motional- does it make me emotional or angry when they do it? (does it push my buttons, is it disrespectful)
  - ❖ **L**ong-term **P**roblem- could this behavior still affect anyone a year from now? (drop in grades, substance use, crime, gangs, withdrawal from family)
  - ❖ **I**'m **N**ot **G**oing there- do I avoid dealing with this because the kids get upset?

  If you answer yes to any of these questions, you should probably set a limit on the behavior or activity.
- **Choose your battles**- don't spend time and energy setting limits that are safe, personal choices for your kids (those that aren't in P.S. I'M HELPING). Compromise often with your children's wishes. Be flexible and give them wiggle room to obey.
- **Insist on good character behaviors.** Expect them to: show kindness, share, show adults respect, usually tell the truth, do regular house chores, say I'm sorry sometimes, not use drugs/alcohol/cigarettes, and not bully, have sex, steal, gamble or do other illegal things.
- Use **family meetings** to set house rules and family routines.
- **Don't allow arguing or debating**. If you set a limit, and they want to say why they don't like it, let them do so respectfully, calmly and briefly (use **open communication**). Then repeat back what they said so they know you heard. Use *"I think…"* and *"I feel…"* when you talk. Then if you decide to stick with your limit, say why. If they continue to state their case, that is **debating (arguing)**. First give your reason again, or say you'll discuss it more *after* they obey. Use a firm voice and steady gaze. Try changing the subject, or our other advice for common debates. If nothing is working, DON'T TALK- JUST WALK. You can give a consequence if they keep talking and won't obey (see skill #5).

Skill #5

PLAN DISCIPLINE AND FOLLOW THROUGH: How to use consequences, teach responsibility and be consistent

And now, what you've all been waiting for…the meat and potatoes…the big Kahuna. This chapter is where we'll show you how to get little Maria and Johnny to do what you want when they don't obey. We'll tell you how to enforce all of those good limits you pick. You'll learn how to plan discipline and be consistent, so your symbol for this skill is a planner notebook.

Some of you may be peeking ahead to this skill, skipping over all the important earlier stuff. You may be telling yourself, "Ya-ya, I'll do special time later, *after* I get Johnny's behavior turned around." If this is what you're thinking, STOP. Please go back to skills one through four and practice them for at least one month first.

The reason we're making such a big deal about this is that discipline success depends on a strong relationship with your kids. In fact, it's the *most* important discipline tool you have. With a strong bond, you won't have to discipline as much, and your kids will often behave because they want to, not because they have to. But when your relationship is strained, kids may push you away and be influenced by other people. They may also push your buttons, get revenge or embarrass you.

Starting a discipline plan without strengthening your relationship is like building a house on a marsh. Just as a house needs a solid foundation, a strong relationship with your kids is the foundation for discipline. A house built on a marsh won't last very long and you'll soon have to do repairs. So using the first three skills will save you so much time and energy. For infants and children 3 years old and younger, please use chapter eight instructions instead.

What is discipline?

Since one of the definitions of *discipline* is "to punish," many parents assume that discipline is hurting kids if they don't obey. This is similar to the old idea, "Spare the rod, and spoil the child." (People often think this quote is in the Christian Bible, but it isn't.) That definition won't help you get good behavior. Discipline is much more than punishment.

 Think of discipline this way to get the best results: **training** children to act according to rules and expectations.

So how do you train kids to behave? One way is automatic—they watch you and imitate how you behave. The other way is to use consequences. Punishments are consequences, but the most powerful consequences are rewards.

Rewards and punishments are consequences used in discipline

Consequences are what you give your kids for either good or bad behavior, in order to enforce the limits you set. A **reward** is anything that happens *after* children do something good to *increase* the chance they'll do it again. Studies show that any behavior you reward will happen not only again, but more often. The flip side of reward is **punishment**. Punishment is anything that happens *after* children do something bad that *decreases* the chance they'll do it again.

Rewards and punishments can be confusing. Parents might think that because they do something after their kids have been naughty, they must be punishing them. But whether these consequences are seen as rewards or punishments is in the eye of the beholder—your child. Just as opera is beautiful music to some and annoying noise to others, whether consequences are rewards or punishments depend on one's perspective.

For example, little Camille has been acting naughty all day. She drew on the walls and pulled your hair. You decide to punish her, so you put her in her room and say that she can't come out until she says she's sorry. You expect her to come out soon. You wait, and wait, and wait. No Camille. Finally, you peak into her room and find her quietly playing with toys. You ask, "Are you ready to say sorry?" She says

"No" and turns back to her toys. What happened? Being put into her room was not punishing—it was rewarding! She got to play with toys! So parents and kids have different perspectives on consequences, and they can change like the weather. Today Camille may be perfectly content staying in her room, but tomorrow she may come out between sobs saying she's sorry. Whether something is rewarding or punishing has to do with what kids think. So figure out what your kids find rewarding or punishing to make consequences work.

Also, some parents think that, in order to be effective, punishments should be painful. But punishment is *anything* that decreases a behavior. So when a classroom gets too noisy and the teacher starts singing the "Barney Song", and the class immediately quiets down, that is a punishment. It's a punishment because the class hates it when she sings (she's tone deaf), and they want her to stop! So they quiet down.

Be realistic about consequences

Nothing can *make* your child act a certain way, at least not for long. As the old saying goes, you can lead a horse to water, but you can't make it drink. But, things can be done to make a stubborn horse thirsty. Using consequences correctly can help make children thirsty to behave.

This part of the chapter is chock full of discipline skills. There is a learning curve for both you and your kids. So don't expect these to work right away and every time. Sometimes bad behavior will get worse before it gets better even when you do everything right. That's just the way it is.

And remember, you can expect good behavior most, but not all, of the time. So **how often do normal, good children obey**? In general, children who are 3 to 5 years old obey about half the time. Children who are 5 to 8 obey about two out of three times, and children who are over 8 obey about three out of four times.

If your child obeys much less than this, start by working on your relationship. If your relationship seems strong, use the skills in this chapter. If you are expecting obedience more often than this, you are setting yourself up for disappointment, and your kids for failure. If your children are obeying about this often, then both of you are doing "good enough."

Use Rewards to Encourage Good Behavior

We usually pay more attention to the behaviors that we want stopped than the ones we want to keep. Naughty behaviors tend to bug us more, so we naturally focus on punishing those. Our whole society seems focused more on punishment. We're more likely to hear from our boss when we do something wrong than when we do something right.

In children, for every bad behavior that can be punished, there is usually at least one appropriate or good behavior that can be rewarded. Childhood learning that comes from being rewarded is more powerful and lasting than learning that comes from being punished. **Any behavior (good or bad) that you reward will happen again.** Using rewards is the best way to change your child's behavior.

Rewards are powerful

They make children feel better about themselves and their parents. They feed self-confidence (or the feeling that kids can do things right) and motivate them to achieve and be good. Rewarding makes good behaviors spread from  one situation to another. Rewards are never given when parents are angry, and they don't leave a bruise or bad feelings.

The two ways to give rewards		
1) Give something good that the child likes		
2) Remove something they don't want (or don't want to do)		
Rewards to use		
Praise	Attention	Privileges
Compliments	Treats	Gifts
Money	Excusing them from	Ending a punishment
Helping with	chores	A fun activity
something they	Eating out	Natural rewards (stay
need to do	Sticker charts*	tuned)

*Sticker charts (a piece of paper on the wall or fridge that you put stickers on for good behavior, and a child earns a reward for a getting a certain number of stickers) can work for small children. But these may be hard to use consistently since you can't add a sticker to the chart for good behavior away from home until you get back.

Attention and affection are powerful rewards

Thank yous, hugs and smiles are all great rewards. Studies show that these are extremely powerful motivators, even more than food sometimes. When parents give a reward like eating out, they give something positive, plus their attention. This makes the reward work even better. Attention is one of the most common motivators gangs use to get kids to join. Your kids won't need attention from others as much if they get lots of it at home.

What is the difference between a bribe and a reward?

Many parents ask this excellent question. A **bribe** is when you give your kids something good *before* they finish doing what you want. It's also when you give (or promise to give) something good when they're misbehaving, because they say they'll stop misbehaving. The classic example is offering candy to a child if she will stop a tantrum, or agreeing to give her what she wants when she threatens to throw a fit. The only way kids should get rewards is by proving they can be good.

A bribe would be giving your children candy *before* you go into a store because they promise to be good while you shop. A **reward** would be to give them candy *after* you're done shopping because they actually were good in the store. Rewarding kids after good behavior motivates them to be good. Bribing makes parenting harder by teaching kids they can get something good for being bad.

Here's an example. Let's say that you're shopping and your children start to wander away, and you say, *"If you kids stay by me until I'm done shopping, I will get you a treat when we're done."* Your kids behave, so you buy a treat in the checkout line. Are you bribing or rewarding? If you said rewarding, ding- you are correct! If you had given or promised them the treat during shopping because they said they'd be good, it would have been a bribe.

Here's another example. Let's say your child is whining in the car and you want the whining to stop. Saying, *"If you're good and don't whine all through errand time, you may play when we get home"* is a reward. He would only be able to play IF he didn't whine the whole time. But saying, "You can play when we get home if you stop whining" is a bribe that rewards him for bad behavior! (Then he'll whine again later to get something else!) It was a bribe because you promised him something to *stop* whining. And he would have been allowed to play even if he stopped for only a minute but whined again later.

How to give rewards—reward early and often

It's best to reward right after children do something good—the sooner the better. This is especially important when you first start using rewards. Let's say you want your son to be neater and stop leaving his stuff all over the house. When you see him pick up something without being asked, reward it right then. Just say, *"Thank you so much for picking up after yourself. I didn't even have to ask!"* Do it even if you don't actually see him pick up, but you know that he must have.

As good behavior becomes more of a habit, don't reward it every time. That could become annoying, and kids need to learn to do things for themselves! But let them know that you notice every once in a while.

Some of you may be thinking, "Sure—I'll reward my daughter when she does something good without being asked, but she never does. I will die of old age first!" If this sounds like you, we respectfully say, "Bull-hockey." Think about the little things. (*"You've got a nice smile."*)

If you have trouble finding one positive thing to praise your child about, you've probably set expectations too high. Or perhaps you're too focused on bad behaviors, or you aren't around your child enough. If you really can't find anything to praise, it's a sign you could use professional help with your kids.

Using money as a reward—allowance

Giving allowance for doing chores is a good way to teach kids responsibility. They'll learn the good feeling that being paid for work gives. Be very specific about what they need to do to get paid. Then be sure that they actually do it and pay them on a regular basis. We *don't* recommend allowance for kids who get almost everything they want and need anyway. Kids with excess money and time tend to do risky things like drugs. And kids who don't have to work for allowance can grow up less motivated to support themselves.

Giving kids more money than they need is one way they can become "spoiled." It's not good for them. So how much allowance should you give? Many parents use a certain dollar amount per year of age. So, a 15 year-old might get $15 per week whereas her 12 year-old sister would get $12. The amount depends on how much work they do, how much money you have, and what your kids are being asked to do with their money.

For example, some parents make their kids buy clothing or school supplies with their allowances. While this can help teach money skills, we think it's too much for children to handle until they're at least in high school. Also, it's best that your child has more choice in what to spend the money on. It can be fine to give teens money to buy school clothes, so if they want a pair of jeans that cost more than usual, they'll have to save for them. Or if you buy them shoes, and they want the most expensive pair, have them pay for the price difference. Have them save allowance for big optional purchases.

Rewarding with money can be a bit tricky. If you give too little, it may not motivate them to do the work. If you give too much, your child may develop unrealistic expectations. If you give your 8 year old $50 a week, what will she expect when she's 16? Start allowance small, to avoid the need to reduce it.

Experts advise against credit cards for kids. Kids will get the idea that money just grows on trees, and won't have a sense of where money comes from and how much they spend.

About money talk and buying kids things

Talking about money in certain ways can build **materialistic values** (assuming that owning lots of things is the most valuable or important goal in life, and can make a person happy). Let's say your children want something, and you emphasize how much it costs and how they better appreciate you buying it for them. That teaches them that expensive things are best, and that when you buy those things, you're doing something really nice. Well, actually, most people think the best things in life are free. Being loved, enjoying nature, good health, friends, time and faith are worth more. Spending time together and giving good attention are the nicest things you can do for your kids.

It's best not to buy kids everything they want anyway. Explain why you won't buy things in ways that **teach them to look for value**. There are two different kinds of value you can teach your children about. One kind refers to what people think is important. Our purchases teach our children about what we really care about. Some parents try to buy the newest or best things for their kids, and lots of them (such as toys or clothing). Instead, some parents emphasize spending money on family activities such as vacations, or on education for their kids.

If your child often wants the newest, most expensive objects, and you don't want her growing up with materialistic values, you could say something like *"You don't really need that." "It's too expensive for us. We need to buy more important things." "It's bad for kids to have everything they want* (see pages 30-32 on spoiling children)*."*

The other kind of value you can teach your children is how much a purchase is worth compared to how much it costs. Teach your kids to spend money wisely by saying things like *"It's not worth the money, since it's cheaply made and won't last long." "You can get other things just as fun for less money."*

Also, waiting for holidays, birthdays or other events to give larger presents makes them mean more. Even when your children spend their own money, you should approve of their purchases. If *you* wouldn't buy them a violent video game, don't allow them to buy it either.

About money and other rewards for school grades

Many kids want to do well in school and don't need more motivation. Other kids don't see the value of good grades. If your children aren't motivated to get good grades, explain that good grades will give them more choice in their careers. Tell them that good jobs are a big part of happiness in adults. If that doesn't work, we think it's alright to offer money or other rewards for grades, in small amounts.

Rewarding grades can help motivate kids to learn the skills they need to succeed in school. Once your child starts to get the good feeling of doing well, and you praise the effort and grades, rewards will become less important. For parents who don't want to reward their children for doing better when they're getting  low grades, we ask, "Would you be willing to go to your job everyday and not get a paycheck? Isn't school the most important job that your child has right now?" For families that don't want to or can't use money as a reward, using gifts, privileges, getting out of chores and other rewards can work just as well.

When using rewards for doing well in school, parents often make the mistake of rewarding too far in the future, like at the end of a semester. Rewarding short-term goals works much better. Give smaller rewards for good grades every month, for instance. Or, reward good weekly or monthly progress reports from your teacher or school. You could reward each good assignment grade too.

You can also reward good behavior in school instead of grades. For example, if your child acts out in class a lot, you could reward on days she doesn't get into trouble (the more days, the bigger the reward). For some children, it works best to reward at the end of each day. Perhaps your child has trouble handing in assignments. Well, we all pay more attention to a piece of paper if it's valuable to us (we're less likely to lose a paycheck than a coupon). So, if she's supposed to turn in a weekly spelling list that gets lost in that black hole between home and school, give a small reward (say fifty cents, or thirty more minutes of play time), if the list is turned in.

Use Punishments to Discourage Bad Behavior

Punishments can be mild and correct a child (called mild punishment) or harsh and forceful (called harsh punishment). While both can temporarily stop a naughty behavior, mild punishments work much better over the long term.

Types of mild punishments

1. **Give your children something they don't like** (time-out, a new chore or responsibility, your disappointment).
2. **Take away something they like—objects, privileges or activities** (allowance, toys, play time, cell phone, TV, games, treats, computer, car, bike, skateboard, iPod, time with friends, hoodie, etc.).
3. **Allow a negative natural consequence to happen.**

Mild punishments to use to correct bad behavior

Add a chore or responsibility—having to work more when they disobey can motivate them to do better next time. Add a chore or two to their usual list, either for one night or all week, depending on the crime. If they mistreat a sibling, they could do one of that child's chores.

Take away a privilege—many things kids take for granted are really privileges. Being able to watch TV, play, ride bikes, use computers, drive a car, use a cell phone, and go out with friends are all privileges. Through trial and error, you'll find which privileges your child cares most about, by how they react when you take them away. Keep using those so your kids know what privileges will be taken away for bad behavior. This motivates them to be good.

Take away an object—something they like or use a lot: a bike, skateboard, cell phone, car keys, toy, snack, favorite clothing item, movie video or others.

Allow a negative natural consequence to happen—this is something they don't like that naturally follows after what they did. Make sure it seems like something that will change your child's behavior and won't be dangerous. Forgetting to bring their homework to school is a negative natural consequence for a child who wanted to turn it in.

Express your disappointment—but without a lecture. Use *"I think...."* or *"I feel...."* statements. Just briefly say, *"I am so disappointed in you. I feel embarrassed (sad, scared, et*c*)."* This works when you have a good relationship.

Time-out—this works for children two and a half to about 8 years old. But it needs to be done correctly to work well.

Instructions for time-out!
Use for children age 2 ½ to about 8 years old.

1. **Have them sit in a boring place**. Location, location, location! Time-out means time out from stimulation. There should be no TV, toys, or music, and no one to talk to. Dining rooms, hallways, or brightly lit basements can be good places. Ideally, use the same time-out chair every time you put your child in time-out. The chair should  be where they can't touch anything, including a wall. Don't use a corner, because they can put their feet on the wall and rock, or touch the wall. If you need to physically put them in the chair, be VERY sure you are calm. Hold them under the armpits and away from you so you don't get kicked.

2. **Tell them why they're going to time-out, and that they can't get out until you tell them to get out**. *"You are going to time-out because you _____. You'll stay in time-out until I tell you to get out."* A simple rule of thumb is to use **one minute for each year of age**. So a 6 year old would be in time-out for six minutes. But research shows that most kids get the message within three minutes, so limit your time-out to three minutes at first. Never end their time-out early, no matter what they do (good or bad).

3. **Don't talk to them or look at them in time-out.** If she's trying to get your attention, or yelling, **talk to the walls.** Say something like *"I can't talk to my daughter right now because she's in time-out. She needs to sit quietly to get out of time-out. I really hope she does—time-out is no fun."*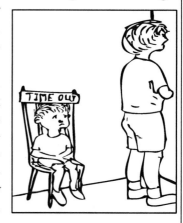

4. **Let them out of time-out only when they finish their time and agree to do something** (like pick up what they threw, or do

what they refused to do in the first place). Then make sure they do it, or else they go back to time-out. For example, if he went to time-out because he hit, have him say sorry (*after* completing his time in the chair) in order to get out. But he can't get out early for saying sorry. If he went to time-out because he wouldn't pick up his toys, he needs to agree to pick them up before he can get out.

5. **After his time is up, say,** *"Are you ready to(pick up your toys,* or *do what I told you to do before you went to time-out)?"* If he says yes, let him pick up his toys and praise him like mad. If he says no, or doesn't pick up after saying yes, he goes back for another time-out. If after a second time-out he still says no when you ask if he's ready to obey, you can either start tacking on minutes (don't go over one minute per year of age) OR say he'll lose something (like a privilege or a toy) if he doesn't pick up his toys.

What if your child is perfectly happy to stay in the time-out chair, so it doesn't seem to work? After making sure all the other steps were done correctly, I asked one mother what *she* was doing while her son was in time-out. She said that she's usually cleaning. I suggested that the next time, she start doing something that her son likes to do. Make your children want to be part of what is happening outside of time-out, so they won't want to stay in a boring chair. Making cookie dough while he was in time-out worked like a charm. He did whatever she asked to get out of time-out. But she didn't tell him he would get cookies if he obeyed, because she knew she shouldn't talk to him in time-out (and that would be a bribe). The goal is to make your kids want to obey and get out of time-out.

What if your kids won't stay in the chair (they get out before you say they can get out)? This will happen a lot at first. Warn them that **they'll have to stay in time-out even longer** unless they get back to the chair right now. If that doesn't work, say, *"Unless Suzie sits back in the chair right now, **she will lose something"*** (a privilege or thing for a while). Talk to the wall, NOT your child. *"Since Billy got out of the chair before he was told, he will not be able to watch Scooby-Doo today unless he comes back before I count to three."*

If you calmly count out loud, and he doesn't sit back down, say,

"OK, he didn't come back, now there will be no Scooby. Now he will lose his favorite toy until tomorrow unless he comes back." Take away no more than two things or privileges, so you can remember and follow through.

If, after you say what they will lose, they still won't obey and go back to the chair, go ahead and take away what you said you would and ignore the time out chair for now. When they complain about losing things, say, *"You didn't stay in time-out, so I said you would lose these things."* Give them a few minutes to react—they may cry, hit you or throw a lovely fit. They might not get upset until later. STAY CALM—take a parent time-out if needed.

Then they **need to do time-out all over if they want their things back**. Say, *"Are you ready to do time-out now and do what I say?"* If they say yes, and they complete time-out and do what you said to get out the first time, they can have their things back. If they don't finish time-out, then make sure you take away their things for as long as you said you would. If they want them back earlier, say, *"Are you ready to do time-out?"*

Don't chase them in order to put them back in the chair—it's tempting but probably the worst thing you can do. The chase can become a very rewarding game. They might giggle while you get more upset!

Instead, try putting them in a different room without much to do (like a guest bedroom). But don't play tug-of-war with the doorknob—it can actually be fun or even frightening for your child. If you shut the door, but your son opens it, leave the door open and tell him if he comes out he will lose something else. You could also put him in a car seat if he doesn't know how to get out of it. Then stay by the car but not in it. For two year olds, you can also try placing them in their empty playpen instead of a chair. You could also have kids sit on a step instead of on a chair. Just don't leave them unattended. There are other techniques that can be used to help keep children in the time-out chair (using a therapeutic holding procedure). Parents should work with a mental health professional when resorting to this.

What if you're out in public? Do the same things. Stay calm and quiet. It may help to whisper what you want in their ear. Good places to have public time-out include your car, a dressing room, near restrooms, maternity sections of stores, or any spot that is less crowded.

It may take a few tries to get time-out to work, but it almost always does if it's done correctly. If your child three years old or older won't complete time-out and do what you say to get out (no matter what you try), it's time to get professional help.

Harsh punishments over-power, hurt, or humiliate kids

Harsh punishments are often done in anger rather than as part of a discipline plan. They include any time a parent touches or threatens to touch a child in a negative way (holding down, yanking, pushing, pinching, shaking, slapping, or hitting). They also include personal attacks and criticizing, insulting, or yelling or swearing at children. Taking away your affection is also harsh. Making kids skip meals, throwing things at them, shoving them, threatening to leave them, or stomping out of a room are also examples.

Many parents have used some type of harsh punishment. It's usually because they didn't know what else to do, or because that's what their parents did. Some parents are firm believers in harsh punishments like hitting. They may say, "My parents whipped me, and I turned out all right." But things are different now. Society's views and laws on child maltreatment have changed. What might have been acceptable punishment 20 years ago may now be child abuse. Plus, harsh punishments are now showing bad results in research studies.

Harsh punishments can trick us into thinking that they work well. That's because they can stop a bad behavior quickly. So parents may think, "Wow, this really works." But the problem is that the naughty behaviors are only stopped for a short time, and then happen again. Harsh punishments don't teach children any good behaviors and don't prevent bad behaviors in the future.

Why harsh punishments hurt parenting

Studies clearly show that **kids raised with harsh punishments have more behavior problems**. They don't develop moral guides to make decisions. They don't learn as well. They're more likely to do poorly in school, use drugs or alcohol, pick delinquent friends, have psychological problems, be aggressive, and have relationship and legal problems. Later on, they're more likely to have suicidal thoughts, physically abuse their own children (your grandchildren), and have lower-paying jobs. Kids who are punished harshly tend to feel bad about themselves. They feel like they're always in trouble and that something is wrong with them. They may say, "You think I'm bad? I'll show you bad." So harsh punishments hurt your kids and actually make your job as a parent much harder.

Harsh punishments weaken the bond you have with your children, and may make them want to get back at you. Hitting and verbally assaulting children not only causes them physical and emotional pain, but it also **makes them angry**. That anger makes them much less willing to behave in the future. Harsh punishment also  teaches your kids that it's fine to physically or emotionally hurt someone when upset.

Children who are used to harsh punishment don't respond as much to rewards and milder punishments. Over time, parents who rely on harsh punishment need to be more severe to get a response. Those parents learn the hard way that it's much easier to scare a 6 year old into obeying than a 16 year old. There is a huge difference between getting children to obey because they love and want to please you, and getting them to obey because they're afraid of you. Parents who use harsh punishments try to get obedience by making kids afraid.

Parents who punish harshly are more likely to be stressed or depressed or abuse drugs or alcohol, and they were often abused as children. Harsh people tend to use harsh punishments. These folks are often angry, irritable, negative, critical and threatening. They tend to yell, argue and be annoyed with their kids. They emotionally abuse their kids by saying things that wear down self-esteem (such as, "You're a lazy good-for–nothing idiot. You always screw up. You're not like your sister, and you make me yell all the time").

Harsh parents have a tough time raising successful kids and their other relationships can suffer too. Perhaps you know a harsh person and know what we mean!

Spanking

Many parents use this for discipline, often because they were raised this way, or because it can stop a bad behavior quickly. Spanking means to discipline a child by hitting him or her with an open hand on the buttocks, arms or legs to cause pain but without causing a bruise or other physical harm. (Hitting a child with an object, instead of an open hand, is now considered by many experts to be child abuse.) Many experts these days consider spanking to be a harsh punishment.

Even though spanking can temporarily stop a bad behavior, there's no evidence that it helps children behave well in the future. Plus, unwanted **side effects** can occur. According to most research studies, aggression and other behavior problems, depression and other mental health problems, and future spouse abuse are all increased in children that were spanked compared to those that weren't. For reasons like these, the American Academy of Family Physicians' website, www.familydoctor.org, states that "Spanking isn't the best way to discipline children."

Some studies have not found bad side effects from spanking, but *only* when used under many hard to define conditions. These conditions included spanking only "mildly" and "occasionally", and only as a back-up to methods that have stronger research support (such as those in this book). And results also depended on what the child thought spankings meant, whether the parent explained reasons for spanking, situations that resulted in spankings, other discipline also used, race, family structure, child age, and the warmth, stress and frustration level of the parent. All these factors influenced how well spanking worked and whether it had bad side effects.

Even with some controversy in research studies, **a few things seem clear**. The highest risk of future problems is found when children are spanked under the age of 2, or at age 6 or older. Spanking children under the age of 2 can weaken their attachments to parents, which can lead to great behavior and emotional problems. Kids who are spanked at age 6 or older not only have more emotional and behavior problems, but they also have lower achievement scores than those who aren't spanked. It is also clear that the more often and more severely a child is spanked at any age, the more severe his or her misbehavior and emotional problems are.

Besides the strong risk of negative side effects, **we can't recommend spanking for the following reasons:**

1. Spanking **does little to prevent bad behavior in the future.** In fact, a child may misbehave *more* after a spanking. Parenting is easiest when bad behaviors are prevented, instead of dealt with once they happen. Spanking doesn't teach good behaviors such as responsibility, and caring for others. But rewarding children for choosing to be good instead of bad *does* increase good behaviors, as well as prevent bad behaviors, with none of the risks that spanking has. **Rewards and nonphysical mild punishments work better** in the long run with children of any age.

2. Parents may **need to use more and more force** to get children to respond to a spanking as they grow bigger. When children are 4 years old, a spank on the bottom might get them to temporarily obey. But spanking won't impress a 16 year old, so parents may consider lashing them with a belt to try to get a response. When this happens, parents often cross the line between harsh punishment and abuse. When a mark is left on a child, it is child abuse. Using more force can also destroy relationships, and make kids act out more because of anger.

3. If other methods like action limits aren't used when children are young, it's harder to get them to work **when kids are too big to spank.** That can make it very tough to discipline teenagers.

4. Spanking **teaches children that it's okay to hit people** out of anger or frustration, including loved ones. It also shows kids that hitting and causing pain is a way to handle problems with family and other people, since children learn from what parents do.

5. Parents who **abuse** their children by leaving bruises and other physical damage often think they are just "spanking", and we don't want these parents to think that what they are doing is okay.

6. Most parents report that their children are angry, sad and have hurt feelings after being spanked. And most parents report feeling very angry, remorseful and agitated when spanking their children. These

aren't pleasant feelings and **can prevent a good, lasting relationship** between parent and child. That close relationship is the single most important thing you need to raise emotionally healthy, well behaved and successful children.

Even if you're using spanking now, you can switch to using the *7 Skills*. Using the methods in this book can work for almost every parent and child, without the risks of spanking. It will take some time for your kids to get used to your new ways, but your efforts will make things much easier in the long run.

Natural consequences

Harsh punishments hurt parenting success, but rewards and mild punishments help train children to behave well. Other useful consequences happen naturally after your child does something. These are called natural consequences. If your child studies hard for a test, he will probably get a good grade. That's a **positive natural consequence** of studying hard. If he chooses not to study hard and gets a bad grade, that grade is a **negative natural consequence**. When done right, natural consequences can work well, especially with teenagers.

But natural consequences aren't all created equal. Some can actually be dangerous. If your teen drinks tonight and then drives, she may die or kill somebody else. Getting into a car accident while drunk is a negative natural consequence. But the severity of that consequence is not what any parent wants. So the tricky part with negative natural consequences is that **you need to control their severity for them to work**. For instance, it would be OK for your child to do badly on a test that he didn't study for, but not for him to fail the class.

Here are some examples of using natural consequences safely. If your child breaks a neighbor's window, you could have him go to the neighbors to apologize and pay for the cost of repairs (what most of us would do naturally). If your child isn't ready for school in time to catch the bus, have her walk or ride a bike to school if it's safe. If school is too far away, your teen can call a cab and pay for the ride, or your child can pay *you* for a ride. If your teen causes a car accident, have her go without a car while the car is getting fixed. She could help pay for repairs and for the increased insurance premiums. If your child doesn't have a job, have her get a part-time job or pay you back by doing more chores. The point is to show your children that even accidents have expensive consequences.

So, using natural consequences doesn't mean parents are off the hook. You can't just sit back and let things happen to get good results. You need to think of what the most likely natural consequence will be after your child messes up, and try to make sure nothing serious happens. You can help your child learn from natural consequences by talking with him or her about making a different choice next time. Say, *"It's too bad that (the bad consequence) happened. Why do you think it happened? What could you have done differently (or what do you think you'll do next time)"?*

You also need to figure out if a natural consequence will change your child's behavior. Say your son has gotten into trouble shoplifting. You have intervened in the past (paid fees to keep his record clean). Now he's been caught vandalizing a building. You could intervene again, but is that in your child's best long-term interest? Perhaps he's on a slippery slope to even bigger problems. Maybe he needs to get the message that mom and dad can't bail him out of everything. No parent likes the thought of a child in court and being put on probation, but maybe that natural consequence is best for this child. After all, probation this year is far better than jail next year.

Natural consequences are often part of a parenting program called **tough love.** This program often focuses on letting whatever is going to happen, happen, no matter how severe it is. Parents often assume that they don't have to do anything. They think their kids will learn the hard way what can happen when they mess up, so they'll be motivated to shape up. An example is to lock the house door when a child arrives home late, even in the winter.

Our problem with this tough love approach is that kids are often set up to fail, because they don't have the maturity and skills to stay out of trouble, and they often won't. They may need to rely on friends who are bad influences. This hands-off approach also makes kids feel rejected, which is often the truth. Parents who use tough love are often so fed up and tired of their child that they give up. If your child repeatedly misses curfew, go out and find him and take him home. Find the consequences that will make him obey curfew in the future and keep him safe. Examples are taking away his transportation, money or other privileges he cares about.

Using both rewards and mild punishments gets you the best behavior

Rewarding good behavior works better to prevent bad behavior, than punishing the bad behavior once it happens. Too many punishments (even mild ones) can wear down the relationship, and stop working over time. So, a successful parenting program is NOT using one mild punishment for every reward. It includes **about five rewards for every punishment** (just a rough goal to shoot for). Remember the relationship savings account?   Using even mild punishment is a withdrawal and rewards are deposits. You need more rewards than punishments to help keep a positive balance.

Action Limits

So! You learned how to pick limits for your children in skill #4. (Remember P.S. I'M HELPING?) You've also learned the best ways to set those limits (tell them what to do), and about rewarding and punishing consequences. This is the exciting part where you'll put this all together to get your kids to obey when they resist. Even good kids won't always obey and decide to be good. Sometimes they'll only obey when you take action by "setting an action limit".

Action limits can fix the two main types of bad behavior

1. You told your child to do **something specific** and **she didn't do** it (for example, she didn't do her chores, or she didn't do her homework before watching TV like you told her to).
2. Your child is **doing something bad that you want him to stop**, or he's already done something that you don't want to happen again.

After describing what action limits are, we'll cover how to use them to fix these two types of misbehavior.

How to enforce a limit by using an action limit

"OK KIDS, ACTION!"

Setting an action limit is when you tell your kids they'll get a punishment consequence if they don't obey (or in other action limits, they'll get a rewarding consequence if they *do* obey). If they don't take action and obey, then you take action with a consequence! You can use action limits to quickly change a naughty behavior happening now, or to prevent one in the future. First, we'll tell you how to set an action limit with a punishment, and then we'll tell you how to set it with a reward.

Punishment Action Limits

Use a punishment action limit if you told your child to do something using our command guidelines (see page 89), and your child still doesn't do it. Tell your child what you want done, and what the consequence will be if it isn't done now.

How to set a punishment action limit

"_____(Child's name)___, you have two choices.
You can __(do what I asked / stop a bad behavior)__
or you can choose __(a consequence)___.
Which one do you pick?"

For younger children, use a visual aid. **Hold up two fingers like a peace sign and say, *"You have two choices."*** If you think they obeyed, check that they actually did and praise them. They avoided a punishment and got a reward instead! The more often you praise good behavior, the less often you'll have to set action limits overall.

What if they won't answer or obey? Then say, *"Pick which one before I count to three, or I'll pick for you."* Your children need to say their choice before you slowly count to three, or you get to pick for them (and you'll pick the consequence, of course). Usually they'll obey because they don't want the consequence. If they don't pick, be sure they get the consequence.

Examples		
"Mark, you have two choices.	*You can finish your homework*	*or you can miss the party tomorrow."*
"Shakira, you have two choices.	*You can mow the lawn*	*or you can pay your brother to do it."*
"Isaac, you have two choices.	*You can turn off the TV*	*or you can lose TV time for a day."*
"Maria, you have two choices.	*You can stop screaming,*	*or you can take a nap after lunch."*

For another example, let's say you've had to ask Maria to come in the house three times, but didn't tell her there would be a consequence for disobeying (you didn't set an action limit). Now she finally came in. Instead of punishing her, tell her what will happen if she doesn't obey you quickly next time. *"Maria, the next time I tell you to come in, and you don't obey quickly, you'll lose your play time the next day* (or some other consequence)." She'll learn to obey and you may not have to wait for her the next time! Setting an action limit earlier decreases how many times you have to ask, gets you quicker action, and saves you frustration.

Five conditions that make punishment consequences work

There's just one more important thing you need to know about punishments. They won't work, and can backfire and make things worse, unless you make sure that five little conditions have been met *before* you punish. Maybe you're thinking, "Oh, say it ain't so"! It may seem like checking five things before punishing will take a lot of time, but with practice, it's quick and automatic. Anyway, they all need to be true for punishment to work. Here they are:

1. Make sure your child knew exactly what he/she was supposed to do.
2. Make sure your child knew what would happen if he/she didn't do it.
3. Make sure your child was capable and able to do it.
4. Make sure your emotions are under control.
5. Make sure the punishment fits the crime.

Now we'll go over each condition. These explanations will include many of the top keys to effective discipline, along with examples. So please read them carefully for best results.

Punishment condition #1: Make sure they knew exactly what they were supposed to do.

Did you use a clear, simple command (see skill #4)? It can help to have kids repeat what you say to make sure they know. *"Now what did I just say?"* Unless you are very sure that your children knew what they were supposed to do, don't punish them. Saying, "They should have known" isn't good enough. When children really didn't know, they'll get angry and lose trust and respect for you. That will lead to worse behavior. House rules you have already set up automatically meet this condition. (That's why we like them.)

Punishment condition #2: Make sure they knew what would happen if they didn't obey.

This means that you set an action limit correctly. Punished kids often say parents are being mean or unfair. But, an action limit lets your children know that they'll get a consequence if they don't obey. All you have to say is, *"You knew what you were supposed to do, and what would happen if you didn't. You chose to disobey, so you chose your consequence."* This teaches them that they are responsible for their actions, not you.

The goal here is getting kids to recognize that disobeying is *their* bad choice, not something you do to be mean. House rules meet this condition automatically—kids should expect a punishment when they break house rules.

Do you need to decide and say which exact consequence they will get when you set an action limit? That works best, but isn't always possible when you need them to obey quickly. You often won't have time to decide whether to take away their phone or give them kitchen duty tonight. Plus, if you are too specific, it'll be harder to remember what you said. You need to be able to set action limits to change behavior even when you can't decide which consequence to give. So, you can use a general consequence in an action limit like this: *"If you* *don't obey, you will lose something (*or, *I will take something away,* or, *you will get an extra chore)."*

If you haven't set an action limit (told them a consequence will happen if they disobey), and they haven't broken a house rule, don't punish them. Otherwise they'll have good reason to think you're being unfair. Instead, say that you're upset at what they did, and they'll get a consequence next time. Of course there are very bad behaviors (like destroying property, violent behavior like hitting someone, illegal things like drug and alcohol use, or starting a fire) that you can't predict or let go unpunished. Go ahead and break this rule in these situations.

Punishment condition #3: Make sure your children were capable and able to do what you asked.

This one's a biggie! It tends to be harder than most parents realize, but understanding it really helps discipline work. **Being capable** means a child is developed or old enough to do something you ask. How do you know for sure that your child is capable of doing something? One way is if you've seen him or her do it many times before. Also check Appendix A. If that table shows your child is old enough to do something, he or she still needs to be taught how to do it first. Remember that kids often won't be able to do things as well as adults.

Being able means kids have the right circumstances to do things you ask. Just because they're capable doesn't mean they're able to do something at a particular time. It's harder for kids to obey if they're sick or stressed during special events or travel. That's why the first day of school or daycare isn't a great time to work on discipline. A 5 year old may be capable of getting dressed alone in the morning, but not able to get his pajamas on when really tired. A 14 year old may be capable of starting her homework alone, but not able to today because she and her friend got into a fight. You may be capable of doing math, but not able to do your tax return right now, because you're worried about your job.

It's really important not to set an action limit or punish for something your child isn't capable or able to do. Take time to teach your child how to do it instead. I once had a mother who insisted that her children be toilet trained before they were one year old. If the children had one accident during the day, they were scolded. If they had two, they were spanked. Despite what this mother thought, one year olds are not developed enough (aren't capable) of being potty trained. This mother hurt her children and planted the seeds for big power struggles with them that came into full bloom in the teenage years.

So what should you do when you know your kids are capable, but they don't do something? Try to decide if they're actively **defying** you (choosing to disobey) or are just not able to do it right now. With a strong relationship, your older children will do what they're told over 70 percent of the time! So if they don't obey, there's a good chance they are NOT defying you. Something else may be going on to make them unable to obey right now.

If you can't understand why your child is acting a certain way, perhaps your child can't either. Kids often are aware that something is wrong, but don't have the words to describe it. Use your talk skills to help both of you understand what's going on. This can help them get ready to obey.

If they *are* defying you (just plain choosing to disobey), be sure you meet the other four conditions before you punish. Then, if your relationship seems weak lately, focus on building that up rather than on discipline for a while. If your child is being defiant, it's a sign he or she needs more good attention, as well as action limits.

Punishment condition #4: Make sure your emotions are under control before you discipline.

Guilt, sadness and fear are common emotions that can make discipline fail. But anger puts the biggest brake on discipline. When we say things in anger, kids remember we were upset much more than what we said (and that makes it hard for them to learn).

Over the years I've worked with many parents who were in legal trouble for physically abusing their children. Hardly any meant to hurt their children, but they did. They got angry and decided to physically punish their kids. Their anger made them lose control and the custody of their kids. Losing control can also cost you your children's love and respect.

One of the best ways to keep anger from getting out of control is to **avoid giving kids too many chances to obey**. Parents often give a command and then wait for their kids to act. The longer parents wait, and the more they ask, the more frustrated they get. Here's an example:

> Parent: "Lucy, it's time for school, please turn off the TV and get your coat on."
> After a couple minutes, the TV is still on.
> Parent: "I said, turn off the TV—we gotta go."
> Lucy: "OK, I know." The TV is still on.
> Parent: "Lucy, come on!"
> Lucy: "Wait, mom!"
> Parent gets mad and yells, "Damn it Lucy, now!"

When parents just keep asking and then yell, kids learn that they don't need to obey until their parents start yelling! But you can avoid this. Just set an action limit after the first time you ask and they don't obey. *"Lucy, it's time for school. Please turn off the TV right now and get your coat on. If you don't, you won't be able to play when you get home."* Lucy will obey more quickly, and your life will be easier.

Punishment condition #5: Make sure the punishment fits the crime.

Parents often wonder how much punishment they should give. The answer is—as little as possible. Start with a small consequence to see if that works. **Start by only taking away one privilege or object for one day, or adding one chore for one day.** Always avoid harsh punishment and making your mild punishment too long or severe. For example, it's usually more work to enforce long groundings than it's worth. Generally, **grounding** shouldn't last more than three days.

It's very important not to take away too many things or privileges, or add too many chores all at once. If you take away everything you can think of at one time, what does a child have to lose for bad behavior? What could you say you'll take away next to try to get your child to behave? In other words, don't say something like, "If you don't obey, I'll take away all your toys, your bike, play time with all your friends, and all your new clothes." Take away one object or privilege first, so you have more options.

For deciding which consequence to use, generally look at the seriousness of the naughty behavior. Is it a repeat offense? Did they do it to hurt someone? Also, it works best to take away an object or privilege that caused the problem. For example, if your son drove his buddies home when he wasn't supposed to, he should lose his car for a while. In addition, if you have already had to punish your child several times that day, you may want to quit there until tomorrow. You might let some little bad behaviors go and just focus on the big ones. Look at all these factors and then choose the punishment.

How to Use Punishment Action Limits for Misbehavior

Now you know how to set an action limit with a punishment consequence, and the five conditions that make punishments work. Now we'll give you important details on how to use punishments to fix the two **main kinds of bad behavior in children**. Do you remember those? The first is when you ask your child to do something and he or she won't do it (like a chore or helping someone or being on time for school). The second kind is when you ask your child to stop doing something that you don't like and he or she keeps doing it anyway (such as swearing or missing curfew or hurting a sibling or taking money from your purse).

Before picking a punishment, ask yourself which type of misbehavior you're dealing with. Then follow the directions described below.

What if your child won't do what you've asked her to do?

Take something away *until your child obeys*. This is how to handle the first kind of bad behavior in children. Let's say you've had trouble with getting your daughter to finish her daily chores for example. First, set an action limit with a consequence in the way that we described earlier in the chapter *("You need to finish all your chores before I get home or I will take your phone away until you do them.")* Now let's say that when you get home, her chores aren't finished. What do you do? You calmly say, *"Your chores aren't done, so you chose to lose your phone. Give me your phone, and I'll keep it until you do all the* *chores you were supposed to do so far this week."* Keep her phone until she catches up on her chores.

Now what if she still refuses to do her chores, or starts but doesn't finish them? **Then add another consequence.** *"Ok, you've already lost your phone. Now if you don't do your chores before dinner, you will lose your radio privileges too. Do you choose to do your chores or to lose both your phone and your radio time?"* If that doesn't get her to do her chores by the time you specified, you can add one more consequence, up to a total of three. *"OK, you've lost your phone and your radio (computer, or car, or toy) privileges. Now you won't be able to hang out with your friends until all your chores are done."*

Only use up to three consequences at a time, and only for a week at the most. More than three consequences won't work any better and will be harder for you to enforce. Write down what you said you would do, so you don't forget. If she doesn't obey, be sure to carry out all the consequences you promised. Then when she complains about not having her phone, or time with friends, or not being able to use the computer even though she needs it for assignments, just say, *"It's too bad that you chose those consequences. You need to catch up on your chores if you want them back."* It may take a few days for her to miss her things enough to obey, but she usually will within a week. Basically your child is **earning back his or her objects or privileges**.

If you have repeat problems getting your child to obey and do something, you could make her earn back her things one at a time. *"If you do your chores every day this week, you can have your phone back. But in order to earn your computer time back, you'll need to do _____ (extra work)."* Or, try different consequences that mean more to her. Then write it down in your planner, so you don't forget! If you chose important consequences to her, chances are that she will decide that doing her chores is worth getting her things back.

If your child isn't obeying by a week's time, it's time to get help from a mental health professional. You could be dealing with more serious problems, such as a badly battered relationship between you, depression, Oppositional Defiant Disorder, or substance abuse.

What if your child refuses to stop a bad behavior?

Take something away *for a certain period of time*. This is how to handle the second type of bad behavior, which is when your child is doing something bad that you want him or her to stop, or has already done something bad that you don't want to happen again. This can include when kids disobey **house rules** or other well established limits.

Let's say you're having trouble with your son hurting your daughter. Maybe he pulled her hair, then scratched her and then finally hit her. First of all, set an action limit. But don't think of these as three different bad behaviors—they're all hurting behaviors that you want to stop, so you can use the same action limit for all of them.

The action limit should state what he'll lose if he doesn't stop hurting her and for how long. Say, *"You are hurting your sister. If you hurt her again, I will take away your bike for a day."* (By the way, it would have been best if you had set this action limit after he pulled her hair, instead of waiting until he hit her!)

Now, let's say that he goes ahead and hits her again (ah, the little darling), and so you follow through and take his bike away for a day. When you give it back to him, say, *"Next time you hurt your sister, I'll take your bike away for two days."* Ah! You've just set another action limit that might stop that bad behavior from happening again. Write it down in your planner and follow through.

You can add consequences up to a total of three, for up to a week, just like we already discussed above for the first kind of misbehavior.

What if your child refuses to go along with a consequence?

In other words, you said you'd take away a privilege or object, and your child refuses to give it up. For example, you told your son he can't go out with friends for a week, so you took his car keys. But he just calls his friend to come pick him up and goes out anyway. Or maybe you took away his toy (or his cell phone), but he refuses to give it to you. Or perhaps you took away computer privileges, but you know he used the computer while you were at work.

In these situations, calmly tell him that he will **lose the object or privilege for longer** if he doesn't obey. If he refuses to give you his favorite toy, say *"You need to give it to me in five minutes or I will take it away for two days instead of one."* Then start counting. Or, do what you can to take the object or privilege away yourself (take the toy, put a hold on his cell phone service, take a computer power cord away, or ask a parent not to allow their child to pick up your child).

You can also add **other consequences for up to a total of three.** These should be objects or privileges you know you can take away because he doesn't have to physically give them to you. For example, if you said, *"You need to give me your iPod in five minutes or you won't get your allowance this week."* If he gives you his iPod, then he still gets his allowance. If not, say, *"OK, you lost your iPod and your allowance. If you don't give me your I-pod in five minutes, there will be no.... (TV, or playing today)."* Don't allow him to bargain! He must give the item to you or he will lose the other things you said he would lose.

What if they aren't learning from past consequences?

Almost all children will decide not to obey action limits occasionally, and so they'll get punishment consequences from time to time. Getting those consequences will teach them that they need to do what you say.

But let's say you've had to give consequences to your child a lot lately, and he or she doesn't seem to be learning from them. And now he or she won't obey an action limit again. First, remain calm! Say, *"Remember what happened last time you didn't obey? Well the same things will happen this time if you don't obey by the time I count to three."*

If saying that doesn't get them to obey, **try using a new consequence or set of consequences**. Remember that consequences need to be things that your child really cares about or uses often. It takes practice to find which consequences will motivate your child to obey consistently.

And that's how it's done! If your child won't obey a certain action limit after you've followed these steps for a week, or if you've tried these methods for a few weeks, and your children aren't obeying action limits most all of the time, it's time to get help from a mental health professional.

Reward Action Limits

Now we'll talk about how to set action limits with rewards instead of punishments. These action limits reward good behaviors so they will keep happening in the future, or they can prevent bad behaviors when you think they may happen in the future.

How to set a reward action limit

" *(Child's name)* ,
if you *(do what I ask / act appropriately)* ,
then you can *(have a reward)* ."

Be very clear what they need to do to get the reward—be short and specific. Don't ask them to do too many things—then they may fail to get rewarded because it's too hard.

Examples		
"Mark,	*if you finish your homework before dinner*	*you can stay up later."*
"Latoya,	*if you mow the lawn today without complaining*	*you can go shopping when you're done."*
"Isaac,	*if you turn off the TV right now*	*you can watch your show when we get back."*
"Maria,	*if you don't scream at me the whole day,*	*you can play outside when we get home tonight."*

Using a reward action limit to prevent bad behavior is much easier than setting a punishment action limit once your child is already misbehaving. And rewards work better in the long run. The more you reward and praise in general, the less you'll need any action limits. Praise them when they do something you ask, or do something good *without* being asked. Also, give the reward only *after* they actually finish what you asked them to do, otherwise it becomes a bribe that hurts discipline.

Don't make rewards too big. As with anything, moderation is the key.

Review the list of good rewards in the box found on page 104. Don't make a reward so big that you have trouble matching it in the future, such as, "Since you picked up your room without being asked, we are going to Disney World for a week!" Also, please review what giving a bribe is so you can avoid doing it, on page 105. Bribing would be to give the reward before they finish their time being good, or promising a reward for stopping a bad behavior in progress.

Giving reward and punishment consequences

Give them right away, or as soon as possible. The best consequences are ones you know you can give right now, especially for younger kids. Praise your 5 year old for using his inside voice at the library while you're still there. Later on, you can praise him again when he hears you tell your spouse. Don't tell your daughter that she won't be able to play with her friends next week—that's too far in the future. Say that she can't play with her friends today, or take something else away today.

If they obey the action limit only for a short time, but then go back to the bad behavior, remind them of the consequence for not obeying. If they continue to disobey or obey only briefly, then carry out the same consequence again. You'll need to do this a lot with younger children.

Do what you say—follow through on consequences! This is the most time consuming part of discipline, so it's often where parents mess up. It's also the most important part of discipline overall. Your children will do best if they know what to expect. If you say they'll get a reward or punishment, they need to get it. Your kids need to believe you or they won't take you seriously. Following through is worth every minute it takes! If you don't follow through, expect discipline to fail over time.

Delaying consequences is not being inconsistent. Sometimes we're too busy at the moment (around other people, at work, disciplining another child), so it isn't possible to follow through right away. Good reasons to delay punishments are: being very mad at your child at the moment, or when punishing right now would embarrass a child in front of friends. A good reason to delay a reward may be that you don't have money today to buy the ice cream cone you promised.

In these situations, it's OK to put off discipline for a little while. Later is better than never. But tell your child why you are delaying a consequence. Then when you do give it, say why they're getting it. *"Today we can get that ice cream cone because you were so good in the car yesterday. Sorry you had to wait."*

Not following through on a consequence can be worse than not setting an action limit in the first place. Delaying discipline for a short while, if you have a good reason, is not the same as being inconsistent. But avoid the "wait until your father/mother gets home" syndrome. Expecting the other parent to discipline for you makes you inconsistent. It also sets up the other parent as someone to dislike or be afraid of.

What to Try When Discipline Isn't Working

First, reread these instructions to make sure you're using action limits correctly. It takes time and practice to get them to work. That's a bummer, huh? That's because kids don't know that parents will follow through on consequences. This is especially true if you haven't followed through before. It'll take following through on many action limits for them to learn that you'll do what you say. It'll take a few weeks to find the consequences that will make your kids take action. Once you get good enough behavior, you won't have to set action limits every day. If you can't get results, here are some things to try.

Build up your relationship. Children who feel close to their parents naturally obey more often. Use the activities in chapter 2.

Use more reward action limits than punishment action limits.

Laugh to yourself, but not at your kids. Seeing the humor in their bad behavior can relieve your stress and anger, and that can make discipline work better. The little munchkins can act pretty goofy when they act out or whine about limits or consequences. Just be careful not to let your child think you are laughing at him. Turn away or hide your face while you smile. Laughing directly at a child who is misbehaving can reinforce the bad behavior and hurt his feelings. He may say, "Stop laughing at me!" Then just say, *"I'm sorry, I'm not laughing at you—just at what you're doing. That can't be my big boy doing that."*

It's normal to feel embarrassed when your kids show their worst behavior in public. You just gotta get over it. It doesn't mean you're a bad parent, and it happens to everyone! If someone notices, say something funny like, *"If you think this is bad, you should see his Dad!"* or *"I'm so excited about her nap today"*

Remove your child from the situation. Sometimes young children get over stimulated, especially in new situations where you really want them to be good (like parties, stores, or special events). They may just need to take a short break in a different room or in the car. Once they settle down, have them practice how they will act before they go back to the situation.

Have a quiet contest when you need things quiet quickly. *"Let's have a quiet contest—whoever talks or makes any other noise first loses. Start on the count of three."* You could even reward the winner.

Double-check your consistency. Are you setting and enforcing good limits? Are you using rewards regularly? Have you really followed through with what you told your kids would happen? Are you having relationship activities as recommended?

Take a parent's time-out. When you're really frustrated, put your kids in a safe place, and say you need some time alone. Go to a quiet place, deep breathe, think, and come out with a plan. This might mean locking yourself in the bathroom or running the kids next door for awhile.

Say that you noticed bad behavior and are planning how to handle it. Give them a warning that you know they disobeyed, and you are planning what the consequence will be if it continues. Say, *"I'm thinking of something to take away if you don't stop like I asked."* This gives them a chance to stop the bad behavior even before you have to set an action limit. This can work like a charm once they learn that you follow through on consequences!

What NOT to Do When Discipline Isn't Working

These things either don't help kids behave or aren't good for you.

Don't sulk around the house or give them the silent treatment. Try not to show your daughter that she's affected your mood and your day, because that can reinforce bad behavior. Hum, sing, chat to yourself, or laugh to yourself instead. Fake it if you have to! Sulkers withhold affection more, and that leads to future behavior problems.

Don't have a temper tantrum. If you show a lot of anger or cry, you could be rewarding naughty behaviors and letting them set your mood.

Don't bribe them to stop bad behavior. You CAN offer a reward *after* they continue good behavior.

Don't give in to pleading, guilt, threats or bargaining for a better deal. Follow through on punishments even when they promise they'll never do it again if you forget about it just this one time. If you believe that one, we've got some swamp land to sell you!

Don't give up. DO keep trying the skills in this book. Following these instructions will eventually work if they are done correctly. If they're not working fast enough, get professional help.

How to Encourage Responsibility and Trust

Using consequences consistently teaches your children that they are responsible for what happens after they do something. They can't blame anyone else when you told them what consequence they'd get for an action. Say your son colors on the wall, and you send him to time-out and then have him wipe it off. If you do that every time, he'll eventually stop coloring on the wall just to see what happens. He'll learn that *he* is responsible for getting punished. And he can take the credit and feel responsible for earning rewards for good behavior too.

Use trust exercises for teenagers

This is another way to teach responsibility to older kids. **Trust exercises** are tasks they can do to show you they can be trusted. Say, *"I need to learn that I can trust you. If you show responsibility, you can gain my trust. The more responsibility you take, the more you'll be allowed to do."* This teaches kids the link between showing responsibility and being trusted.

Move from small responsibilities to bigger ones. You might give your son ten dollars, tell him to go buy milk, and bring back the change and receipt. If he does, say, *"Thanks, good job,"* and give him another bigger job later. Or, tell him to be home by 10 PM. If he isn't, say *"You aren't taking responsibility, so you can't go out for awhile until you earn my trust again* (by doing more trust exercises).*"* Good kids will call when running late, and if it only happens occasionally, that's ok.

So what happens when kids behave so badly that parents learn not to trust them? Often these parents don't give opportunities to earn back their trust, so it never happens. No matter how badly your children behave, you can still teach responsibility and gain back trust using these exercises—and your seven skills.

Consistency in Parenting

This is the **most important part of discipline** and the most common area parents come up short. You could be the most loving, rewarding parent with a great relationship. But if you aren't consistent, you can still have trouble.

Consistency is how similarly you deal with things over time. It's how predictable you are, and how often you follow through on what you say. The more predictable your children's world is, the better. If you tell Joey that you'll take him to the park and then don't, you're being inconsistent. If you get mad at the kids for watching TV before doing their homework one day, but not the next, you're being inconsistent.

Parents are often inconsistent because life gets in the way. And being consistent takes work! Maybe you promised to take Joey to the park before you realized that you had to work this weekend. Perhaps you didn't discipline for watching TV that day, because you were too tired to notice that they hadn't finished their homework yet.

It's impossible to always be consistent, and luckily, you don't need to. Your life would be way too strict and boring if you were. But too little consistency creates the most problems with discipline. Some parents are consistently inconsistent! You'll know you need to be more consistent if your kids aren't behaving well enough (see pages 6 and 103 to review healthy expectations for good behavior), or if your discipline skills don't seem to be working. You know you are being consistent enough when your kids can tell you what will happen after they have misbehaved (they'll get a consequence).

How being consistent makes parenting easier

Consistently following through on limits and consequences makes **kids behave better.** On the other hand, inconsistent parenting is strongly linked to behavior and other problems (like breaking rules, aggression, poor grades, anxiety, depression and substance use). It sure is tempting to let misbehavior go for now, isn't it? Yah, especially when you're tired of dealing with it. BUT, letting it go now just makes it much harder to deal with later. If you spend the time and energy following through now, it'll pay off big time down the road. Following through takes practice. So give it a few weeks before expecting improvement.

Consistency also **teaches kids self-control**. If you give them consistent limits, they'll learn that some behaviors aren't acceptable, even if they've never done them before. If you consistently tell your three year old to only draw in her coloring books and not on your walls, she'll be less likely to paint graffiti on public property as a teenager.

As we said, consistency **teaches children responsibility.** It also helps children learn good behavior much faster. Think of how much harder it would be to learn how to get to the post office if you took a different route each time. Sure, kids who grow up without consistency can eventually learn things, but it takes much longer. If Dad always takes away the bike when a helmet isn't worn, the child will wear the helmet.

Consistency **helps lower a child's stress** and makes the world feel safer. If Mom always comes to pick a child up as she says she will, the child won't worry that she won't come.

How to be more consistent

Think and plan ahead. Choose your battles and your limits ahead of time. What are the kinds of things you absolutely do and don't want your children doing at this age? Use P.S. I'M HELPING to help you decide. Then decide if a behavior

violates those limits. If it does, set action limits or house rules to correct it. If you start consistently stopping these behaviors, they will eventually stop themselves.

Don't set an action limit unless you feel sure you can follow through on giving the consequence. It's better not to set an action limit than to not follow through on it. Parents often make empty threats to their children ("If you don't shape up, you'll be grounded for a year!") Your kids need to learn that if you say you are going to do something, you'll do it. It should be pretty rare for something to keep you from carrying out a consequence. (We already talked about when it's alright to delay.)

Have practice sessions for your kids to learn good behaviors. You can delay trying to fix a behavior today by working on it later. Practicing decreases the need for discipline, and makes it easier to be consistent. Try to anticipate when your kids won't behave, or when you've had trouble before, and practice before the next time it could happen. Practice when you aren't stressed, and make it fun—you can be silly and they'll still learn. You can practice table manners, making conversation, meeting new people, and appropriate behavior at your workplace, at religious services, and in the classroom. You can even practice dealing with disappointment: *"We're at the store looking for the new toy I promised you, and they don't have it. What will you do?"*

Try to use the same consequences that you know work. It's best if your kids expect the same things to happen. Through practice, you'll find the best consequences for different situations. Try to get to the point where you remember those consequences easily. But, limits and consequences will need to be changed over time, as your children's interests and abilities change.

Be consistent AND flexible with discipline

Consistency doesn't mean every time your child does X, you have to do Y. You don't have to use an action limit or put her in time-out every time she yells. You only have to *if* you *told* her you would. Consistency just means reacting in a similar way. When she yells, instead of an action limit, you could just say it's hard to have fun with her when she yells. Ignoring a behavior one day and punishing it the next isn't similar. Let's say your child remembers his homework, so you tell him how mature he's getting. The next day he remembers again and you give him a high five. You consistently praised him but were flexible in how you did it.

You can make some **exceptions to limits or consequences by being flexible** and still be consistent. (Thank goodness!) Here are examples.

- You said he's too young for roller blades and then you see his friend using them. It now seems safe, so you cancel the limit.
- You said no bike riding for two days, but Grandma is coming and she loves to ride with the grandkids. So you have your child do extra chores instead, and explain that this change was made only because Grandma's visiting. (You did it for her, not the kids.)
- You decided your limit or punishment was inappropriate, or could be bent this time, so you changed it. Lighten up—no one does it right all the time! Just say, *"I've had a chance to think about it more and have decided on a better decision on that limit (or consequence)."* Try to give a reason and make it clear that this won't happen very often.

If you find yourself often changing your mind, spend more time planning limits and consequences before giving them to your children so you can be more consistent.

Don't let **guilt** be a part of your discipline decisions. Let's say a consequence for your daughter was missing a dance, and you feel really bad. You still shouldn't let her go, but you could surprise her later with a little something nice. Just don't tell her it has anything to do with the consequence. It's just because you love her or to brighten her day.

What if you've been inconsistent so far? There's still time! Think about the two or three things your kids do or don't do that trouble you the most and start there. Plan discipline and promise yourself you'll carry it out. You can even ask an adult to watch and let you know when you're not. In a family meeting, describe bad behaviors, tell your kids that your inconsistency has been bad for them and what your plan is.

Consistency between different caregivers

While consistency starts with you, it doesn't end with you when other people take care of your kids. Your child will be better off if all caregivers are as consistent as possible, especially at home. If you and your partner can't agree on how to handle things, discipline fails.

When one parent tells the children to do something, and the other parent says they don't need to, it gives confusing, mixed messages. Kids as young as 4 will take advantage of this, playing one parent off of the other. One parent may say yes more often, and when kids figure that out, they may ask this "softer" parent for things after the other parent says no. If your child does this often, when she asks to do something, ask her what your partner said. Then check with your partner to see if that's really what happened. Take away a privilege if she doesn't fess up to asking another parent or caregiver first.

Communication is the answer. Normal parents will disagree over discipline. Relatives and day care providers can also disagree. Talk to each person about what you think should happen if your child does something and why. If anyone is upset, calm down first. Find things you can agree on, or find compromises where you both get something you want. Agreeing should be easier if everyone reads this book first.

Don't let your children hear these discussions. The more kids hear caregivers argue, the more they'll misbehave! Discuss it in private, as long as your child's health isn't being threatened at the time. If you and your partner hardly ever agree on discipline, there may be something wrong with your relationship—see a counselor. If another caregiver refuses to become more consistent with what you want to do, then become even more consistent yourself doing what you think is best.

Look at you. You made it through the meatiest skill yet! We now would like you to please fill out our little consistency survey, since it's so critical to success. Rate each statement in the table below according to how often it is true: seldom or never true, sometimes true, usually or very often true. Circle the number in that column with a pencil. Answer according to what actually happens now (not what you plan to do, or the way you think things should be). Start with your oldest child and add up the columns to get your total score. Then erase and start over for your next child, and so on.

		Seldom or never	Sometimes	Usually or very often
1.	This child does what he or she is told to do without much delay.	0	1	2
2.	When threatened with punishment, this child will do what needs to be done.	0	1	2
3.	This child understands what "no" means, even if he/she argues.	0	1	2
4.	This child is good at getting around the rules.	2	1	0
5.	When I give this child a chore, I end up doing it for him or her.	2	1	0
6.	My spouse/partner and I disagree about how to deal with this child's behavior.	2	1	0
7.	This child trusts me to do what I say I will.	0	1	2
8.	This child is well behaved when away from home.	0	1	2
9.	It is hard to figure out how to deal with this child's behavior.	2	1	0
10	If this child is sorry, I let him/her off easier.	2	1	0
11	It's easier to discipline this child when I'm in a good mood.	2	1	0
12	To get this child to obey is more trouble than it's worth.	2	1	0
	Total points for all three columns: First child _____ Second child _____ Third child _____	Column Total	Column Total	Column Total

The higher your score, the more consistent you are with your kids. The best possible score is 24. If you scored that many, look and see if you misunderstood any questions. Most good parents won't score quite that high! The goal is to keep your score as high as possible, hopefully around 20 or above. If you got different scores for each child, think about why and how you do things differently. Repeat this survey again later to see if you are getting more or staying consistent.

Now that you're a master or mistress of picking limits and enforcing them, the next step is to learn to balance this control with support of your children. Please read on!

Skill #5 PLAN DISCIPLINE AND FOLLOW THROUGH:
Use consequences, teach responsibility, and be consistent

- Use mostly rewards. Prevent bad behavior with **reward action limits**:
    "If you __(obey)__, then you can have__(reward)__."
- **Reward** early and often- catch them being good, reward **after** they obey.
    1. **Give something good**—attention, praise, allowance, hug, treat, gift.
    2. **Take away something they don't like**—end a punishment, cancel a chore, help them with something they need to do.
- **Don't bribe** (don't give or promise them something *before* they finish obeying or to get them to stop misbehaving).
- To set a **punishment action limit:**
    "You have two choices. You can__(obey)__, or you can choose __(punishment)__. Which one do you pick?"
    If they don't obey, hold up two fingers and say,
    "Pick which one before I count to three or I will pick."
    If there is no action while you count to three, carry out the punishment.
    "Ok, you chose to __(punishment)__."
- **Use only mild punishments**: Take an object or privilege away. Add a chore or responsibility. Say you're disappointed. Allow a negative natural consequence to happen.
    Time-out—ages 2 1/2 to 8. *"You're going to time-out because.... You can't get out until I tell you to get out."* Use a boring place, talk to the wall only, require them to do something to get out (obey), make getting out look good.
- **Make sure of five things before punishing your children:**
    1) They knew exactly what they were supposed to do. 2) They knew what would happen if they didn't. 3) They were capable and able to do it. 4) Your own emotions are under control. 5) The punishment fits the crime.
- If they refuse to obey **when you ask them to do something**, take something away until they obey. If you need to **stop a bad behavior** or keep it from happening again, take away something for a certain period of time. You may add consequences up to a total of 3, for up to a week.
- Make **natural consequences** work by controlling their severity and using ones that should change behavior.
- **Follow through with your limits and consequences!** Think and plan ahead. Have practice sessions. Use the same consequences that work. Respond in a similar way but be flexible. Talk with other caregivers about discipline.
- **What to try if discipline isn't working:** Build up your relationship. Use a different consequence(s). Laugh. Remove your child from the

situation. Take a parent's time-out. Have a quiet contest. Double-check your consistency. Say you notice what they're doing and are planning a consequence if it doesn't stop (*"I'm going to take something away."*)

- **What NOT to do if it isn't working**: Sulk or have a tantrum, give up, bribe them, give in to pleading, guilt, threats, or bargaining, use harsh punishments (don't hold down, push, pinch, shake, spank, hit, or threaten to hit them; don't attack their worth; don't insult, yell at, or swear at them; don't withhold affection or meals, throw things, shove them outside, or say you'll leave them).

Skill #6

BALANCE YOUR SUPPORT AND CONTROL: How to optimize your parenting style for good behavior, independence and resilience

If you're a computer user, support and control may not sound like parenting words—they're what you need for software and a tab on your keyboard. But we're not talking about computers here, or ladies' undergarments either! The words *support* and *control* nicely sum up in a nutshell the two things that kids need from parents.

Supporting your children means being positively involved in their lives, giving warmth and affection, and being tuned into and supplying what they need. It means accepting them and encouraging them to be individuals. It's what you do to help them grow up emotionally healthy and happy. Using the first three skills helps you provide this support.

Controlling your children means providing limits, discipline and supervision. It means expecting things from them, such as that they will get more mature with time and that they will stay part of the family. It's what you do to influence their behavior. Skills #4 and #5 help you provide the control and consistency your children need.

Some parents spend more effort on supporting their kids, and don't use much control. Some parents do it the other way around. Parents who use medium amounts of both support and control make their job the easiest and get the best results. That's why your symbol for this skill is a balance.

What's a parent to do to find that good balance between support and control? And when does discipline go too far so that a child's self-esteem and chance for success are lowered? Or when is a parent being too lax so that the child isn't learning responsibility? Let us explain.

A **parent's "style"** reflects the kind and amount of support and control he or she uses. We'll describe parenting styles so you can see what style you use now. Then we'll tell you how your style affects you and your kids, and how to modify it for the best results. But first, let's start with the low-down on ways parents control their kids.

Controlling Your Children:
How to Have Healthy Expectations

The first way parents control their kids is by setting limits on behavior. But kids need breaks from having to be good and meeting our expectations, just like we need breaks from our jobs. So it's important not to give unnecessary limits and or make expectations too high.

Allow your kids to make safe personal choices

Parents have many expectations, from what kids achieve to how they dress. Many of these aren't really required to grow up successfully. That means your child has some choice in these matters. When kids are allowed to make some choices about their day, they feel in control of their lives. This control helps them feel confident and happy.

Use P.S. I'M HELPING from skill #4 to set healthy limits on what your kids do. If a behavior doesn't fall into one of those important categories for which to set a limit, it seems like a safe, personal choice to allow (even if you wouldn't choose it). So, you might allow your kids to wear flip-flops instead of shoes. But allowing preteen girls to dress in scanty, sexual styles is not an appropriate or safe choice, for instance. Allowing safe personal choices is part of choosing your battles and letting your kids move toward independence. It's a key to avoiding over-control of your children. This is especially important for teenagers.

Besides setting limits, there are other ways that parents control their kids. Here are ways that control can go overboard and backfire.

Look at what you expect from their activities

Activities in and outside of school (like clubs, drama, music, religious youth groups and sports) can help children make friends, have fun, gain confidence, and learn responsibility. But parents need to ask themselves, "What do I expect from my child's involvement in this activity?" Do you expect your child to be the best? Team captain? First chair? Lead singer? Valedictorian? Even if your child is a great athlete, a gifted performer or a genius, you may set him or her up for failure or unhappiness when your high expectations aren't met.

Many times parents' high hopes come from their own desire to be good at something. Sometimes parents get self-esteem or pleasure out of how well their kids perform. If this sounds like you, you may be considering what your child wants last. Expecting more than your children can or want to achieve can even lead them to lie and say they did things they really didn't do to make you happy. Pushing them to excel can also make your children think they need to succeed at any cost, even by cheating. Plus, expectations that are too high can lead to low **motivation** (thinking there is no reason to try since they can't meet your lofty goals), as well as anxiety and low self-esteem (thinking they aren't good enough for you). Trying to control your child's performance can badly batter your relationship.

You may hope that your children will get involved in certain things. But, children often resist what parents have in mind! If they are resisting something you really think they should do, have good reasons to start the activity, and go easy. For example, it's OK to insist on some piano lessons to see if they like it or to prepare for another instrument. It's OK to throw a football around sometimes to see if you can spark his interest, but you'll soon find out if it's really his thing. If it isn't, then drop the ball! We believe it's OK to insist on religious youth group participation (with flexibility to miss), if it's a part of your family's tradition and faith. Finding a flexible, fun experience makes it more likely they'll continue to be involved. Insisting on swimming lessons is fine, because that's a useful life skill. If they signed up for a year, class, or season of something, having them finish it teaches them to honor commitments.

After trying it for a while, if your child says he doesn't like a sport, instrument, hobby or whatever, you won't change his mind. So ask yourself why you are insisting he continue. Dreaming of a child doing it or wanting it yourself isn't a good enough reason. Insisting for reasons like these can hurt your relationship. It'll also be hard for your children to do well, and they'll probably quit later anyway.

Good reasons for insisting that a child continue a group activity would be avoiding boredom and giving a child something to do that he or she has talent for. After all, it's good for kids to be involved in some type of supervised activity with other kids. Motivating kids to do things that will add to their career options (with extra money or privileges) can be fine, but only if they agree.

What about expecting them to do well in sports?

Sports can be great for physical fitness, making friends, teaching discipline, gaining confidence and keeping kids busy. But children who feel pushed to achieve often feel that love and attention are based on how well they do. Kids will resent parents who seem to love or praise them only when they do well. This can ruin a relationship forever.

"YEA! OUR BOY WILL BE THE NEXT JOHN ELWAY, I JUST KNOW IT!"

I once worked with a 12 year old who was a four-time junior national champion in her sport. She was competing all over North America. When we met, she was training for another national competition. She was also a nervous wreck. Her parents brought her to see me when she failed to qualify for nationals. While there were still two more chances to qualify, her father was convinced she had failed because she was mad at him. Because of this, he had not spoken to her in a week.

The daughter said she had a lot of trouble sleeping. She needed to do many things before she could fall asleep. These included lining up her shoes according to their height, making sure there was nothing under her bed or in her closet, looking out her window and blowing four kisses to her dog, and then turning her light switch on and off twelve times while she hummed a song. She had to perform these rituals in this order every night. She couldn't perform this ritual the night before her last competition and she thought that was why she didn't qualify for nationals.

In meeting with her parents, I shared my concerns about what the pressure was doing to their daughter. I suggested they let her take a break from competition for a few months. Her father insisted that she could not take a break, even if it hurt her. He stated, "I was never good enough to compete in this event. My daughter is. She is good enough to go all the way. She will, no matter what it takes." Soon after we met, they moved to another state. I have yet to see the daughter's name listed as a member of the U.S. Olympic team. This father's pressure was hurting his daughter, maybe for life, just because of a sport.

Good attention to your kids means attending their games, concerts or other activities whenever possible, and helping make them fun. It doesn't mean letting them know how disappointed you are when they lose, or telling them mostly how they can improve. It's best for kids if you want them to try to do well, and to feel successful as competitors even if they aren't successful in winning a competition. It's best if you want them to have fun and feel good about their effort, their commitment, and what they *have* accomplished. The drive to succeed (motivation) has to come from within the child—you won't be able to make it be there. We also suggest avoiding coaches or instructors who emphasize performance over everything, or who use personal attacks or humiliation.

School grade expectations

Tell your kids that school helps get them where they want to go in life. More years of education means higher salaries. School helps give them enough money to live on, without being dependent on you when they grow up! Good grades give children more choice in their careers, and having such choices is a big part of happiness.

But more important than actual grades is that children are taught *how* to learn and are encouraged to love learning. Good learners who are motivated can do about anything they put their mind to. But putting too much emphasis on grades can lower a child's self-confidence and desire to learn.

We suggest expecting your children only to try as hard as they can and do their best. For some kids this will mean almost straight A's, and for others it will mean mostly C's. For most, it will mean a mixture of A's,

B's and C's. And you really can't assume your child didn't try hard enough just because she didn't get an A. You can be sure of this only if she didn't turn in assignments or missed class, or you know for a fact she didn't study.

It's a dangerous thing to expect a child to always get straight A's. This sets up good students for anxiety and failure when they get a B, for goodness sake! B's are good! For those kids who push themselves to get straight A's, and think nothing less is acceptable, we believe that it is sometimes important for them to get a B. We call this a "therapeutic B." Once a string of A's has been broken, the child can relax a little and begin to focus on really learning the course content and not on a letter grade at the end of the course.

Show your kids that you like to learn by learning together. Talk about how studying is like solving a puzzle, or a mystery, which is like playing a game. Emphasize learning from mistakes, and that everyone makes them. For example, after your child gets a bad grade on a term paper, emphasize learning how to write a good paper, not the grade. That's the best way to help her do better next time. If your child is really learning, the grades will usually be good enough. By the way, kids' intelligence accounts for only 25 percent of how good or bad their grades are. **Grades are determined mostly by** other things, such as access to information and help, motivation, study skills and effort.

Talk about the fact that **a lot of kids cheat** to get good grades, and that's not OK. Cheaters don't learn. Tell them you would rather have them get a bad grade than cheat to get a good one. Cheaters won't always be able to cheat, so they'll eventually fail and not know how to make the grade on their own. Penalties for students caught cheating are getting higher. Putting pressure on kids for good grades increases the chances they'll cheat. Emphasizing the grade instead of the learning also does.

About neatness and order in the home

Typical homes with kids are, shall we say, a slight bit messy (OK— ours sure is). Part of good parenting is teaching children how to take care of themselves and run a household. Basic home training with **chores** includes picking up after themselves, bringing their laundry to the washer and running it, dusting, vacuuming, kitchen, lawn, trash and bathroom duties. It works best if your kids share chores equally, rotating who does what. A time guideline for chores is 20 to 30 minutes on school weekdays with more on the weekends.

Chores are an important part of learning responsibility. Teaching respect for other people's things is important too. For instance, they may need to ask permission to use something, and return it. But don't expect kids to do things as well as you would.

Bedrooms are their space, and we recommend not getting into power struggles about how they keep their room once they are in junior high. It should be clean enough so there's not anything unhealthy like rotting food around, and so they can find the stuff they need.

The fact that kids can't be as neat as parents can cause a lot of stress. This is a conflict that can hurt relationships. Parents who put a lot of effort into how things are done by others in the household, including neatness, organization or cleanliness, often find themselves feeling frustrated. Children in very neat households often feel criticized, because they can't do things as well as their parents want, and they often don't see the need to either. They can also feel bad when it seems like the house is more important than they are. This home conflict is tied to depression, low self-esteem and eating disorders in children.

A family home needs to be just organized enough to be user friendly (being able to find stuff you need) and clean enough to be healthy and safe. Try to shift your attention from how neat and organized your children are towards their character. Also, are you having fun, and laughing with them at home? Are you spending most of your time learning and playing with them? How your child feels about being home with you is more important than having the house the way you want it. When your kids leave the nest, you can have things your way.

Psychological control must NOT be used with children

This is like playing mind games to get kids to do what you want. It hurts children and makes parenting unsuccessful. Examples are withdrawing affection, belittling or putting kids down, trying to make them feel guilty, criticizing or giving them the "silent treatment" when they misbehave, all to try to change their behavior. It includes telling kids, "You don't love me," "You're ungrateful," or "You'll be sorry" when they disobey

Psychological control blocks children from learning to control their own behavior and emotions, and keeps them dependent on their parents. It keeps children from becoming independent and developing self esteem. The use of psychological control is linked with childhood depression, anxiety, behavior problems, drug use and truancy, so you'll want to avoid using it.

Supporting Your Kids:
How to Make Your Support Healthy

When you think of supporting your kids, it may give you icky thoughts of still paying for their food and rent after they leave home. But what we'll talk about here are ways to support them when they're young, so you *don't* have to support them later! Many parents wonder how much they should be involved in their child's life and where to back off. Parents can actually be overly supportive and involved. Throughout this section and the next, we'll show you what this looks like, and how you can build self-esteem, responsibility, resilience and independence in your children.

Help your child find organized activities to do with others

Being involved in supervised activities in or outside of school is very important to a child's development and education. These activities help children develop social skills, responsibility, friend circles, and self-confidence. They can also add to career and school choices.

Kids who aren't involved in clubs, music, team sports, drama, religious or community service groups tend to hang with friends who do the same. These kids miss the chance to learn to get along and work with others, including adults. Getting these children involved in activities prevents two of the big causes of teenage problems: boredom and isolation. Without group activities, kids can isolate themselves and start to think differently than most other kids (and not in good ways).

But avoid scheduling too many activities

Getting kids involved in group activities is a good way to support them. But over-scheduling your child can lead to stress and trouble succeeding. The American Academy of Pediatrics has recently stated that American kids are over-scheduled and has expressed concern. Kids need a little time by themselves almost every day, when nothing is planned. There should be enough time for talk, play, homework, reading and chores most days. Cut down on activities if there isn't.

A good rule of thumb is to have only one or two activities outside home and schoolwork at a time. Cut back if your children's grades drop or they often have to miss class or family activities. Ask yourself these questions to try to figure out whether a child's activity is worth the money, energy and time it takes everyone.

1. How much does he really enjoy it, or do *you* mostly enjoy it? (What would he say if you said he needed to quit? Does he only like it when he does well or wins?)
2. Will she use the skills she's learning when she grows up? (Can or will she possibly do this as an adult?)
3. What would he be doing instead? (Good things like homework, chores, learning another good skill, and playing? Bad things like computer games, being bored, watching TV, getting into gangs?)
4. Is she really learning skills like time management and responsibility, or do you mostly take all that on yourself?
5. Is the activity building confidence, or helping make good friends?
6. What does it take away from your other children's activities or the family?
7. Can your child keep her grades up, do chores and have down-time?

How to know if you might be an overly involved parent

Too little supervision or involvement with children is called neglect. The flip side is too much involvement in your child's life. Both are damaging to your child. (You are probably thinking—these guys will never be able to make this one clear. Ok, it's a toughie, but give us a chance.) **Some signs of over-involvement** are:

1. Your child complains you're almost always with him, and wants to do things with his friends or by himself.
2. He says you don't let him make any decisions.
3. It bothers you when he thinks differently or wants to do different things than you do.
4. You expect him to be your friend and counselor by listening to you talk about your problems.
5. Your teenager isn't maturing and taking care of his own problems because you are doing too much.
6. You are being intrusive. (You'll learn about this on page 182.)

Over-involvement lowers self-esteem and the chance to learn from mistakes. It can cause depression and anxiety in children.

I once saw a 19 year old male student who took an overdose of medication in a suicide attempt. During treatment, he said that he had issues with his mother. He said that she would never leave him alone. During high school she would often show up when he was at a friend's house and cry when he told her to leave. She even made a big scene when he wouldn't save the last dance for her at his senior prom! At home, he never seemed to be alone, since she always wanted to be with him. She wanted to know every detail about his days. This is an extreme example of a mother's over-involvement that drove her son to attempt suicide.

If your involvement embarrasses your child, stop it

Your child may ask you to leave when you drop her off somewhere. Spend enough time to meet the adults who are supervising and make sure it seems she's in good hands, and then go. If you often help in an activity or class, and your child doesn't want you to, then stop. Back off on physical affection in public if your kids seem uncomfortable.

Don't DO your children's homework, but help them with it

Teachers work very hard to teach our children, but the time they can spend with each student individually is short. You can help by continuing the teaching at home.

When helping with homework, Do NOT give your children the

answers, but do **help them figure out how to get answers** if needed. Review homework and point out errors that need to be fixed. Start by asking them what facts they already know that could help them find the answer. Then ask them what they think they could use, or where in a book they could read, to help. Give them some hints if they aren't sure, let them work on it some more, and come back and check later. Help your kids to recognize the good feeling that comes from figuring things out for themselves. Even if an answer to a problem would have been better with more of your help, if your child's answer is good enough, don't change his answer to your answer.

If you show them how to do their homework, make sure they understand by asking them to explain what you did. Ask them to answer the question again (or answer a similar one) without help. Then you'll know they learned how. Once they can do homework well enough by themselves, help only if they ask for it. But watch their grades so you know when they need help. If you can't help (because you can't remember or didn't learn that stuff in school!), get them help elsewhere.

We also recommend that kids do what we call "summer homework" and read over the summers to keep their knowledge fresh. Summer homework is schoolwork that parents or schools give to students to do over the summer. It may include reviewing math, grammar, vocabulary or other subjects such as history. In addition, find teaching moments when you're together. For example, if you pass over a state line on a road trip, see if you can name all of the United States together.

When to back off on praising your kids

Can you really go too far with praise? You bet your sweet bippy! It's possible to praise kids too often or in ways that hurt them. Praising most 7 year old boys for using the toilet isn't necessary. But praising them for raising the seat may be!

Start by not exaggerating or going overboard with compliments. Exaggerated compliments are hardly ever true, and it's important that your kids think you're being honest. Saying, "You're the best" at something, can be bad for children. Few people are ever the best at anything. And even if they really are, it usually doesn't last for long. If children think they are the best at something, they can get hurt or lose interest once someone better comes along. So be honest with your praise. Tell them that the most successful people from business to sports know that they can always improve. A good exception to this is complimenting your child just for being yours: *"You're the best kid in the world to me."*

Instead of saying, "You are the best drawer" say *"What a neat drawing. I really like how you put the colors together."* Instead of "You are the smartest kid" say, *"You are doing so well in school. I'm so proud of my bright daughter who works so hard."* Instead of "You are the most beautiful" say, *"Not only are you beautiful, but even more important, you are also a great person."*

Try not to limit the types of things that you praise. If you usually praise only a couple of your child's qualities, she may come to think that those qualities are all that matter. For example, if a daughter grows up often being told how pretty and skinny she is, she may believe that looking pretty and being skinny are very important things. Then she won't feel good about herself when she gains weight. This can lead to depression and eating disorders.

And about **intelligence**…please go easy on telling your kids how smart they are! This can discourage them from working hard, and lead them to think that they don't have anything to learn from others—including you! And, as you'll see in the teen chapter, book smarts have little to do with making good decisions. There are many more important things about your children than how smart they are, like their emotional health, good character and happiness. Good grades are nice, but success is just as much due to how well they get along with people, feeling happy and supported, working hard, and loving to learn.

Support them in a healthy way when they're sick

For short illnesses, get them back to school or playing as soon as possible. Kids may notice if they can get away with bad behavior when they're sick. Or they may even pretend to be sick to get out of punishments, homework or uncomfortable situations. In some families, children think they mostly get good attention when they're sick, so they'll act more ill than they really are.

 If you suspect they aren't really sick, ask about things going on in their life. Discuss it, help them cope, but get them back to school! If you're not sure if your child should be in school, call your school nurse or doctor for advice. When your children are not obviously ill, they should not be watching TV, movies, playing games or being with friends when they stay home. Make this time boring, full of naps and quiet time, so they'll want to be well and get back to school or play.

Avoid criticizing their weight or other body traits

Frequent criticism makes children believe that they are worth less. Being criticized about something they don't feel any control over leads to poor self-esteem, depression and anxiety. So avoid saying negative things about your child's body shape. Comment on good things about your child's body. For example, *"You have pretty, shiny hair," "You have nice legs (muscular or shapely)," "You carry yourself well," " I love your nose," "You have such a great smile," "I love the shape of your hands," "I love your laugh,"* etc.

But it's important to address health problems like obesity. Address it from a health and not a beauty standpoint. Childhood obesity can lead to adult obesity, heart disease and diabetes. We are now seeing much more obesity and diabetes in children than ever before.

Talk sensitively about being overweight. Don't sound critical by saying something like, "You're getting fat". Instead, say something like *"I notice you are having a problem with your weight"* and point out that this can make your son or daughter sick. Make an appointment with a health care provider for advice, which may be better coming from a medical professional than from you. Teach good habits like eating a healthy diet (less junk food, fast food and soda; and more fruits, veggies and grains). Get your children into the habit of regular exercise to get healthy. If you're overweight also, you could learn to eat healthy and exercise together—make it a family project.

How and when to tell your kids about sex

You're feeling light headed and queasy. You're starting to sweat, and hope you won't chicken out. It's time for…the birds and the bees talk! It's time to tell kids about sex when they ask questions, or if they say they know already. (Then they may have gotten inaccurate info.) Usually early grade school (age 8 or second grade) is a good time. Ask them if they would like to learn about what sex is. If they say no, then wait a few months. Also, teaching kids about sex is something that needs to continue after the first "talk." Answer questions as they come up, and bring things up yourself over time.

Here's how the first sex talk could go. Say that sex is a fun, pleasant activity between two adults. It is touching each other's private parts in ways that feel good. For kids younger than 8, we suggest skipping the details on intercourse, as it can be too frightening. Just say it's also a way we make babies. Tell them it's OK for them to touch their own private  parts, but it isn't OK for anyone else to touch them except the doctor. Those parts are special and only for themselves until they're older.

By age 11 or so (sixth grade), children need to know how sexual intercourse causes pregnancy. Use medical words, and say that intercourse is where the man puts his penis inside the woman's vagina. Don't be silly, but matter of fact, like teaching a class. Girls will commonly wonder if it hurts. Say, *"Not when you've grown into a woman and want to have sex, because your body will have changed."* Young teenagers need to know everything else about sex, including that all sexual activity is sex, and the what the risks of having sex are (see chapter 9).

Give similar support to your girls and boys

Don't say things that make kids think their abilities or interests are any different because of their gender. This can dash their chance to learn to take care of themselves, and make them more dependent on others. For instance, if a boy thinks he doesn't need to learn to take care of a household, he may not be able to when he lives alone. Or, if a girl thinks she doesn't need to know how to hold a job outside the home, she may find herself staying in a bad relationship just because she doesn't have the skills to make it on her own.

Having different expectations of boys and girls also limits their potential. Boys can grow up to be excellent caretakers of children and the household. Girls do grow up to be engineers, CEOs, senators and doctors. Give all your kids a strong start on the road to maturity by teaching them how to take care of themselves and a household.

Good Ways to Support Their Resilience

Resilient people can overcome challenges and obstacles, and bounce back from mistakes and disappointments without giving up. They are happier than less resilient people and aren't as likely to hurt others when upset. The most important way to help your children be resilient is to **show them that you value and appreciate them no matter what they do, just because they're yours.** Using your relationship skills really helps. Notice and compliment their accomplishments, even small ones. Here are other keys to resilience.

How to help them cope with disappointment

Talk about how there will always be things in life that are out of their control (like what other people do). It's best not to waste energy on those things. Say how it's good to rely on others for support. Also, help them recognize when their goals aren't very realistic, so they don't keep getting disappointed when they fail to meet their goals. Find opportunities for your kids to succeed so they gain self-esteem and confidence.

Remind your children that nobody is perfect, and everyone gets disappointed sometimes when they discover they can't do something well. Discourage your kids from talking themselves down. Emphasize their strengths (such as being helpful, being fun to be around, or being willing to try new things and enjoy them with a good attitude, whether they're good at those things or not). Talk about weaknesses as things they may be able to slowly improve if they get help. It doesn't work to just keep telling them to try harder when they don't have enough interest or talent to do something well. That can make them feel like losers, since you think they should be better just by trying.

Sometimes it's hard for parents to know whether their children aren't doing something well (such as a musical instrument or sport) because they don't have the talent for it, or because they just don't *want* to do it well. **Kids who want to excel at something that they don't have talent for** tend to be frustrated and discouraged when they fail. If you aren't sure about your child's talent (natural ability), ask an instructor or coach.

Let's say that you aren't sure whether your son didn't make the varsity hockey team because of lack of talent or rather lack of effort. The coach says he doesn't seem to have much talent but tries hard. If your son says he's frustrated and wants to improve, try getting him help. If after practicing more and getting extra instruction he still doesn't improve, telling him to just try harder won't help since he probably lacks hockey talent. But since one doesn't have to do something well to enjoy it, let him continue to play if he still likes it and his expectations are realistic. If it's just frustrating and disappointing for him, encourage him to move on to something else. If you keep pushing him to try, not only will he not improve, but he'll lose interest and even act irritated about playing.

Kids who don't want to participate in an activity often don't put much effort into it, whether they have talent or not. They also tend to give up more easily and to be irritable and whiny about defeat. If your child used to be good at something in the past, but now isn't successful, she may have lost interest in the activity, or she may not have enough talent to compete anymore. Ask your child, *"Is this something you like and want to do better?"* Also ask instructors or coaches about talent and effort.

To find out if she just isn't trying hard enough to succeed, you can try offering her a reward for showing improvement. If she seems to really want the reward, but can't do well enough to get it, then she probably doesn't have the talent to do better. If she improves enough to get the reward, you'll know she could try harder *if* she wants to. Pushing her in an activity she doesn't like won't help her improve, and she'll probably just give it up later anyway.

Avoid the blame game. Help your children see disappointments as chances to learn, and not failures. Discourage talk about who else is at fault and blaming someone else. Feeling like a victim can be a lifelong habit that keeps people from success and happiness. This makes a person weak and powerless to change things for the better.

Don't let them expect special treatment in life

Successful kids grow up with healthy levels of self-esteem but realize the world doesn't revolve around them. Other kids, however, grow up feeling entitled to special treatment (which isn't healthy). They think that guidelines, rules, policies and schedules are for everyone else but them. We suspect this happens more when parents allow or encourage this attitude.

Explain to your kids that policies and rules are made for a reason: to make something better, stronger or safer. Society has laws, and schools and jobs have policies for good reasons. People who don't understand this expect exceptions in school or work—and that makes them less successful. These folks are more miserable because they are often fighting the system. They have trouble getting along with others. They also have trouble being a boss or parent, since that requires making rules and enforcing them. Teach your kids that being special doesn't get them out of following the rules.

Teach your children to delay gratification

Kids who grow up getting things they want quickly have trouble working toward goals. For instance, they may not have the patience to stay in school and may drop out to work instead, giving them fewer career options and less money over the years. Make sure there are times your kids need to wait for things. Have them save allowance to buy big things, reward only after they totally finish a task, and wait for special occasions to give bigger gifts.

How to teach children to solve problems

When your child has a problem, let her talk about it first, and just listen. Use your talk time skills. Listen without criticizing or discouraging her. See if she can come up with a solution. If her plan is reasonable and safe, praise her for working it out and tell her to go ahead with it (even if it isn't what you would do). If you think what she picked won't work, or she doesn't like her own solution, ask questions that will lead her to a better solution. Do NOT just give her your answer unless she asks for it. Say that most problems get better with time.

For example, let's say your daughter mistakenly told two different friends (Beth and Bill) that she would see a movie the same night. She wants to go with Beth, and so wants to lie to Bill by saying that she's sick. Ask her how Bill would feel if he saw her at a movie with Beth that night. You could suggest she just tell Bill about the mistake (it's no big deal, happens to everyone) and make new plans for later. If she follows her plans anyway and her solution turns out to be a mistake, help her learn from it by talking it over. Try not to say, "I told you so." (We know—that can be hard.)

Let them see how you handle your mistakes

Let them see you turn a mistake into a chance to learn or change for the better. Here are examples. *"I should have listened to you, sorry. I'll listen better next time." "I knew there was a bill lying around. I should have looked for it—now it's late and I have to pay more. I'm going to put all our bills in one place from now on." "Man, I should have checked the time—my mistake. I'll be more careful next time."*

Let your children do many things themselves

Doing too many things for your kids is actually bad for them—yeah! Kids with parents who do too much for them won't learn to do things for themselves. Doing this tells your children that you think they can't do things right. If kids don't think they can do something, they'll be less likely to try. Having kids do things to take care of themselves develops responsibility and independence.

LET **ME** DO IT !

When your child wants you to do something that you know he or she is capable of doing, say, *"I know you can do that if you want to."* Obviously, it needs to be something you have seen your child do before. For example, your 4 year old son wants you to help put on his pants even though you have seen him do it many times. Use this chance to teach independence and say, *"I know you can put your pants on if you want."* If he still resists, then say, *"I guess you're choosing not to play yet, since you can't play until you're dressed."*

All Parents Have Their Own Style... of Parenting, That Is

Parenting style relates to how much parents control and support their kids. Different styles place more importance on control or support. Our names for the four main parenting styles go by what they emphasize. Parents usually use one style most of the time, but occasionally draw from a different one. Hold on to your hat—we're now going to give you a chance to find out what style you use and what it means for you and your kids.

Please read our descriptions of the four parenting styles carefully. Then decide which one is most like what you do. Maybe place marks by things that sound familiar. The description of your top style won't match you exactly. After you decide which one is your *most* common style, try our advice for it.

Keep in mind that it can be very hard for parents to accurately see what they're doing with their kids. Parents tend to report doing what they *want* to do, or think they *should* do, and not what they *actually* do. Sometimes what kids think you do is more accurate (too bad we can't check what your kids think here). It's also natural to defend what you do, and it's hard to get feedback. But it'll make parenting easier and more successful if you're open to learning.

The parenting styles are described by listing each style's approach to certain parts of parenting. It may help to ask relatives, friends, or partners to see which style they think you use to get the truest picture. Let's start by looking at two commonly used styles.

Controlling Parenting Style

This style focuses much more on control than support of children. It doesn't mean there is *no* support; there's just much less support than control.

- **Relationship**: Parents using this style feel they usually know what's best for their kids, and that their kids should know what they want. They're often disappointed, frustrated and angry with their kids and let them know it. It's easier for them to show affection when their children perform well.
- **Control**: Parents tend to give frequent, detailed instructions and give a lot of commands. Obedience, respect, work, tradition and order are emphasized. Parents may try to make kids feel bad or guilty when they misbehave.
- **Discipline**: Parents have solid expectations for behavior. They expect kids to obey without question, and feel no need for discussion. They try to stick to their expectations no matter what their children say. They are able to tell their kids what they think without sugar coating their words, to the point where their kids may be embarrassed or scared. They use more punishments than rewards. Physical punishments are used more often in this style compared to other styles.
- **Participation**: Parents often believe that their kids can't make good decisions without help. They participate much more in their child's activities if they like the activities themselves.
- **Communication**: Parents often use lectures instead of open communication. They often feel they need to yell to get their kids to listen. They tend to criticize their kids, even in public, and often give loud commands.
- **Independence**: They expect their kids to grow up quickly. Children are valued more if they think and act like their parents. Parents often expect kids to take up their beliefs, and family tradition is greatly valued. Parents don't like when their kids have different

values and beliefs.

- **Monitoring**: Parents strictly monitor what their kids are doing. They may hover over their kids, frequently correcting them. They tend to take on the roll of a drill sergeant.
- **Other names for this style:** authoritarian, or "It's my way or the highway."

Kids raised with the controlling style tend to be more unfriendly, uncooperative, unpopular, and self-centered than other kids, and less interested in school or other organized activities. They tend to be more withdrawn, showing less responsibility, motivation and happiness. They often get hostile or childish when stressed, and are less helpful to others. Research shows a clear link between this style and behavior disorders in grade school children. Anxiety and depression are common, since these kids feel they have no control over life. They are less able to take care of themselves than others, relying more on their parents financially when they are grown up.

Teenagers raised this way rebel more, which often means drug abuse and other delinquent behavior. It can cause kids to look for support outside of the family, and they are likely to pick delinquent friends for this support. They tend to resist parents' input and advice. The controlling parenting style is associated with higher teen marijuana usage compared to other styles. Kids who think their parents use this style believe more in **self-determination rights** (they want to make their own decisions on where they live and with whom). Kids often feel like they aren't important to their parents and feel controlled and criticized. This style results in the lowest school grades, even when mixed with other styles. It's best to stick with one style most of the time—but not this one!

Advice for parents using mostly the controlling parenting style

A lot of parents use this style, and you may have been raised this way yourself. But society is different now than when you were growing up. Chances are you care about your kids and want them to do well. You are correct that children need direction and control, but the control you're using is outweighing your support. You may think your kids are fine, and may disagree that you're controlling more than supporting.

You may think that what you're doing is best and that things are all right. You might think, "If it ain't broke don't fix it." But your children are probably having, or will have, problems. And that means more trouble for you. If you continue to use this style, you'll have to discipline more often and your kids won't be as emotionally healthy or successful as they could be. Your relationship will suffer.

Things could be better for you and your kids. If you want well-behaved, happy, successful kids that feel close to you, then work on changing your style more toward the balanced style. Combining the controlling style equally with another style still has worse results than using the balanced style instead. Use your seven skills to make life easier. Concentrate on the relationship building skills #1–#3, as well as on open communication (see page 94) and flexible limit setting as described in skill #4. Review how to avoid very high expectations here in skill #6, as well as how to use rewards and only mild punishments in skill #5.

Permissive Parenting Style

This style focuses more on support than on control of children. Very little control is given to children compared to the amount of support they get.

- **Relationship**: Parents are warm, and highly accepting of who their kids are. They believe in fulfilling their kid's desires by giving them most everything they need or want. They may try to be their children's friends.
- **Control**: Parents provide very little restraint or direction. They don't have many expectations of their children. Few demands and limits are given.
- **Discipline**: Parents use very little discipline and punishment. They tend to let misbehavior go, or don't follow through on consequences. They may give kids what they want, or even bribe them to stop misbehaving. Parents often find discipline and being consistent hard. They may give long, repeated explanations to their kids for why they should behave.
- **Participation**: Parents center life around their children, often at the expense of their own needs and desires. They may believe that kids

need to learn from their own experiences, and parents shouldn't interfere. They trust their kids to make good decisions.

- **Communication**: Parents tend to let their kids make most decisions instead of giving advice. They don't often tell kids what to do. Their kids often debate and argue with them to try to get things their own way.
- **Independence**: Parents think "kids will be kids" and don't require much mature behavior. Kids are generally allowed to do their own thing.
- **Monitoring**: Parents try to watch out for their children's safety. They use a low level of monitoring of what the kids are doing and who they are with, especially as they get older.
- **Other names for this style:** lenient, under-controlling, or lax. We didn't want to name it "supportive style," since this would give the impression that it works well, which it doesn't. Think of the permissive style as giving permission. This style gives more permission and more support than is good for a child.

Kids raised with the permissive style tend to have good moods, but act immature. They tend to be **impulsive** (rush into activities without thinking), interrupt others, and have trouble lowering their voices. These kids tend to act spoiled and self-centered. They're less curious, responsible and able to rely on themselves than other kids. Teenagers tend to be aggressive, independent and rebellious. They have trouble controlling their feelings and making good decisions on their own behavior.

Using the permissive style leads to many of the same problems in children that using the controlling style does. These include higher marijuana use and belief in self-determination rights (thinking they should decide where to live and with whom). Children raised with either the permissive or controlling styles (or with a combination of the two styles) grow up less likely to support themselves financially. The not so great results using the permissive style show that there really are good reasons why kids shouldn't get everything they want, and why they need consistent discipline and direction.

Advice for parents using the permissive style

You want good things for your children, and are a loving parent. But your kids need more than your warm affection and attention. They need more direction, limits and consistent discipline. You may not be doing this so far because you're uncomfortable with conflict. Or, you might be afraid that your children will get mad or reject you. You may not want to make the effort, hoping your kids will grow out of misbehavior. Maybe you were raised this way, and since you think you turned out alright, you think that your kids will too.

But as we said, things are different now than they were 20 years ago. American kids have more money, free time and access to substances today, and are exposed to more sexuality and violence than ever before. There are increasing trends in cheating, lying and entitlement in today's teenagers. Therefore this style is more dangerous than ever. It may work all right when your children are younger, but they'll need more structure to stay successful. There's a fine line between using this style and neglecting your kids by not giving them the control they need.

Things will be better for you and your kids if you use the *7 Skills* to move towards a more balanced style. Using discipline may seem scary if you're not used to it, and your kids will resist at first. Setting action limits will soon take care of that. Concentrate on skills #4 and #5. Your kids will benefit much more from limits than from gifts and privileges. In fact, your kids may stay immature if you don't expect much from them. Also, be a part of your child's decisions. The parts of their brains that make decisions are not fully developed, and they need your guidance. Teach them responsibility and expect them to mature. Also use skill #7 for closer monitoring of their activities.

The helicopter parent—a bad controlling and permissive style combo

This might be the closest thing to the "mother hen" in stories. These well-meaning parents hover closely over their children (like a helicopter) even when they're not needed. They pay extremely close attention, in a way that is overprotective. They hover over their child's every decision in a way that is overly controlling. They rush to prevent any failure or discomfort, and do too much for their kids, in a way that is overly supporting.

There's no problem with giving frequent advice, but when parents actually do things their kids should do themselves, it hurts the kids' development. More parents may be using this style because of e-mail and cell phones (it's so easy to stay in touch now). The cell phone's even been called "the world's longest umbilical cord"! Parents may hover to keep their children close and dependent, to avoid letting go. But yet these parents often report low self-esteem and sadness in themselves, whether their kids are doing well or not.

Most helicopter parents have good intentions, but end up doing harm. Almost-constant supervision interferes with children learning how to solve problems and make decisions. It delays maturity and a healthy transition into adulthood. That's because kids aren't given chances to fail or succeed on their own. They aren't given enough opportunities to resolve conflict, and deal with problems or failures themselves. Children need to learn how to cope with hardship to be successful in life. They need to learn from mistakes.

As far as education, national PTA studies show that a parent's involvement has a lot to do with a child's grades early on. But when helicopter parents stay very involved in high school and college, it keeps kids from learning responsibility and self-reliance. (Parents should still help their kids avoid dangers like illegal drinking and drug use, failing or dropping out of school, and other unsafe situations.) Helicopter parents often have very high expectations of their kids, including good grades and other achievements. Kids raised this way often think they are loved only when they do well.

Helicopter parents often don't hold kids responsible for their actions, and even handle kids' problems with the school or authorities themselves. Children raised this way may be more anxious because too much was done for them, and they're afraid of failing or making mistakes. They may feel inadequate to do things on their own. These things can lead to irresponsible behavior, such as not completing jobs or assignments because they seem too difficult.

This parenting style may also lead children to think they deserve special treatment. It could promote selfishness, feeling entitled or even narcissism. These kids may grow up thinking that, "People need to do things for me. It's all about me."

You may be a helicopter parent if you do things like this:

- Demand special things or treatment for your child.
- Write essays or do homework for him or her (or take over school projects).
- Frequently offer teachers help they don't want or protest to teachers about grades.
- Put the block in the hole (or the ring on the post) when your small child is trying to.
- Answer questions yourself when someone asks your child something.
- Feel ashamed when your child fails.
- Take over a conflict your child has.
- Monitor your child's personal e-mail.
- Bother coaches for more playing time or directors for a solo or leading role.
- Are preoccupied with the details of your child's activities.
- Go with your child to interviews for jobs or scholarships.
- Fight with an employer who wouldn't hire or give your child the hours she wanted. (Helicopter parents have even started butting in on salary negotiations for their adult children's jobs!)

Parents using this helicopter style have also been known to:

- Choose a child's college even though there was a similarly priced one he liked better.
- Complete his applications for him or hire others to do it.
- Say things like, "*We're* applying here."
- Check up on her at college several times a week.
- Organize her schedules.
- Help with college homework.
- Contact professors to try to change a grade.
- Show up at the dorm every week to bring food or pick up laundry.

Helicopter parents often assume they're welcome at any meeting or class, head to a child's college or job to fix any problem, try to get a child into a job or college even after the child has been rejected (instead of helping her see that she still has good options), or make wake up calls after she moves out. (How will she ever learn to get herself up?)

Helicopter parenting raises kids who have trouble becoming independent, responsible adults prepared for life in the real world. Don't let your kids get used to you taking care of things for them. Kids need opportunities to be frustrated by hard tasks, so don't help them too much. Give your children plenty of chances to do things themselves, even if they fail, and even if you could have done better. But continue to use P.S. I'M HELPING limits to keep your children safe and help them become happy, successful adults. Until they are adults, move out or go to college, it is still necessary to know who your children are with, generally what they are doing and where they are for safety's sake. Now let's move on to something that works much better.

 Balanced Parenting Style

This style uses medium doses of both control and support of children.

- **Relationship**: Parents are warm, affectionate, and emotionally close to their children. They give good attention regularly to their kids. Children feel accepted and loved even when they're naughty or different. Children think that their parents try to do what is best for them. Parents show empathy for what kids go through growing up, and respond to their children's needs.
- **Control**: Parents control with firm and clear limits that are flexible and appropriate. They expect their kids to obey most, but not all, of the time. They don't allow kids to debate them out of decisions. No psychological control is used.
- **Discipline**: Parents use more rewards than punishments, especially praise. They punish in ways that aren't harsh. Consequences are given consistently and calmly. They tell kids what they expect ahead of time, show patience, and apologize when they're wrong. They try to judge their kids' actions fairly. When they get mad or frustrated, they control these emotions and

don't punish out of anger.
- **Participation**: Parents have high interest and actively participate in their children's lives, even in activities that they wouldn't have picked themselves. They avoid over-involvement and over-scheduling of their kids. They are more involved in their kids' education than parents using other styles.
- **Communication**: Parents use a lot of open communication. Kids are encouraged to share their opinions, and be a part of decisions. Parents explain reasons behind rules and discipline, to show how everyone benefits. Parents tell their kids what consequences will be for misbehavior before they discipline.
- **Independence**: Parents encourage independence in safe ways. More mature behavior is expected as their children grow. They allow kids to make safe, personal choices.
- **Monitoring**: Balanced parents closely monitor where their kids are, whom they are with and generally what they are doing. But parents avoid being intrusive (see page 182), and often compromise with their children. They explain good reasons for not allowing something.
- Other names for this style: authoritative and… the winner!

The balanced parenting style has been shown by many years of research to have the best results. **Kids raised by parents using the balanced style tend to be** self-controlled, cooperative, friendly, helpful, happy, and motivated to achieve. Using this style gives you the best chance to produce emotionally healthy children that behave and do well in school. It's associated with the highest school grades and fewest behavior problems of all four parenting styles.

This style creates kids that have better work habits, healthier self-esteem and higher abilities to support themselves as adults compared to those raised in other styles. Kids raised in this style use drugs less often than kids raised in other styles, and are least likely to do other illegal things. They show more leadership, trust, respect and responsibility. They also tend to have well-rounded friends. Balanced parenting leads kids to ask for their parents' help to make moral decisions. A study even showed that girls raised this way are less likely to be sexually active early. Children are more influenced by their parents, and are less dependent on peers! Now that's what we're talkin' 'bout!

Advice for parents using mostly the balanced style

First, remember how hard we said it is for parents to recognize what they do with their kids. There is a natural bias to report doing what you think you should or want to do, even if you actually aren't. It's interesting that many parents tend to rate themselves as balanced, when their kids think they use another style.

If you really think you are using a balanced style, good for you! Try your hardest to keep using it. Continue to take care of yourself so you stay prepared for success (skill #1). Keep paying good attention to your kids (skill #2), using the Talk to Teach guidelines and staying calm with your kids (skill #3). Keep using effective discipline (skills #4 and #5) and review what to do when your kids try to debate you. Learn how to keep outside influences from ruining your success in the next skill.

Neglectful Parenting Style

This style uses little control or support of children.

- **Relationship**: Parents tend to be detached from their kids and their responsibilities. They aren't warm, affectionate or responsive to their children's needs, and don't show empathy. They often struggle with their own mental health, and often use substances.
- **Control**: Parents don't place many demands or limits on their children.
- **Discipline**: This is very inconsistent—parents may use no discipline or they may use excessive and harsh punishment. They don't reward or praise their kids much.
- **Participation**: Parents are mostly uninvolved in their children's lives, and have little interest in their school, activities, health or happiness. This is very inconsistent, from superficial involvement (just trying to look like a good parent) to no involvement.
- **Communication**: Parents may not communicate at all or may share inappropriate things about friends, marriage or job problems with their kids. Parents tend to be needy and mostly talk about themselves. They make promises that they can't or have no intention of keeping.

- **Independence**: Children are forced to be independent to try to get what they need to survive.
- **Monitoring**: Parents often fail to supervise their children. There is little concern for safety, so children are often found in dangerous situations.

Kids raised with a neglectful style are often aggressive and antisocial. Poor grades, school discipline problems, and criminal behavior are common. Alcohol and drug abuse, and serious mental illnesses are also common in these unfortunate children.

Advice for parents using the neglectful style

Your kids need much more support and control than you are giving them. Seek professional help now. Early intervention is the key to helping you and your kids. Contact social service agencies, or a mental health center, school, or doctor's office to get hooked up to support services. You don't have to say you're afraid you're neglecting your kids, but just that you need help with parenting, your stress, or your kids. It's better for you and your kids if you ask for help, rather than to have someone report you. Use the *7 Skills* the best you can, and keep trying.

What the law considers child neglect

We think all parents should know this, so they'll know if they are in danger of being arrested and/or having their kids taken away. We'd also like you to learn it so you can report suspected neglect. In general, you are neglecting a child if you purposefully don't give the care he or she needs, and it results in danger or harm, even though assistance was available. Parents often don't know how much they're hurting their kids by not taking care of things. They usually don't neglect their kids to be mean. They're often overwhelmed, without parenting skills and support. Neglect is the most common way that parents mistreat their children in America.

There are different kinds of neglect. **Physical neglect** is not providing adequate food, clothing, hygiene, sleep, shelter or supervision. Outsiders may find the house uncomfortably dirty (with rodents, animal feces, broken glass or other health threats), or the child may be dirty or often sleep in class. Inadequate supervision means not paying enough attention to what children are doing or who they are with, so they're not safe (including abandoning or kicking a child out of the house).

I once worked with a mother who took her 3 and 5 year old children on a vacation to Disney World. Hotel security found the kids wondering around at 3 AM the first night. Their mother was found passed out and drunk in their room. This neglectful mother's trip to jail cut the vacation short.

Educational neglect is not enrolling them in regular or home school, allowing many unexcused absences, or not getting them special help they need. **Emotional neglect is** withholding affection, exposing children to violence like spouse abuse, letting them use drugs or alcohol, encouraging criminal behavior, and delaying psychological care. Ignoring (not looking at or talking to), rejecting (not touching, often criticizing or humiliating), isolating them from other people, and playing on their fears to scare them are all examples. **Medical neglect is** refusing to provide medical care, even though money or assistance is available.

How much discipline is abuse?

We'd also like you to know what the law says is abuse. **Physical abuse** is physically hurting a child on purpose (not by accident). It's also when someone *could* have severely harmed a child by doing something on purpose. Physical discipline that leaves a mark is abuse; this includes hitting or restraining a child in a way that causes red marks that last 24 hours, broken bones, bruises, bite marks, or in any other way that requires stitches or other medical care after discipline. Child abuse is punishable by law.

Spanking with an object such as a hairbrush, wooden spoon, belt, paddle, or tree branch is now considered by experts to be abusive. You're putting yourself at risk of going to jail if you are doing this. That's because you're much more likely to cause a bruise or other damage, since you can't tell how much force you're applying to your child's body with an object, compared to your hand. Other forms of child abuse are locking kids up, putting them in a closet, physically restraining them by tying them up, and making them do physically demanding things such as pushups.

Mental or emotional abuse can be even more damaging. It means causing psychological damage to a child with frequent negative attention and actions. Every parent occasionally loses it and regrets saying something, and that isn't emotional abuse. The things listed under emotional neglect are considered abuse when they are severe and used consistently. Belittling, humiliating, ridiculing, shaming and threatening harm are included. The unfortunate children suffering this kind of abuse are usually being abused or neglected in other ways also, including sexual abuse.

What increases the risk of child abuse or neglect in the family?

The risk is higher with parents who were abused, use drugs, allow domestic violence, have few parenting skills, are poor, have few good friends or little family support, and have very high expectations for their kids. Having chronically ill, hyperactive, or spirited children also increases risk. For mothers, more education *lowers* the risk. Parents who can control their emotions and handle stress are less likely to abuse their kids.

What to do when you suspect a child might be abused

Occasionally you may see a parent begin to lose control and potentially hurt a child. If you see that happening, it is your civic duty to say something.

Your goal is simply to let this parent know that someone is paying attention. Say something simple like, *"Boy, kids can sure be a handful. I remember those days."* (Or *"Mine sure can be."*). It helps to say something good about the child (*"What pretty eyes your child has"* or, *"Your little girl sure seems to have a healthy curiosity about things."*) You could also offer to watch the child for a few minutes while the parent takes a moment to regain control. Act like you understand how hard it is to be a parent, but don't say anything critical! That could make the parent more aggressive with the child or you.

Sometimes people aren't sure if they should say something, because they don't know if the parent's behavior is that bad. When in doubt, it's usually best to say something rather than hold back. If parents seem to be a bit rough with their child in public, you can be sure they'll be much more severe in private.

We all pay a hefty price for the high rates of child abuse and neglect in America! About a million children a year suffer abuse and neglect in this country. Many more cases go unreported. **Abused kids who don't get help** are often angry and destructive, have job and relationship troubles, and abuse their own kids. Drug and alcohol abuse are common among them also, as is emotional illness. They are more likely to become criminals.

Children die every day as a result of neglect and abuse. If you suspect that a child is being abused or neglected, it really helps him or her if you report it. Please report it to your local county child protective service agency, the police, or abuse reporting hotline in the phone book. You can even report without giving your name. People can't find out who reported them. The National Abuse Hotline for help or reporting is **1-800-4-A-CHILD** (1-800-422-4453). Each state or county also has its own hotline.

You now have expert knowledge about the best parenting style to use with kids. Using this balanced style will get you the best results and make your job easier. Read about the styles again from time to time, to increase the chance that you will stay balanced. Coming up next—the skills to combat the newest threats to successful parenting!

Skill #6 BALANCE YOUR SUPPORT AND CONTROL:
Optimize your parenting style for good behavior, independence and resilience

- **Help with homework**: Don't give the answers, but teach how to find them.
- **Don't praise in ways that hurt**: Don't exaggerate compliments, tell them they do everything well, or that they are the best or smartest. Do say things like, *"You're the best kid in the world to me—I'm so lucky."*
- **Think about what you expect from your child's activities** and whether they're worth the money, time and effort for the child and the whole family. Avoid over-scheduling your children.
- **Teach kids to be resilient**: Teach how to solve problems and deal with disappointment, but not by blaming others and playing the victim. Let them do things themselves, and convince them that you value and appreciate them just because they are yours. Discourage talking themselves down. Don't label them as only having certain abilities. Show them how to turn mistakes into chances to learn. Emphasize the importance of following rules, policies and laws.
- **Focus on your relationship and enjoying home life** rather than the organization and neatness of the home.
- **Use the balanced parenting style for best results**: Use medium control and support. Give good attention regularly. Set clear, firm limits using P.S. I'M HELPING. Try not to limit safe, personal choices. Give consequences consistently. Use more rewards than punishments. Apologize when you're wrong. Keep anger and stress under control. Check what you think about their behavior to avoid misjudging it. Use open communication. Be involved and monitor for your kids safety. Use only mild punishments and meet the five conditions first (see page 122).
- **Report suspected abuse or neglect**. Also **say something to parents**: something good about the child (*"She has good energy and spunk—that's good for girls," "He's bright—you can tell"*) and something supportive (*"Kids sure are a lot of work—but life would be empty without them, huh?" "My little girl does that a lot. She's much better after her nap. I just try to laugh."*). Do not threaten or criticize parents who may be abusive. Just make them aware that you notice them.

Skill #7

KEEP A CLOSE EYE ON THEM: How to monitor and manage outside influences to prevent problems

Who would have thought that boys would ever wear their pants clear below their butts—on purpose! Back when we were growing up, boys wore pants tighter than the law should've allowed. And girls were embarrassed to show their underwear in public. Now bra straps aren't hidden, but shown off! Why do kids follow fashion trends anyway? We suspect it isn't because they think it's attractive. It's because other kids do it. It's part of their quest to be cool (or hot, as the case may be).

But kids can be influenced in more lasting and dangerous ways than fashion faux pas. There are other people and things that can destroy your best efforts to raise them to be successful, happy adults. Using the first six skills greatly cuts the chance that your children will have behavior and emotional problems. But you can do all these skills well, and you can still have trouble if you don't monitor and manage things that greatly influence your children.

Monitoring your children is essential for parenting success

Let's start by talking about how to best monitor your children. Your symbol for this skill is eye glasses. **Monitoring** is what you do to find out what your children are doing, where, and with whom. Asking questions of your child, their 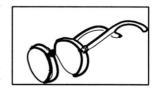 friends and their friends' parents, as well as supervising activities, are all recommended ways to monitor.

The research is very clear—when parents monitor well, children have better grades, and are less likely to pick up bad habits from peers, use substances, and be involved in crime. The best possible results take place when kids freely tell their parents what is going on and what they are up to. This is most likely to happen when your relationship is in good shape, and you use open communication.

Although monitoring is necessary for raising good kids, excessive monitoring can hurt parenting. Researchers have a name for this—they call it **intrusive parenting.** Think of it as "intruding" into a child's life or development in harmful ways. Intruding can cause older children, especially teens, to feel that their parents are being too controlling, or interfering in their lives, for no good reason. This can lead kids to rebel against their parents, and do risky things. It cuts off communication and hurts the relationships between parents and their kids.

How to know if you are monitoring too much by being intrusive

Check if you are doing any of these intrusive things, and read the comments on how you could do things differently.

1. **You are involved in things that your children have shown they can take responsibility for themselves.** For example, your child consistently turns in homework on time, but you still ask when he needs to turn in assignments and check that he does. Keep in mind that monitoring isn't the same for every child and for every activity. It isn't like a set speed limit that is always the same. Monitoring should be flexible. If your child has shown that she is responsible in a certain way (she does her chores without you asking), then don't check on her chores every day. But, if she hasn't done her chores consistently, then continue to check daily until she does.
2. **You solve problems for your child, or do things for him that he should be doing himself** (or learning to do by himself). Examples include laying out clothes for a high school student, or telling kids how to handle social situations when they don't ask for help. Children, especially teens, want and need to be able to decide and do many things themselves. Use P.S. I'M HELPING to decide if you need to get involved in something that your child is doing.
3. **You invade their privacy without good reason,** like listening to phone conversations, reading e-mails, or barging into their room without knocking. This includes being involved in activities when it

isn't necessary, or when your child doesn't want you to. It also means often asking for every little detail about events in their lives, from schoolwork to conversations. See guidelines for searching their rooms on page 261.

4. **When they play, you don't let them figure things out or do things the way they want to.** This includes giving a child continuous directions, or interrupting play to try to stop it or change it when change isn't necessary. Doing this hurts learning, especially in young children.

5. **Your kids don't have alone time or "down time"** to do their own things, because you are so involved in their lives. Even small children need down time to play in a safe place on their own while you keep an eye on them.

6. **You restrict their clothes, friends, schoolwork and activities in unnecessary ways.** Teenagers see these things as partly personal choices. It's best to allow your teens to make safe, personal choices when possible (see page 146). It's also best to compromise often—try to find the middle ground on most things that your teenagers want, instead of flat out saying "no." If something they want isn't found in the P.S. I'M HELPING reasons for setting a limit, you probably can allow it.

7. **You use a controlling parenting style.** Adjust to a balanced style.

8. **You use psychological control.** You may not even realize it. Review what this looks like on page 151, so you can avoid using it.

Now that you know how to avoid being intrusive while you monitor your children, we'll tell you how to manage outside influences. It can be hard to tell how dangerous something is or what to do about threats to your kids. This chapter will help you make a circle of safety around them while helping them become independent.

We'll show you how to support your child's health and happiness by controlling exposure to some things until adulthood. How and when children find out about the bad things and adult issues in the world can change their lives. The biggest threat to a parent's ability to control this is the many forms of media that children are exposed to. But first, we'll start with another huge influence on how our children turn out—other kids. We'll explain how these and other influences can make your job much harder, and how to manage them to make things easier.

How Other Kids Affect our Children

Our success as parents can be greatly affected by who our children interact with. And today, children can have almost constant access to other kids using **cell phones** and the internet. Many professionals are concerned that this constant access may make friends more influential to children than ever before.

Texting is becoming more popular, and allows kids to frequently communicate with each other without even talking. This makes it much easier to "say" regrettable things that would have been hard to say in person. Another concern with texting is that large amounts of time may be taken away from other things that kids should be doing, including listening to parents. Not allowing texting can save you money and make your job easier. Now let's talk about the ways kids influence each other.

Peer pressure: what it is and what it can do

A child's peer is anyone about the same age, and may or may not be a friend. Peer pressure refers to how kids affect what other kids do. By its name, it seems to mean that kids are forcing others to do something by pressuring them. But the **most common type of peer pressure** involves NO pressure on a child who actually *wants* to do what other kids are doing. This is the biggest way that peers change what kids do.

The way it works is that a peer group can change what is "normal" or desirable for all kids in that group. In other words, just by being with certain kids, children can change their mind that something is OK to do, even though they used to think it was a bad idea. Like wearing pants low! Because they aren't mature adults yet, even good kids can start to think that having pink hair, using drugs or stealing are "normal" things to do, especially if they identify with kids who do those things. The good news is that peer pressure works the other way around, too. So being around kids with good habits and ideas can lead a troubled child to change in a good way.

The first way you can combat this kind of peer pressure is to **"test reality" with your kids**. That may sound like a lab experiment, but it's not. It just means talking to your kids about how bad behaviors can mess them up (like drugs or crime), and about how healthy, successful people don't do those things. This may even mean saying, *"Please don't make the same mistakes I did."* The other way to fight peer pressure is to keep your relationship strong so your kids will talk to you, are open to your advice, and care about what you think.

The other type of peer pressure is when your child is teased, dared, or pressured by threats to do things that are bad for him or her. To fight this, have frequent judgment-free talk times so your kids feel comfortable telling you things. Also talk about how to resist pressure, and practice with them. Figure out how to say "no" strongly but politely. If your child is asked to go break some windows, smoke, or bully someone, he could say, *"No, not my style," "I gotta go, dude" "I'll really get in trouble," "That's not cool," "No, thanks anyway," "The stuff makes me sick man," "My parents would kill me,"* or whatever seems comfortable.

Why friends and peers are so important and influence kids so much

As a normal part of starting to separate from parents, children need other kids' approval. So friends become important for support, self-esteem and fun. Trying to become an individual can take different routes for kids. Some try risky things. Others get defiant, dress weird, or take on interests or opinions that differ from those of their parents. If you're Republican, they may say they're Democrats just to be different!

You'll probably remain their biggest source of support if your relationship is strong, and you use a balanced parenting style. If your relationship is troubled, your child's buddies can become much more important than you are. When that happens, friends will influence how your child behaves more than you do! This is one of the reasons that the type of friends your child has is so important.

How to help your children pick their friends

Friends can have a huge influence on what your kids think, and how they behave. Since your children want to be accepted by kids they hang out with, they'll be tempted to do things the other kids do, even if they don't want to, just to fit in. You have the right to help your children be with kids who are generally good for them and we recommend doing so. (Generally good kids to us aren't involved in illegal things, in trouble at school, disrespectful or mean.)

Here are some ways to help your kids make new friends. Suggest they ask someone over after school or on a weekend. Offer to drive and feed them. Or, if they don't want to do that, ask if you can call a parent yourself to help your kids get to know each other. Volunteer in class or other activities to get to know other kids. Perhaps someone nice from work, the neighborhood or place of worship has kids the same age as yours. You could invite a family over for dinner. Talk up kids who may be a good friend (*"That Lisa is funny. I wonder if she'd want to come over some time."*) Also, get your kids involved in supervised activities with other kids.

Teach your children social skills. If your children seem to have trouble making or keeping friends, watch them play with others. Make gentle comments if they're doing something that makes it hard to play. *"I noticed that you didn't give the other kids a turn—that's no fun for them. They may not want to play next time."* Or, give the other kids a turn yourself, so your child sees how it's done. Say something if your child says rude or mean things, makes fun of others, bosses everybody around, doesn't share or take turns, doesn't let other kids choose, gets upset at teammates, whines, cries easily, quits when he's not winning, or blames somebody or something when he loses. Teach him to say nice things to other kids, like *"Good job, try again."* Have practice sessions to see if your child gets it. Shy kids may need more time to make friends. Hang back from helping if they don't want it.

What if your child feels rejected when someone doesn't want to be friends? Say something like, *"It's too bad for her that she doesn't get to be friends with you, because you're so fun and nice."* Tell her it happens to all of us. Explain that friends come and go in life, and that's why family is most important. Tell her that she'll have lots of other friends, and will always have you.

How and why to cut back on friend time

If it seems like spending time with friends is more important to your teenagers than time with you, that's normal and by itself isn't that concerning. As long as you feel their friends are a good influence, help them get together. Kids can resent not getting time with friends. But emphasize that family and school come first. There needs to be enough time for chores, homework and family activities. Including friends in family activities can help you get to know them better. It may help you and your child have more fun together. But there's a difference between trying to be fun with your child's friends and trying to be one of them.

But are you worried your kids are spending too much time with friends, or friends are becoming too important or dangerous? Here are ways to tell. **You may need to cut back on your child's friend time if:**

- You are afraid to talk to your kids or tell them what to do because of how they'll react.
- Your kids avoid you.
- There isn't enough time for chores or homework.
- Your children seem annoyed that you want to be with them because they *only* want to be with friends.
- They're being disrespectful.
- Their grades have dropped.
- They are picking up unhealthy attitudes or behaviors.
- They seem willing to do anything to be included in a group of kids.

If any of these things are happening, sit down for an honest talk and plan more relationship building and home time. First explain why you are concerned. Say something like, *"I'm worried about you, and see you changing in unhealthy ways. How are you doing? I want you to know that you and the family come first, before friends."* Say you aren't taking away their friends—you are just cutting back on time with them. Explain that buddies will come and go, and most people move on to other friendships after high school. They might not ever talk to these people again after graduation! Say you care and won't allow friends to hurt them (drop their grades, break up the family, or give them unhealthy attitudes).

After explaining why you are cutting back on friend time, plan activities for your child several days in advance. Enforce plans with consequences. Let's say you want your teen to come home after school instead of going home with Fred or hanging out at school. You could say, *"I need you to come home after school tomorrow. If I call and you don't answer, or I find out Fred is there too, you can't get together this weekend at all."* Don't be afraid to drop in or have someone else check.

How to tell if friends may be a bad influence and what to do

Get to know your children's friends early. Try to make accurate judgments of them, or your kids will resent it. Watch them hang out the first couple of times. Teenagers will get mad about too much watching, so when you feel like it's a safe friendship, back off. Pay attention to friends over time, as good kids can turn into troubled ones.

Kids who act mean, want your kids to lie or sneak away and do private things, bad mouth their parents or you, or do poorly in school can be bad influences. Also, if your child is picking up bad habits and says, "Everyone is doing it," it really means that "almost everyone I hang out with is doing it." Then he's probably around someone who is endangering him without him realizing it. His friends may be changing what he thinks is important, normal or good. Studies clearly show that if a child's friends are doing drugs or other risky things, that child is at high risk of doing the same. If your child's friends are doing illegal or immoral things, it's time to help him or her find new friends.

If you decide you need to draw your child away from another kid, do it slowly. It's best to help your children change their minds on friends themselves. Tell them why you're concerned. The goal is for them to see that your point of view is in their best interest. Comment on a friend's bad behaviors. *"Joe was really mean to that other kid. That's NOT cool—I think he tries to get attention that way. I wouldn't want to be his friend unless he was nicer."* *"I wonder why your friend needs to look and act so differently than other kids, and why he doesn't think school and family are important. I'm worried that he's changing the way you think too."* Try to make it tough for them to be together. Change schedules, or get your child busy with something or somebody else. Or say they can only be together at your place when you're around. Monitoring your child's activities can help buffer the bad effects of dangerous friends.

Make sure you have good reasons to **suddenly forbid your child from being with someone**. Things that fall under P.S. I'M HELPING are good reasons to limit being with a certain friend. These could include threats to your child's personal safety (a friend is in a gang or drives while drinking), violations of Important Morals or Manners (your child is more disrespectful or irresponsible after being around that friend), or things that could create long term problems for you and your child (hanging out with a friend who thinks drug use, drinking, gambling or dropping out a school is okay for kids to do).

If you decide to forbid being with a friend, tell your child that you will not allow her to see this friend for now. Tell her it's because you love her and are concerned. Enforce it with an action limit if necessary. Talk about how to politely tell her friend (*"My Mom says we need to take a break. I'll really get in trouble if I don't."*) Help her see other people and spend extra special time with her yourself. Warning! If your child is very upset because she can't see somebody who may be using drugs, it could mean your child is addicted. For more information on drama, relationships and weird teen thoughts, see the teen chapter #9.

Teach how to deal with being teased

Teasing is to slightly embarrass somebody, often by trying to be funny. All kids tease and make fun of others sometimes. So yours will get teased, too. But when kids get teased a lot, they lose self-esteem and expect more bad treatment. This leads to bad relationships and possible trouble with behavior or grades. When kids aren't taught how to deal with teasing, it can lead to lifelong anger, and even crime. Most school shooters were apparently repeatedly teased or bullied. But teasing won't affect your children much if they know how to deal with it.

Tell your kids you don't allow making fun of others, and suggest how to help their friends stop doing it. Let's say your daughter's friend has been teasing a girl on the playground. Your daughter could say, *"Hey, that isn't cool, let's leave her alone,"* or *"You know, that makes me feel kind of sad. Let's do something else."*

If your kids are teased, tell them that it happens to everyone. For what sounds to you like mild teasing that hurt their feelings, say that it isn't cool or nice, and explain that kids do it to get attention. Then tell them to ignore it and pretend they didn't even hear it. Or your children could try being **assertive** by saying, *"I don't like to be teased—please stop that."* Or they can try making up something nice to say back, or talk to the wall about something totally off subject. This is very disappointing to the child doing the teasing! Teasers will often give up if they can't get your child upset, since it's just no fun anymore.

If another kid says	Your child could say this
"You wear that shirt every day—it's ugly."	*"Yah dude, when is it time for lunch? I'm hungry."*
"Your picture looks stupid."	*"Thanks—yours looks really good too."*
"Your Mom is fat."	*"Your Mom looks nice."*
"You're dumb."	"I know you are, but what am I?" (NO—we are just kidding!) Real answer: *"Thanks!"*

What to do about bullying

A bully is someone who repeatedly threatens to hurt, or does hurt, another person physically or emotionally. A bully really means to hurt someone, but a teaser usually doesn't. Bullies exert power over people they see as weaker, using threats and put-downs. They are often angry or insecure kids trying to get attention and build themselves up by bringing others down. But some bullies are just mean people who enjoy hurting others. Kids are more likely to become bullies if they're harshly disciplined or are around other mean kids. Bullies are four times more likely to become criminals than other kids and have higher rates of mental illness and drug use.

Most of us have seen bullying happen. It tends to happen in places where kids aren't supervised enough. When adults allow a child to be bullied, that child can grow up with depression, deep anger and low self-esteem. Two thirds of people who shoot kids in school were apparently bullied. Gangs may use bullying to get children to join.

Defend your children with knowledge. Tell them why bullies do things and how to stay away from them. *"Just walk away when they come by you, never defend yourself with a weapon, and always tell the teacher and me if something happens."* The days when you can just teach your child to fist fight to protect themselves are gone. Children can get suspended just for hitting back, and bullies may carry weapons. If another kid says he'll beat your child up, or that he'll bring a weapon to school, report it immediately. Remove your child from school until you feel comfortable that the threat is gone.

Often kids will not talk about being bullied. They might think it's their fault, or feel ashamed or afraid. If you think your child is being bullied, ask him if he knows anyone who gets teased. Then ask if he himself has been teased, and get the details. If it sounds like bullying, tell him it isn't his fault and he doesn't deserve it. Talk to his teachers or principal about it, and reassure your child that it will stop. Don't put your children down for being concerned (they're just kids).

Now let's go on to another major threat to successful parenting—what our kids see and hear in the media.

The Media Are a Huge Influence on Our Children

Media that spread information or entertainment are everywhere! Television, movies, magazines, music videos, other videos, news including newspapers, the internet, books, advertising, video and computer  games, phones, pictures, radio, CDs, and DVDs, are all media that our kids are being exposed to more than ever. And media content is changing in dangerous ways. Today's media show more violence, sex, substance use, commercials, and terrorism than ever before.

Children in America watch an average of three hours of TV each day, and spend about six hours a day with all forms of media! Holy buckets—that takes up almost all the time they have outside of school and sleeping! These are hours taken away from homework, chores, reading, family activities, sports, musical instruments, and other creative and physical activities. In the 1950s, television was thought to be a way to bring families together. Today, family members often watch different shows in different rooms for hours. Average American children now spend more time with the media than their parents! That's one reason media have such a strong influence on kids.

Kids are very influenced by what they see and hear

Unlike adults, children tend to believe that what is shown in the media is like real life. That includes how characters act and relate to people. The more children see something acted out on a screen, the more they expect their lives to go that way. In addition, since kids are like sponges, they're more likely to approve of and do the things they see! Kids have less experience and thinking skills than adults do. Just because you can tell the difference between fantasy and reality doesn't mean your kids can. That may be why research shows that being exposed to media is strongly linked to many problems in children. Brace yourself. We think you'll be surprised.

Violence in the media and children

We don't want to bore you, but just glance at these numbers. By age 18, average American kids will have seen 200,000 total acts of violence including rape, murder and physical assaults on television alone. They'll see 16,000 murders acted out on a screen. Why should you care? Well, research clearly shows that seeing violence **increases aggressive and violent behaviors** in kids. These include fighting, threatening or actually hurting someone, bullying, and getting physical when upset. (By the way, threatening to injure people or damage property is considered violent behavior just as actually doing these things is.)

People *learn* to be violent and aggressive—they're not born that way. The more violence a child sees (especially when he's young), the more he thinks violence is a good way to solve problems, and get what he wants. He also expects others to be more violent. Seeing real or pretend violence also makes kids desensitized to it. That means they're less likely to react to violence, and be less sympathetic or helpful to victims. Psychologists worry that our whole society may be getting desensitized to violence. As we allow more of it, it has to be more extreme to get a reaction from us.

And get this! **Children younger than 8 years old can't always tell if**

something they see on a screen is actually real (as in a news broadcast) or pretend (as in a play). Children who see violence are more afraid they'll be hurt. Viewers of all ages can have flash backs of violent scenes long after the show is over. Many times these scenes aren't needed to tell the story, but may be the only thing that people remember, especially younger kids. Seeing violence, real or not, may result in intense fear that can last for years.

What does long lasting fear do to children? In other words, why should you care if your children are exposed to things that scare them for a long time? The reason is that it can make even teenagers have long-term sleep problems, nightmares, anxiety and depression. Also, children with long lasting fear don't do as well in school or activities. They are less motivated, use substances more, and have untrue, unhealthy views of life.

How the media show violence

Most TV shows and movies have violence in them. Children's shows actually have more violent scenes per show, but the violent scenes are milder. Most violent scenes show less pain and harm than would happen in real life. One third are even shown with humor (like people getting hurt is funny). Carrying a weapon is usually made to look normal and people with them more powerful. The violent person usually doesn't get punished, and the good guys do the violent thing half the time. This may be why some kids think that violence is justified for things they believe in. School shooters often say they were justified, and did it to solve a problem, or show people how they felt.

 Movies and cable TV show more gory details than network TV. There seem to be more torture scenes recently (it's shocking to us that anyone would find watching torture to be entertaining). Of course, children should never be exposed to that kind of violence.

One fourth of music videos contain violence, weapons, alcohol, or tobacco use. Many of them show women as objects for sex (you know, there is nothing worthy or interesting about women except for their bodies, which can be used for sex). Lyrics can even contain graphic murder and rape content.

News stories are full of violent crimes, with more graphic words and pictures than ever. **Children aren't developed enough to emotionally handle this!** Watching the news can give children intense fear, anxiety and nightmares. Professionals are also concerned that watching these scenes may make kids admire weapons and believe that violence is a good way to solve conflict. Kids who watch a lot of news believe there's more crime than there really is, and that they'll almost certainly become victims of crime.

Coverage of terrorism and natural disasters can go on for hours. The more kids watch (or even see pictures), the more anxious they get. It's the unpredictability of all this that is the most harmful. That's why kids need to get back to their routines quickly after something bad happens to a family or community. Getting them back to class and routines gives them the sense of security they need. Just talk about world events briefly and assure them you'll always take care of them. Children who witness real violence (like domestic abuse or gang violence), suffer the most damage to mental health and behavior.

What about violence in video and computer games

It's amazing that the average teenage boy plays video games for thirteen hours a week, and the average girl plays five hours a week. Playing violent video games has been proven to **increase aggression and pro-violence values, and decrease sympathy for victims**.
The more kids play, the more they fight, the lower their grades are, and the more they get into arguments with parents and teachers.

Experts are also worried that violent games may **change the decision making part of the brain** in teenagers, possibly forever. The part of the brain that makes decisions and controls impulses is less active in kids who play violent video games, even when they're not playing. And there's a window of time in childhood that the brain needs to learn to do these things. It's much harder to learn them once the window is closed with age. Kids who play violent games may miss the chance to learn to talk to people, create, solve problems, and resolve conflict in other ways. So they may make more violent decisions as adults.

We're afraid there's more bad news. Games can be addictive.

Addiction means not only does someone *want* something, but he or she *needs* it to avoid uncomfortable withdrawal symptoms. **Withdrawal symptoms** are excess anger, irritability, shaking, or feeling upset, uncomfortable, or anxious. They even happen to addicted children when they can't play.

Other **signs of addiction** to watch for are lying about how much they play, not wanting to do much else (even being with people), and trouble with grades. Kids who play a lot of games are more obese, and become gamblers more often. Quality, non-violent games in limited amounts could be a good way to develop hand-eye coordination and learn about interesting topics.

Seeing sexual scenes affects children

Sex, sex, sex! (If you were dozing off, hopefully we have your attention again.) Sexual content in media is increasing and getting more explicit all the time. This includes kissing, referring to sex, implied or actual intercourse, and implied or actual sexual touching. How much do kids see? The average American child sees 14,000 sexual acts or situations every year on TV alone.  Popular teen shows, on the average, actually have more sexual scenes than other shows.

But what may be fine for adults to see is not good for kids to see. One reason is this: **Media usually show teenage sex as normal and common, and don't show any risks.** Even 12 year olds say they feel pressured to have sex by media messages, and think that everyone is having sex but them. Studies have shown that kids who see a lot of sexual situations are more likely to think that sex without commitment is fine. And get this—**teenagers report that the media is their biggest source of information on sex!** So, if you don't talk about sex, you're letting media answer your children's questions (such as when to have sex, with whom, whether they need birth control, and what else could happen to them if they have sex).

Professionals are concerned that sex is often shown as risk free and happening outside of stable relationships. Remember how we said that kids tend to think what they see is normal? Well, this leads to unhealthy thoughts and behavior. A study showed that the more young teens saw sexual content, the earlier they had sex, and the more partners they had. That's right—**looks like if your kids see more sex on a screen, they'll have more sex**. They'll also think that more of their friends are having sex. Well, when teens think their peers are doing it, they'll do it earlier too. Kids who have earlier sex have more partners, infections and unplanned pregnancies.

Media other than TV and movies have unhealthy sexual messages as well. Most females shown in video games are partially nude or doing sexual things. Seems like almost all racing games have big-breasted women in bikinis pushing their butts out and waving flags! A typical music video has young men (who may or may not have good character, looks or talent) performing surrounded by barely dressed young women, who all act like they want to have sex with the singers. Well, girls exposed to music videos are much more likely to be in favor of premarital sex. A common cover story on women's magazines is about how to please men sexually (not the other way around). No wonder decreased sex drive is so common in adult women! They grow up with these messages that men are more important to please than themselves.

Pornography is now easy for kids to see on the internet. It can even appear in pop-up ads. The way that kids see adults interact can be very disturbing, and change what they think is normal for sex and relationships. Seeing sexual acts is most damaging when the acts show women being harmed or when children are involved in the sexual acts.

Media use actors and models with unusual bodies

Kids today are assaulted by unnatural and unusually attractive bodies everywhere in the media. Models today are often sickly thin. Remember that kids think the media is a mirror of what is normal. Girls and boys are more unsatisfied with their own bodies than ever before. This is especially a problem for girls, because female characters are often unusually attractive, and men often aren't. Girls may think this means that their bodies have a lot to do with how happy and worthy they are (which isn't true). Since very few of us have swimsuit model figures (or if we do, we don't for long), this thought leads to depression, low self-esteem, eating disorders and even substance abuse. It can cause long lasting unhappiness and relationship problems.

How women are shown acting sexually also leads girls to believe that acting sexual is important for success (which it isn't). And boys who watch media characters may think life is better with six-pack abs and bulky chests. A body may look nice for a while, but has nothing to do with being a good friend or mate!

Tell your kids that lasting happiness isn't a function of body type. Even movie stars with beautiful bodies are often unhappy people. Those folks even pay to have their bodies changed. Tell your kids to concentrate on other things that make them happy or successful like their schoolwork, music, sports, hobbies, friendships, faith and family. For all body types, eating healthy and exercising make us feel good and have more energy.

Kids today see more alcohol, tobacco and drug use

Despite our public ads telling kids to "just say no" to drugs and alcohol, it seems like media are telling kids to "just say yes"! Even prime time TV shows often refer to cigarettes, alcohol and drugs. Showing actual drug use is common in movies and music. Experts believe that kids get media messages that smoking is cool and alcohol is glamorous and harmless.

Watching all media increases a child's chance of using alcohol and tobacco. Kids who watch over four hours of TV a day are five times more likely to smoke than those who watch less than two hours, even if their parents don't smoke.

How to Decrease Media Risks to Your Children

The good news is that there are things you can do to decrease the media dangers to your children. The American Academy of Pediatrics (AAP) recommends that **children be limited to one or two hours of** quality entertainment (non-educational) media each day. This goes for teenagers too. Educational media should be checked for violent and sexual content that may scare children (history shows, for example, can have disturbing graphic violence). This can be hard to keep track of, so many parents find it works best not to allow any non-educational media during school weeknights, or certain days of the week.

The AAP also recommends, and we heartily agree, that **TVs and the internet NOT be allowed in children's bedrooms**. (That includes teenagers!) It's so much harder to control how much and what they're seeing there. And **children younger than 2** should not be watching  TV—they should be doing other things that develop the brain (talking, playing, singing, and having books read to them). **Children younger than 8** should not see or read about violent things, or watch the news. For older children, limit news watching *and* watch it with them if possible. Reassure them that violent things probably won't affect them.

Basically, keep your children's exposure to violent and sexual material minimal. But **don't just rely on rating systems** as a guide. Parents think there's more violence and sex than the ratings say. For instance, parents often think that PG-13 shows aren't alright for teenagers to see. V chips in TVs can block programs, but these use the unreliable network ratings. And beware—a more mature rating may make your child want to see it more. For games, most with E ratings contain some violence, where you have to hurt someone to make points. Most all T (teen) games reward players for wounding a character.

Be especially careful with movies and cable TV because, although there may be limits on what can actually be shown according to ratings, there are almost no limits on what's hinted at. A child can imagine violence and sex easily. **Imagining things can be just as damaging** to a child as seeing them acted out.

We also recommend limiting so called "reality shows", where kids can see people judging others and relating in unhealthy ways. These shows also tend to highlight extreme behavior in people. In reality, most of these shows do NOT reflect reality. Remember that children learn from what they see, and think that what they see is like real life. As far as movie rentals, there are many unrated versions available. These could contain the most graphic and disturbing images and talk.

Watch and listen to things with your kids. Turn off shows that seem inappropriate. Seeing things together can be a great way to start a discussion. Ask them what they think and feel about things they see. Make comments or ask questions, like *"Do you really think there is love at first sight?"* Listen to their answer and then tell them what you  think. *"I think it's impossible to really love someone you don't know, but you can be very attracted. It takes a long time to know if you'd really be happy together."* *"They hardly know each other but they slept together. Seems like movies show that a lot."* *"That boy singing is surrounded by a bunch of girls who act like he's a god or something. He could be a real jerk. Those girls don't seem to think much of themselves."*

Watch that your child doesn't identify with violent characters, since he'll imitate them more. Seeing people rewarded for violence (getting a thrill, being looked up to) is the most dangerous thing to see. Teach your kids better ways to resolve conflict than violence, like cooling off, talking and compromising.

Listen to their music (even if you have to force yourself). Rap and hip-hop music lyrics include more violence, negative acts against women, alcohol and drug use than other music, according to research. A study of girls who watched mostly rap videos showed they were three times more likely than other girls to have hit a teacher, been arrested, or had sex with multiple partners. (Their behavior may not be due to the videos, but to their  environment including the videos.) Kids who listen mostly to heavy metal are more involved than other kids in smoking, drugs, cheating in school, alcohol, sex, truancy, and stealing. So listen to their music, and offer to replace dangerous CDs with safer ones.

Limit their video and computer game time so your kids have time to do and learn other things. The brain is still developing in childhood, mostly through new experiences. If their experiences are limited mostly to games, parts of the brain that do other important things like make decisions, interact with people, solve problems and create things can go undeveloped. Basically, if kids don't use parts of their brain during childhood, they may never be able to use those parts. Also watch for signs of addiction.

It's best if **games are played at a central place** in the home (it's easier to see how much and what they're playing). Beware! M rated games have the highest amounts of damaging violence and sexual behavior, so we don't recommend letting your kids play them. Play new games together. Comment on how the game differs from real life, such as how an act that doesn't hurt a character in the game could actually kill or put someone in a wheelchair, and there'd be a lot more pain and blood. Comment on the half dressed women they see. *"I don't know anybody that looks like that. She looks goofy."* If your child is aggressive (hurting or threatening to hurt other people or animals), or starts reenacting violent scenes or talking like the characters in violent games, you need to take away all violent games NOW.

Beware of the internet. Many kids use it for school assignments. But over half say their parents know little or nothing about the websites they've been on. Three fourths of teens have seen pornography. One fourth have visited a hate site. Your kids can shop  with your credit card, gamble, illegally download music, order alcohol, buy guns, and learn how to build bombs on the internet. They can even find inaccurate sexual information. Pedophiles and sexual predators are actively seeking out young victims on the internet. They lure children into giving personal information and then try to meet with them to commit sex crimes against them. Most victims are 13 to 15 year old girls who meet their offenders in a chat room. Most girls know that these people are interested in having sex, and may feel close to the offenders after the fact. Children with conflicts at home are more likely to be victims.

Try to limit the time your kids are allowed online and the sites they visit. Try non-educational sites together first to check the content. **Don't allow the internet in their rooms** but only in a central place so you can better monitor use. Use parental controls on your computer or other software including pop-up blockers. Warn your kids *never* to give out personal info or pictures. It is now possible to find out where someone lives with as little as a phone number. We also suggest not allowing chat rooms— explain that they may be talking to an adult who would like to hurt them. Make sure they're getting your attention, affection and acceptance at home, so they don't feel they need to get it from a stranger. Personal websites or community sites can cause lots of trouble for kids, like wasting hours each day and creating drama. When you can't monitor, you can hide a power cord to stay in control.

Tell your kids about the risks of gambling and that even kids can get  addicted to it, even on the internet. *"Getting addicted to gambling means you can't stop, even when it takes all your money, makes you lose your job and drives away your friends and family."* Explain that ads trick people into thinking that most people win. Almost five percent of teens already have a gambling problem!

Teach the truth about advertising. Commercials and ads are made to make money, and can twist the truth to trick people. Ads try to convince people they want or need something they probably don't. Teach your kids not to believe everything they hear. For instance, just because a product has a money-back guarantee doesn't mean the product works. Commercials also promote unhealthy eating habits, and watching a lot of TV is linked to obesity and diabetes in kids. Commercials during sports shows now have more violent and unsafe behavior than ever before. Skip them when possible.

Kids will insist that media don't influence them, but studies prove that they do. So, good enough parents today decrease the bad influence of the media on their kids. If you forbid something, try to replace it with something similar that is better for them. If your son wants to rent a horror movie you don't approve of, help him find a scary movie that is more appropriate. Don't allow your kids to argue or debate you, but try to compromise. It would be great if kids bragged to each other in the video store, "My mom didn't let me see that one—too gross." "Oh yea, my dad wouldn't either."

It can be tempting to plop the kids in front of a video when you're busy. But resist letting media be a frequent babysitter or role model for your kids. If, despite your best efforts, your kids end up being exposed to something you don't feel is good, use this exposure as a chance to discuss your concerns about what was shown or about media in general with your kids. Try to find things to watch and play that have positive messages, or that provide harmless fun, like board games and cards.

Today's kids see and hear so much media, it seems like they could be raised by screens more than parents (TV screens, movie screens, computer screens, telephone text message screens, game system screens, etc.). Violence or sex on a screen may be pretend to you, but it's real enough to change how your children act. There's a big world out there full of interesting people and things to see and do. Media may be necessary in many adult lives, but try to limit their influence on your children's lives.

Substance Use in Children

What Marijuana Does to Kids

Pot is called by many names, including weed, mary jane, grass, hemp, hashish, THC, herb, or cannabis. It is the most common illegal drug used by teenagers. Marijuana is not the same as it was in the 1960's, 70's or 80's. Through selective breeding of plants, it now has **five times more active ingredient** than before. This means pot smokers, especially those with teenage brains, are more likely to get addicted. It also means it has more severe and long lasting effects on the brain than it used to. Using pot is now linked with long-term memory, motivation, concentration and coordination problems. The effects can last long after the drug wears off. Studies show kids are less alert, slower to respond, and have more problems in school when they smoke pot. It has also been linked to anxiety, panic attacks, depression, and symptoms of schizophrenia (seeing things that aren't there and hearing voices).

People **can become addicted** to pot just as they can to cigarettes. There's more risk of getting hooked the younger a user starts. But even occasional users can have withdrawal symptoms, and need higher amounts to get high. Pot is also considered the **gateway drug to other drug use**. In other words, most people addicted to other drugs started with marijuana. The earlier and the more often kids use it, the more they'll use other drugs too. Be aware that if your child's friends are using drugs, your child is probably using also. Kids use more often when other family members do also.

Marijuana contains a mixture of toxic chemicals that cause bronchitis, and some cervical and prostate cancers. Smoking pot during pregnancy is associated with many cancers in the baby, as well as possibly permanent bad effects on the baby's brain. There are lots of other dangerous substances out there—please see the teen chapter.

How to lower the chance your kids will use substances

Educate them on all the risks in grade school. According to the American Academy of Family Physicians, "Kids who aren't properly informed are at greater risk of engaging in unsafe behaviors and experimenting with drugs." So make sure your kids can tell you what alcohol, tobacco and drugs do to the body, and to people's lives. For example, kids need to know that if they use drugs, they'll be with more dangerous people, and will be much more likely to do jail time. Using any substance, including cigarettes, can limit the type and number of friends they have, the life partner they find, and their success in school and life. They may become addicts that will do *anything* to keep using.

Be involved in your kids' lives. Also, don't use harsh punishments or permitting or controlling parenting styles. Kids who ask for time alone with other kids are *more* likely to have sex and use drugs. So, limit the amount of unsupervised time spent with other kids—and that includes dating! Give them time to be with friends around adults you trust.

Get your children involved in supervised activities—these could be school, community service, or religious activities. Kids who are involved in these activities show fewer risky behaviors than kids who aren't. Kids who say that religion is important and participate in religious activities are less likely than other kids to do risky things, according to a recent study. They have lower rates of early sexual activity, smoking, alcohol, truancy, marijuana use and depression. Limit exposure to media (you've heard this before)!

If you smoke cigarettes, you might tell them you're addicted and would quit if you could. If you're trying to quit, tell them you'll keep trying. Say that they'll have a better, healthier life, stay younger looking, and have a lot more money if they don't smoke. Please don't expose them to second hand smoke—there is no good excuse for this. Second hand smoke causes most of the same health problems that smoking causes.

Moderate use of alcohol in adults has benefits like preventing heart disease. But many adults choose not to drink for good reasons. If you drink alcohol, explain that adults can tell better than kids how much is too much. Teenage brains can get addicted more easily. It works best to say you expect them to wait until adulthood to decide whether to drink, so they're not as likely to get hurt. If you drink, you can show them what responsible drinking is with your own behavior (such as not getting drunk, and not drinking and driving).

Keep your kids away from people that use drugs. **If you find out that your children are using** substances, tell them you won't allow it, you're worried about them and that you'll help them stop. Set action limits with consequences. If that doesn't work, take away everything they need to get more of the substance (their car, computer, phone, money, user friends and unsupervised time), until you know they've stopped for at least a couple weeks. They may have a temper tantrum, but much worse things will happen if you don't seize control now. Then watch to make sure they don't use again. Contact your doctor, mental health professional or social services for help if problems continue.

Other Outside Influences and Risks to Your Children

Gangs

Why do kids join gangs? To belong to a group, or because of peer pressure, boredom, failing in school or jobs, being afraid and needing protection, or low self-esteem. Kids say they first like the attention, friendship, money, respect, and being able to talk to others about problems. But then some gangs will seriously beat kids up before letting them join. (Nice—where can we sign up?) Kids don't figure out the problems gangs will cause until later: getting arrested for theft, vandalism, drugs, weapons, assault or even murder, and that they're often not allowed to get out once they join. Sounds like the song "Hotel California"—you can check out but you can never leave!

To cut down the chance your children will join a gang, start talking about gangs in early grade school (kids join as early as age 9). Spend time with them every day, and give them lots of affection and good attention. Make them feel special because they are yours, and show them good morals by how you act. Help them with schoolwork or learning disabilities so they can do alright in school. Tell them to walk away from gang members. Know who your kids are with, help them find good friends and set firm curfews. Move away if you must. Keep your child active in school, music, sports, worship, community, home and family activities. Plan a better future together by making your child's education a top priority.

Guns in the home

About half of all US homes have a gun in them. So even if you don't have one, your child could come into contact with one at another home. One study has shown that when boys were tested by having a handgun placed where they could see it, most touched it and fired it, even if they had previous gun safety instruction. According to safety regulations of the NRA, children should be told what to do when they see a gun. *"STOP, don't touch, leave the area, and tell an adult."*

Guns should be stored locked up, without ammunition, in a way you're sure kids can't get at them. But according to the National Center for Health Statistics, over one half of handguns in homes with kids are stored improperly (are loaded, have ammo stored with the gun, or aren't locked up). If your child visits a new home, it's recommended that you ask if there are guns and how they are stored.

Most guns are bought with the good intent of protection. But a person killed by someone using a home gun is 43 times more likely to be a family member than an intruder. Firearm injuries are the second leading cause of death in 15 to 24 year olds, and the third most common cause of death in 10 to 14 year olds. Half of inner city high school boys and one fourth of girls say they know how to easily get a gun. People in homes with guns are three times more likely to be murdered and five times more likely to commit suicide. Plus, just so you know, thousands of teens kill themselves with a gun every year.

Sexual harassment

Yes, this can even affect kids. It's when someone else does something that is related to the sex of your child, making him or her feel uncomfortable or embarrassed. It includes touching, pinching, patting, grabbing, talking about the body sexually, and making sexual gestures, comments, and jokes. It can lead to fear, depression, and school and body image problems. It is illegal. Experts recommend telling kids about this around fifth or sixth grade. Explain how it's different than letting someone know that you like them (which is just flirting). Have your kids tell you when anything like this happens.

Sexual abuse

This can be uncomfortable to think or talk about. But we must to keep our children safe, since a secret exposed loses its power. Sexual abuse is involving a child in any sexual activity: vaginal or anal penetration with or without an object, oral-genital contact, genital-genital contact, fondling (touching their genitals or forcing them to touch); exposing them to pornography, prostitution, or adults engaging in sex including masturbation; and encouraging sex acts with other children. It's one of the cruelest, most selfish acts of power used against a child. It is morally wrong. Molestation is similar and includes threatening to do these things.

Child sexual abuse hurts children and robs them of their childhood. It is unfortunately very common. At least 100,000 children a year are sexually abused, and many cases aren't reported. Fifteen percent of college students report they were sexually abused. Abused children often grow up to be depressed adults who may abuse children themselves or commit other crimes. They often seek out sexual partners early, and have trouble with relationships. As adults, they often choose bad partners, and may allow abuse because they don't think they deserve better. The earlier abuse is found and treated, the better.

Keep your children safe by having a talk about their private parts, starting as early as when they are toilet trained. You can call genitals by a different name: private parts, girl parts, boy parts, special parts, the parts that are covered by underwear, parts that are different between girls and boys, or where we go pee and pooh-pooh from. Say, *"These are private and only for you to touch."* By the way, touching their own genitals is normal and healthy for children (masturbation).

Asking about sex, looking at nude pictures, and showing interest in sex is common and normal in children. Acting out sex or having detailed knowledge about sex is not normal. Playing doctor (showing and touching genitals) is not concerning in grade school or younger children of about the same age. Just redirect them to other activities if you find them playing it. If older kids babysit for you, be aware that some children are given drugs or abused—even sexually—by older siblings. If you have suspicions, ask your children details about what they did when you were gone.

Tell your kids to say no if someone other than a doctor tries to touch their private parts. Say it's never OK for someone to frighten or pressure them into sharing their bodies. Abusers will often tell lies to keep kids from telling. They may say that a parent will get hurt or in trouble, or will be mad if the child tells. Say that you want to know if someone tries to touch them, and about the lies they might be told. If your child says that someone has touched him or her, or talked about doing it, comfort and thank your child for telling you. Say, *"I believe you. It's not your fault. I will protect you."* Report it to child protective services or police—only reasonable suspicion is required. Keep your child away from the suspect.

Know who your kids are with and generally what they're doing

People who want to hurt children can be anyone—daycare providers, babysitters, family members or friends, coaches, boyfriends, girlfriends, or religious people. But family and friends most often commit sexual abuse, not strangers. It usually happens when children are left in the care of a family member, family friend or boyfriend.

To keep your children safe, leave them only with people you know well enough to have a feeling of trust. There is usually safety in numbers—kids are safer in a group, and around more than one adult. For babysitters, be sure to call several references. Thoroughly investigate daycare centers and homes. Check on your kids often by popping in unexpectedly until you feel very comfortable that your child is safe. Make sure your children seem happy, normal and comfortable after they've been with someone. Get to know your child's friends well and meet their parents. Someone you are dating or living with is probably not a safe choice for childcare until you've known and trusted him or her for years.

Carefully teach stranger danger

When your children are old enough to have a conversation with you, tell them that there are some people who try to hurt kids, but that you'll keep them safe. Do NOT give details about what happens to kids that are abducted—it isn't necessary and can produce long lasting fear. Explain what a stranger is. *"A stranger is a person you don't know well. Strangers can look nice or mean. They can look like someone's grandpa, grandma, dad or mom, brother or sister. Some strangers are a danger."* Explain that it's never safe to go up to, talk to, take anything from, or help a stranger, unless you are there and give permission. *"It's never OK to go up to a car unless you know the person in it very well."*

Unfortunately, studies show that after kids are told about stranger danger once, they still go up to cars and strangers! So occasionally play a little game to remind them. You could talk to a check out lady and then ask your child if she is a stranger. (Correct answer: yes, because we don't know her well.) Ask, *"If you're playing in the park, and somebody asks you to help him find a puppy, what should you do?"* (Say no and run to you.) Ask, *"You're walking home from school and a man you've seen before calls your name from a car and asks you to help him. What would you do?"* (Say no while walking away.)

Teach self defense in a non-scary way

Once you think they can understand, you could say, *"It hardly ever happens, but sometimes adults try to hurt kids. I'm going to tell you what to do so it can't happen to you."*

Say something like this, *" If someone tries to take you, scream loud and run to me or another big person."* A pediatrician in our community tells kids to be a screaming octopus, *"Wrap your legs around theirs so they can't walk."* *"If you can't run, then hurt them so you can run away—just like superman. Hit or kick their boy parts, poke their eyes with your fingers, smash their nose, bite them hard or hit the front of their neck where it sticks out. Ka-pow! Bam! Don't believe anything they say. Remember everything you can about them and their car. You can even make the car crash by steering crazy or pushing the pedals to get them in trouble. You can pull out wires or grab the gear shifter and pull on it* (show them how*). Now that you know this, you'll stay safe. I'm so proud of you for learning this big girl/boy stuff."*

Don't let discomfort keep you from teaching what kids need to know to get out of a bad situation. Make it light and don't be afraid to laugh and entertain them by acting out what you'd do if an adult tried to take or hurt you. Do something fun afterward and praise them for learning how to stay safe. Reassure them that you'll never let anything bad happen to them.

Limit the kind of decisions you allow your children to make

It's impossible to be with your kids and watch what they're doing all the time. Children need to develop independence and decision making skills anyway. But children's ability to make good decisions is limited. That's mostly because of inexperience and the fact that their brains are not fully developed yet. This skill—lucky #7—enables you to make good decisions about outside influences on your children, to protect their safety, success and happiness. Using this skill helps kids learn to make good decisions on their own.

The power you have as a parent

You have the power to strongly affect your children's behavior, emotional health and happiness. By learning and using the *7 Skills for Parenting Success*, you know you have what it takes to seize that power and give your children the best possible beginning in life. Be a good enough parent by occasionally asking yourself if you are prepared for successful parenting and a strong relationship, paying attention, calmly talking to teach, seizing control, planning and following through with discipline, balancing your support and control, and monitoring and managing outside influences on your children.

We think parenting is the most important and demanding job there is. We hope you'll find that using these methods makes life with your kids much less stressful and much happier. While it's important to use all seven skills, you don't have to use them perfectly to get good results.

Congratulate yourself for your efforts and for getting help when you need it. We believe you'll see your work pay off as your kids grow older. When they become parents, they may even ask you for parenting advice! If you'd like, clip out the chapter end summary cards, hang them on your fridge, carry them with you, or put them on your nightstand to review whenever you need them.

If you have teenagers, infants or toddlers, we'd like to show you some additional important information and skills in the next two chapters.

Skill #7 KEEP A CLOSE EYE ON THEM: Monitor and manage outside influences to prevent problems

- **Monitor** who your children are with, where they are, and generally what they are doing, **but avoid being intrusive.**
- Children need friends—help them find good ones.
- **Manage peer pressure:** Keep your relationship strong, test reality with your kids (ask them what they think about things and tell them what you think), and help them learn polite, strong ways to say no to other kids when they don't want to do something.
- Teach your kids about teasing and bullying and how to deal with them.
- **Limit exposure to media**—Limit TV, movies, games, music videos, computer, magazines, etc. to two hours a day. Exceptions are non-violent, non-sexual, non-scary educational material, sporting events, parties, and family game or movie fests.
- **Children younger than 2** should not watch TV. **Children younger than 8** should not watch the news or see or read about violent things.
- **Limit exposure to violent and sexual content**—Don't trust ratings. You decide what your children see. **Watch and listen to things together and talk** about them. M rated games are most dangerous. Check music to make sure lyrics aren't violent or sexually explicit—replace concerning ones.
- **Don't allow TV or internet in their bedrooms.** Computer/video games and the internet are safest in a central place so monitoring is easier.
- Teach internet safety—about predators; never give out personal info; no chat rooms. Limit instant chat with friends so they don't waste time or create drama. Use pop-up blockers. Limit non-educational sites to ones you've seen together, use monitoring software or use suggestions from your internet service provider.
- Teach the truth about advertisements—they are made to take your money and can mislead and trick you.
- Teach the dangers of gambling, pornography, addiction, guns and gangs early.
- **Have zero tolerance of alcohol, drugs and tobacco.** Ask your children to tell you the dangers of substances.
- Teach your kids about private parts, stranger danger, and self-defense.

Chapter 8

START SUCCESS EARLY: How to give you and your baby or toddler a great start

There is probably nothing that changes life more than bringing a new baby home. Life with a baby can be so rich, even with the high costs to your wallet and lifestyle. Crying, sleepless nights, smelly diapers, bottles, and cuddling fill the early days. Then during the toddler years, it may seem like all you do is chase after them, clean up messes and run damage control. But how you care for young children strongly affects how well they do in the future. What you do matters… a lot!

 If you use certain skills when they're little, you can give your children a good start on the way to emotional health and good behavior. You can also help them learn, and build strong attachments to you.

The skills we'll outline here are for parenting infants (babies from birth to about 12 months of age) and toddlers (from 1 to 3 years of age). For medical questions from bottles to rashes, please let your health care provider guide you. And for help with common challenges, from toilet training to separation anxiety, see chapter 13 for advice. This chapter will focus on how your interactions with your infants and toddlers can set you up for successful parenting later.

First of all, as infants grow, they are able to do more and more things. That's because of three things that develop. As their brains develop, infants learn more and more. As their bodies develop, they gradually get more control over how they move. Their behavior also develops over time, so they can make little decisions on what they want to do. Does this all happen automatically? Yes, but parents affect how it happens very much.

Responding sensitively to your baby is most important

Parents affect development most by how they respond to their little ones. By responding, we mean communicating with, reacting to, and meeting a baby's needs. How sensitive parents are when they respond to an infant predicts how well the child does at age 3 and well beyond that! The best development happens when parents respond sensitively throughout childhood. Responding to your little ones in a sensitive, caring way simply means being in tune with what they need and giving it to them. It means supporting what they're interested in doing.

Sensitive responses teach infants that they can control what parents do

It's actually very good when infants think they have some control over their parents! But, we said "some." They obviously can't totally control what you do. But the control they can have is very important to their health. When infants learn they can control some things, they learn that they can make things happen. This motivates them to learn, and try to do things themselves. That helps them develop and feel worthwhile.

Giving little children some control even makes them more likely to ask for help when they're older and stressed, instead of withdrawing. But children who feel that everything is out of their control learn to feel helpless in this world. Feeling helpless makes people depressed and anxious.

Giving some early control also helps children behave. (We know it's hard to believe, but it's true.) The reason is this. Young children who feel they have no control over what their parents do learn to fuss for what they need. They act out more to get what they want. But children who are very neglected will stop fussing and interacting with people because they know they won't get any response.

Consistent responses are also very important

What is the next most important thing besides responding in a sensitive way? Consistently responding to your baby is the answer. That just means responding to what a child does in a similar way. This helps a child feel that she can control things that happen to her. There's that control thing again—it's very important to your little child. You know you're being consistent when he or she expects what happens next, or is very surprised when it doesn't happen as usual.

Of course, your little ones can't control your family that much. When you need to care for other kids, or go to work, you will. Letting little children have some control doesn't include letting them do dangerous things or wreck the house, of course. Always reaching for their hands when they try to touch an electric outlet, and saying *"Danger, owie"* is a consistent response that teaches not to touch it. Sometimes you'll respond consistently *against* what they want. That gives them a sense of control too, by learning that their parents will consistently protect them.

Consistent, sensitive responses help your baby attach to you

When children are securely attached, they feel that their parents always protect and care for them. This really helps them develop, think and learn. When babies bond well to a parent, they're more independent by age 1, and obey a lot more often when they're 2 years old.

How to Respond Sensitively to Your Little Child

Talk to your baby every day in a warm, sweet voice

One of the first ways you can sensitively respond is by talking to your infant in a gentle way. Talking to infants early and often is critical for raising healthy, well-behaved children. Talk to her even before she understands. Starting the very first day, look in your baby's eyes, smile, and talk quietly to your baby. Use a sweet, musical and warm tone. A normal tone of voice (like talking to someone at work) is not warm enough.

Say things that show you want and approve of your baby. Use small, loving words and short phrases. Repeat them gently, over and over. *"You're such a pretty baby, Mommy loves you. Yes, Mommy loves you."* *"What a big baby boy you are—I've been waiting for you."* This is the first way you start an attachment between the two of you. This bond will grow as your baby learns to recognize you, and keeps hearing loving things.

Continue this warm, positive talk every day through the toddler years

This helps them learn the sounds and mouth movements they need to read and speak some day. Talk to them in the car, in the house, while you work, in the store, and everywhere. Smile and laugh a lot! Do it even when you don't feel like it—it may actually be most important then. Tell stories. Sing songs—they don't know or care if you're a bad tenor, or even tone deaf! Sing to them until they say, "Daddy, no more singing!" (Don't laugh—that happened to us.)

When they make noises, repeat their sounds and words back

Repeat back your *baby's words* or sounds in a gentle, sweet voice. Smile. This encourages them to say more. One year olds usually start to say single words, like "baba" or "mama." Two year olds usually can say a couple words at a time, like "me help," or "yum juice." Repeat what they say and add more words, such as, *"The juice is yummy. It tastes good."* This shows them how to say words better, and gives them good attention.

Ask them lots of questions

Ask infants little questions, like *"Did you have a fun day with grandma?" "Do you like your new blankie?"* Even if they are too young to answer, this gives them attention, and teaches them talking noises. They'll learn names like Mama, Dada, sister, and brother better if you use those names instead of him, her, and I. *"Mama loves when baby smiles."*

When your toddler can answer questions with yes or no, nodding or pointing, allow plenty of time for him or her to answer. Listen carefully, and look at them if possible. Say good things about what your child tries to say. *"Oh really? That's interesting, I like that." "Wow, you said a big word—good girl!"* When they ask you a question, always answer and use simple words. When they can talk, have them repeat new words and say, *"Good job"* if they say anything back (no matter how badly they said it).

By age 2, toddlers can start to understand what you're saying. Have little conversations. Warm talking between a 2 year old and a parent predicts social and school success more than anything!

Being cheerful helps you and your little ones

Research shows best results when small children are around adults who are in a reasonably good mood. (Oh, boy—seems like this may take a little faking sometimes!) If other adults think you have a positive personality and attitude, your kids do better. Depressed parents are more critical and harsh, and their kids have more trouble with depression and behavior problems. That warm voice we talked about is especially important when your little child is upset or you are upset.

Also, try to never ignore your little one, even when you are overwhelmed. No matter how you feel, try your best to keep talking to him or her with a sweet voice. If you feel very upset and don't feel in control of your emotions, take a **parent time-out**. Just put him in his playpen or other safe place and come back in a minute or two when you feel calmer.

Avoid showing negative feelings toward your little child

This is very damaging. Some parents do this with body language (brushing off, not looking at, or shoving a child), or with words ("you little brat, pain in the…, what are you whining about? I wish you would just hush up"). Showing no emotion to a small child can be just as damaging as showing negative emotion. If you often feel that your little one is annoying or bothering you, it's a sign that you need help.

Be physically close

Gently touch, hold, kiss, and cuddle your baby many times every day. This helps babies develop and bond. Smile at them, look into their eyes, pick them up, bounce them gently, rock them, put them to your shoulder, rub their backs, and tickle them gently. As your toddlers start walking, add hugs, pats on the back, and hand holding.

Your small children need many of these physical touches EVERY SINGLE DAY. Smile when they touch you. When they smile, smile back. Nurturing touch is very important to a child's development. But it's also important to recognize when you're touching too hard, or your child doesn't seem comforted with your touch, so you can stop then.

Hold your toddler (1 to 3 year old) when he wants you to (if you're not too busy or holding other things). Remember that when small children can often control what Mom and Dad do, they are more secure and develop better. So let *them* tell you when they want to be held or to get down. They'll eventually get interested in things they can't do while you hold them, so you won't have to hold them forever.

You can't spoil children by giving them the physical contact that they want. And sometimes you'll need to hold them when they don't want to be held, to keep them from danger or making a mess. When you need to get something done, it's fine to leave them in the playpen for a short time, even if they cry. Rub her head, tell her you'll be right back and then soothe her when you return. That is our advice for toddlers. You'll find different advice for dealing with crying infants (from birth to about 12 months old) later in this chapter.

Other important physical care includes daily baths, diaper changes and good nutrition. You can help their physical development in other ways too. Give your baby tummy time when she plays starting at about 2 months (but according to the American Academy of Pediatrics, or AAP, you should never place infants on their tummies to sleep, but on their backs instead). This helps her develop neck muscles for crawling. Help her stand and walk when she seems ready to learn. Give her a quiet, warm, and clean place to sleep. Watch what she's doing at all times—she can get into danger any minute. Cover outlets and close off stairs.

Your child should never be around cigarette smoke, since it increases the likelihood of infections and illnesses, like sudden infant death syndrome. Please follow other safety and health recommendations from your health care provider.

Respond when they want to eat or drink

To develop well, babies must feel that they can get what they need without struggling. When you meet their needs and wants, they learn that their world is predictable and soothing. Children who learn that they need to yell, fuss, or cry to get what they need will misbehave to get what they want when they're older.

The earliest chance babies have to control things is by getting fed when they're hungry. The American Academy of Pediatrics (AAP) and other organizations recommend feeding babies whenever they're hungry in the first year of life (on demand). We heartily agree. Breastfeeding has been shown to be best, and there are fewer complications and more months of breastfeeding when it's done on demand. The AAP has stated, "Newborns should be nursed whenever they show signs of hunger, such as increased alertness or activity, mouthing, or rooting. Crying is a late indicator of hunger."

On-demand feeding seems to help babies feel secure and attached. But hunger and pain interfere with attachment to a parent. Hopefully, you'll start to recognize when baby is hungry before he or she fusses. Of course, babies may have to wait a short time if you're busy. Scheduled feedings, on the other hand, are linked to problems in babies such as low weight gain and dehydration. Parents who insist on getting their babies on a feeding schedule for their own convenience should do it only slowly over a period of months. Every couple of days, you could expect a baby to wait a few more minutes to eat, for instance.

Gradually start feeding schedules at 1 year of age. Toddlers should join the family at mealtimes. When they can sit in a high chair, feed them during the family meal even if they don't seem hungry, so they get used to being there. But if they seem hungry before or after the family eats, feed them then also. Also follow your doctor's recommendations.

Sometimes you may need to feed him when he doesn't seem hungry so he gets enough nutrition. Plus, when a fussy baby who normally feeds well rejects the breast or bottle, he's not fussing because he's hungry. Try to soothe him some other way to avoid over-feeding him.

Good nutrition habits start early—when babies first start to eat food. Make new foods available and appealing, and give rewards for trying them. Do *not* force young children to eat something they don't want. This will set up power struggles over food—not a good thing.

Respond to their distress signals

Understanding this next thing is a big key to early parenting success: **infants and toddlers communicate by showing emotion.** This is true not only before they can talk, but when they're just learning to talk. That's why infants and toddlers cry or fuss when they're upset! So crying and fussing are common and normal.

What's more, when they're fussy, they're often trying to tell you something. Try to figure out what will help your baby feel better. They may be tired and need to be rocked to sleep. They may be hungry and need to eat. They might just need a little attention and need to be held. They may have a tummy ache or messy diaper.

Sometimes you won't be able to figure it out because it's due to a fussy temperament or colic. Studies show that responding sensitively to an infant's distress predicts school achievement at age 6 better than how much she's encouraged to learn! So you'll get best results by not brushing her off when she calls out or comes to you for help or comfort.

If your little infant cries, don't always pick her up

Research has shown that children learn and do better if parents didn't always pick them up when they fussed as infants (from birth to about 12 months). So when your babies cry, sometimes just talk sweetly and touch them gently, or put them in a baby swing and smile at them. How fast you respond (say you have a 2 year old having a tantrum at the same time) is not as important as the fact that you do respond. Again, the advice is different when they grow to be toddlers. Many experts agree that when your child is old enough to reach up to you because he wants to be held, it's good to hold him when possible.

Show your little child empathy every day

Empathy shows that you care about what happens to them. Try to imagine what things would be like in their baby shoes, so to speak. That helps you respond better. For example, say *"That must have hurt. I'm sorry you hit your finger. Momma will kiss and make it better."* This works a lot better than saying, "Don't be a cry baby." Saying things like that makes them think that you don't care, and that they're not worth much. That will lead to more problems that you'll have to deal with later.

Now that we've covered what helps little children develop and attach to you, here are ways to help them learn. Responding to what they're interested in is the key.

How to Help Little Children Learn

Let them explore things they reach for

When your little one wants to see something, let her see and touch it if it's safe and appropriate. Not letting her touch it can interfere with learning. Try not to be overprotective or block what she wants to do without a good reason.

Of course, good reasons for not letting her touch or see something would be keeping her safe or protecting other people or their things. If they've got something that isn't safe or appropriate to play with, say something like, *"Careful baby, scissors are sharp,"* or *"That's Daddy's—not for baby."* Take the dangerous item away when you say this. Also, show siblings that you watch out for them by keeping the baby from messing with their things.

Parents who really restrict what their little children do have trouble responding sensitively. Those parents often can't see that their children have needs and interests different from their own. Little children whose needs and interests aren't supported won't be motivated to listen and behave.

When possible, let them look at things for as long as they want

When your little child is busy checking something out, don't try to switch his attention to something new. He'll learn better if he can keep playing with things he's interested in. This makes it easier for him to figure things out. It also motivates him to try new things. And get this— research shows that parents who do this have toddlers who obey more! Asking little kids to look at new things when they're into something else confuses them. Their little brains aren't ready to do this yet. Wait for *them* to switch their focus to something new. They will when they're ready.

When they want to see something that is safe and appropriate, **show them the object, name it, and describe it.** Use short, easy words. Do it even before they can understand. *"You want the red car. It's a nice red car—let's push it and see if it goes."* Ask a question about, or comment on, what your child does. Or suggest that she do something related. *"You want to see the wrapper? Here's the shiny wrapper. The wrapper makes a funny noise. Does it taste good?"*

If they aren't interested anymore, they may look away. When they find something new to look at, do the same thing with the new object. If they're tired, they may yawn, or nod off. Try to notice these cues that they need a rest. Figuring that out can avoid fussiness.

When they aren't looking at something, show them new things

The time to show them new things is when they aren't into something else. Research shows better speech and intelligence in small children when parents encourage looking at new things, and noticing what is happening around them. Almost every day, point to pictures and objects. *"This is orange juice—it's orange and good for us."* *"That's a guitar—it has strings."* Say the words over and over, even when they can't understand yet. Ask them questions about things, even if they can't answer. Act as if you enjoy the item. Laugh with them when something happens (the ball hits the bell, the stack falls over). Talk about things you are thinking about. *"It's cold outside, burr, cold outside."* *"Baby has a pretty dress—pretty dress."*

What about toys?

Some of us have had mega piles of toys in our homes at some point. But too many toys hurt learning. They over-stimulate and distract kids from exploring what they have. Children only need a few toys at a  time that they can safely play with. That's good for your wallet, too! When you hand baby a toy (or hold it for her if she can't hold it yet), touch it, describe it, and name its parts. Let her put it in her mouth if it's safe and clean. Infants explore and learn about things by putting things in their mouths. Show how it works the first time and return it to her if it's dropped.

 Try to have toys that are made for their ages. To lower your stress, avoid toys that can make a big mess. Electronic toys that move themselves aren't good for learning in little children. Toddlers are often more interested in stuff they can play with around the house than fancy, expensive toys anyway. Larger plastic items, like food storage dishes, or pots and pans they can put in their mouths are great. Toys are better if they make noise, have different shapes and bright colors. Avoid plastic bags or toys with small parts that can choke children.

Let them choose how to play with things

As long as it's safe, let them choose how to play and do things as much as possible. Letting them do things their way teaches them to solve problems and builds self-confidence. By the time children have reached age 3, the more parents have been helping them finish things, the less they can solve problems and learn by themselves. So, when he's trying to fit pieces of a toy, don't help unless he hands them to you.

Telling them what to do when they play doesn't give them a choice, and can make them feel like they're "doing it wrong." There's nothing good about telling infants and toddlers that they are doing things wrong. Give them a choice between two activities sometimes. *"Would you like to play with your trucks or your dolls?"* Don't take away something they're interested in, unless you need to. Also don't punish or scold them for what they do with something you allowed them to play with.

Do go ahead and gently tell them what to do for safety, to protect others, or for teaching good behavior. *"Please pick up your bottle and give it to Momma." "We don't hit—hitting hurts."*

How to show them how to do something

So, if they can't figure it out, how do you show them how things work? Just give them little hints or demonstrate part of it. Showing how to do something the first time is fine. If they need help, try not to take over and finish it—that shows them that they can't do things. Just make suggestions. *"Go ahead, try another slot for the block, it might fit, good job,"* instead of, "Put the red block in the red square hole, otherwise it won't fit." If he hands the block to you, you can put it near the red square hole, and then hand it to him and fit it through together. Just help him start, giving a little help along the way, but don't take over.

To make things easier for your little one to do, set things up in advance. Help infants feel successful by doing this a lot in the first year. Break down tasks into little steps, so they can work on just one at a time. For example, with a stack of rings on a peg, have them practice with only the biggest one first. As they can do more alone, help them less. In fact, *don't* help when you think they can do it themselves (even if it takes them a while to figure it out). Just say, *"I know you can do it, just try again."* Find harder games when something seems easy for them.

Give toddlers lots of chances to do things themselves

Toddlers gain confidence by seeing that they can do things, which motivates them to do more. If something they want to do seems unsafe or impractical, try to substitute something they can do instead. For example, your son wants to push the stroller, but you're in a hurry and need to do it yourself. Just let him push it later when you aren't in a hurry.

Respond when they do something new—praise them!

If they try something new and good, like trying to roll over, sit, or clap, say something. *"Good baby rolling over. Do that again."* *"What a good clapper"* (even if hands barely touch together). This encourages learning. Praise just for trying something, even if they can't get it done or do it well. *"Daddy likes how you try to get the spoon in your mouth."* Praise makes them want to try. The more specific you are about what they did, the better it is for learning.

Read books, sing and dance with them

Start reading together as soon as your baby can sit on your lap, and do it often. Read simple books with lots of pictures. Let them touch the book, put it to their mouth and try to turn the pages. Point to pictures, and name and describe the things you see (*"blue boat, blue boat"*). It's normal for toddlers not to sit still for a whole book, so just do what you can. Listening to classical music can have good effects on learning. And dancing together to gentle rhythms can be fun and help you bond.

Use routines

Daily routines that include naps decrease your stress, which is good for both of you. Using a flexible schedule increases the chance your baby will get the sleep, food and attention needed, and you'll get time for yourself. It helps you fit in good learning activities, like the library, zoo, or play-dates with other kids.

Be careful not to force them to learn early

Studies show that parents who try hard to teach little children so they'll know more than average (like showing flash cards and quizzing them) tend to be less nurturing than parents who are more relaxed about learning. They don't respond to their kids' needs as well. So try not to focus on your little ones' brain development over their emotional development.

Forced teaching only makes a short-term difference in school anyway. Other kids catch up later. If you're forcing your child to look at something instead of letting her look at what she wants to explore, it can actually hurt her development. BUT, you *can* safely increase your child's learning by giving quick positive feedback for trying things. *"What a big boy trying to do that. You'll get it with more practice."*

You can use the skills in this chapter to help them learn.

Encourage toddlers to be social

Normal toddlers are self-centered and freely tell you their needs and interests (often with great emotion!). Children gradually learn how to get along with people by watching others, including you. In the first two years, go ahead and instruct them how to be social. *"Say bye-bye," "Give Grandpa a hug because we're leaving," "Share your crackers with brother, please."* Encourage them to play, laugh, share, and smile at others. Praise them when they do. Show them how to touch other children gently. Say, *"Mommy is touching the little girl so nicely," "Gentle, we touch gentle."* When you give kisses, tell baby, *"Nice kisses for baby."*

When your kids are about 3 years old, stop giving them *as much* social instruction with other kids. At that age, controlling social skills too much can become a problem. Let them go up to another child themselves and see what they do. Interfere only for safety, aggression (hitting, biting, etc), bullying or to teach sharing. Notice and praise good things they do (like talking, playing together, sharing). If they're not interested in playing with someone, start to play with the other child yourself. Most kids will want to join in. If your child hardly ever wants to interact with you or other children, it may mean there is a developmental problem. Then you should see your physician.

Don't allow your little ones to watch television

Many kids these days will spend most of their free time with screens— game, movie, computer, phone and TV screens. Don't let your toddler start this habit so young! Small children should spend very little time in front of a screen. In fact, the American Academy of Pediatrics recommends no television for children younger than 2 years old. They need to be moving, touching, hearing and learning from people, books, nature, music and toys.

If you're still going to let them watch television or movies, don't trust that a show for kids is alright unless you check it out first. Even cartoons show hitting or otherwise hurting people or animals. It's safest to let kids watch shows that you've already seen and approve of.

Early Discipline

Small children need sensitive responses much more than discipline. But, limit setting is an important part of teaching good behavior early. A limit is like a rule. **Setting a limit** means to not allow them do something, or to expect them to do something else. Setting behavior limits from an early age helps keep them safe and teaches them a big fact of life: There will be limits on what they're allowed to do. But this needs to be done very sensitively at these young ages.

After children are about a year old, they can start to understand when you're saying something good or bad about what they're doing. But they still can't understand well enough to follow a discipline plan like those in skills #4 and #5, so don't try. Just do what's in this box instead.

Before your children are 2 years old, limit what they do only for:

1. Health and safety reasons.
2. Protecting people's things (including yours).
3. Teaching basic manners (like no hitting).
4. The good of the family (like keeping routines and your sanity).

If you decide your child's behavior isn't good, just:

1. Take him or her away from the situation, area, or person, or
2. Take away the object involved, or
3. Redirect his or her attention to something new.

You may need to do more than one of these things. Don't give long explanations why what they're doing is bad- they just won't get it. Don't raise your voice. Just quietly say, *"Oh, oh, that is Mommy's. Play with this."* Or say, *"Daddy doesn't want to see it break,"* while taking a fragile object away. Don't bother saying "Stop it" – it won't work since they won't understand. Just calmly do one of the above three things.

Don't expect small children to know what is all right to play with. They can't tell if something isn't safe, will ruin the furniture or cause you trouble. They will be persistent (a good trait to have) and still want interesting things. But you're the parent, so you decide. Also, there are a few behaviors in a 1 or 2 year old that you may need help changing, such as hitting, biting, or temper tantrums. See chapter 13 for tips.

Starting when they are 2 years old, they can understand more of what you want. But they still can't do what you say very well. Normal 3 year olds only obey half the time! Allow them plenty of time when you tell them to do something. Make sure they are capable of doing it (they are old enough). Check Appendix A if you aren't sure. Use the talk to teach guidelines for giving children commands (see Chapter 3).

If your 2 year old doesn't obey, and he or she has done what you asked before in the same situation, you can try setting an action limit. But that may not work until they are 3 years old, and that's normal. You could also just stick with the suggestions in the box above for now. Reward them often for good behavior. Use only mild punishments, like time-out. But time-out only works starting at about age 2½. If you use time-out, and they won't stay seated in a chair, you can try placing them in a playpen instead. Don't use a crib for time out, otherwise they may think of punishment when they go to bed at night.

Be consistent with your limits

Every time baby does something you don't like, try to react pretty much the same way. If you pick up the bottle and keep it for a while every time he throws it on the floor, he will stop throwing it when he wants to keep it. Then when he throws it, you know he's just playing and you can keep it. If every time she reaches for your coffee, you sweep her hand away and say, *"Messy, that's messy,"* she'll stop reaching. Even when your little ones are pretty dang cute, don't laugh at behaviors you don't like—that can be rewarding and make those things happen more often.

Crying and yelling is normal for infants and toddlers

Remember how we said little children communicate by emotion? That means they normally cry and fuss to get attention and try to get what they want. And **normal toddlers only obey commands half the time** because their little brains and bodies aren't ready, or because they just choose not to! Yah, we know. That means when children are 2 or 3, life can get tough. Many people call this "the terrible twos."

Well, when kids that age choose not to obey, they are just doing what is part of normal development, called **actively disobeying**. Toddlers usually actively disobey just by saying, "no!" and continuing doing what they're doing. But normal toddlers sometimes get really mad when they  actively disobey. Lucky us! Don't stress yourself out trying to fix this normal behavior. It will go away eventually.

Expect and celebrate your toddler's struggle for independence

Between ages 1 and 2, healthy children start to struggle for independence. A good sign that this is happening is when they actively disobey. So, **it's good that your child starts to resist you and refuse to do what you say!** Expect it, and don't be angry or disappointed because they're doing something good for their development. By the time kids are 3 years old, they can do what their parents ask *most* of the time. We said *most* of the time (not *all* the time) now!

Praising good behavior is the best way to avoid bad behavior

When your child does something good, even when you expect it, say *"Daddy likes it when you...* (put your cup down on the tray, smile, talk)." *"Good boy, picking up your socks."* Praise with words even before your little child can understand. *"You are so sweet, touching her so nicely"* (sharing your blankie, giving a cracker). They will get the idea that they're doing something good from your attention and gentle voice.

Be patient with them

Children don't naturally know how to behave. They'll try something several times before understanding that it's not allowed. They'll need many reminders too. Their memory is not very developed yet, but improves with time. Start teaching basic limits now, and you can do much more when they're older using the *7 Skills*.

Never shout at, shove, shake, yank, hit, spank or push them

Since children learn how to act by watching their parents, doing these things teaches them to do the same to you and other people. Also, research studies clearly show that **children who are physically punished under the age of 2 disobey more, are more aggressive and have more emotional problems**. That's because physical punishment can interfere with the attachment of a small child to a parent. So even though spanking at this age can quickly stop a bad behavior for now, it increases the chances for severe behavior and emotional problems when children get older. Please see page 116 for more information.

Avoid saying bad things about little children when they disobey

Children notice a rejecting tone and it's enough to hurt their development. Please don't scowl at them, scold them or be critical. Try not to talk with an angry or sarcastic tone, even when putting them in time-out. Avoid saying negative words, like *hard, difficult* or *bad* about your little child. He's probably just acting normal for his age, trying to get what he wants and needs. We've heard parents say things like, "He's my mean one." Little children don't misbehave to be mean— they don't know what being mean is yet. They act out because they don't have self control yet, and that is normal.

Avoid saying the word *"no"* to your little ones

Kids learn to say what they hear. So when your little children do things that you don't like, avoid saying the word "no." That way they won't learn to say "no" to you as much Try saying *why* you don't want them to do something instead. *"Oh, oh, danger," "Icky, big mess," "That's owie for baby," "This is only for Mommy," "We don't...," "Babies don't...," "We need to...."*

Baby-proof your home to avoid setting some limits

Use protectors and gates to block off dangerous things, or things you don't want messed up or broken. Move things that are inappropriate for babies to touch until they're older. Have plenty of safe objects around that they *can* play with.

About crying and colicky babies

Most babies cry up to an hour at a time every day the first three months after birth. Newborns are usually quieter in the hospital, so this can be quite a shock when you get home! **When a baby cries, see if you can figure out why** (hunger, wet diaper, something hurting, tiredness, too warm or cold). Try to soothe or distract her (hold or bounce her or use a baby swing).

But don't pick up infants every time they cry (before 1 year of age, and when they're too young to reach up to you because they want to be held), so they learn to soothe themselves. Let them cry for a few minutes when you lay them down to see if they can put themselves to sleep. If not, rock them a little and try again. If your baby cries much more than usual, check with your doctor.

Babies with colic cry longer and more intensely than other babies. Having colic means crying usually more than two hours at a time, pretty much every day. One in five normal babies has colic, usually starting at about 2 to 4 weeks of age. No one knows for sure what causes it, but it is known that cigarette smoke makes it worse. Fortunately, colic is just temporary. It usually lasts only until the baby is 3 or 4 months of age. By the way, colicky babies do not have more behavior problems than other children when they're older.

The intense noise from colicky crying can be annoying (like nails on a chalkboard). Plus, babies with colic usually can't be soothed, no matter what. Ugh! It can turn any parent into a basket case, and these babies are abused more often than other babies. It's normal to feel angry, but it isn't normal to act on it by hurting your baby. Remember he or she can't help it, and it isn't your fault either.

These things can help you cope. Treat the crying as a distress signal. Try to figure out what will make it better (even if you can't). The more sensitively you respond now, the less she'll cry as a toddler. Try carrying her around on your arm with her tummy down. Don't over-feed her. Follow your doctor's advice. Take several short breaks a day. Lay her on her back in the crib and go where you can't hear her for a few minutes. Wear headphones, listen to relaxing music, or use ear plugs.

This isn't the time to worry about bothering other people for help. Ask someone to take the baby for a while for your baby's sake. Take baby outside or for a ride in the car. If you've reached your limit, you NEED to take a break. If you don't, you have a high risk of abusing your child. If you ever feel like hitting or throwing her, lay her down in a safe place and call for help from family, neighbors, friends or a social service agency.

The parent giving most of the care to any baby needs to be listened to, praised and thanked. He or she needs breaks to be able to keep giving good care and avoid burnout. Other parents in the family should frequently take over for a few hours. Also use a baby sitter, or share babysitting with friends and relatives you trust.

Temperament

All babies are born with personality parts, called temperament traits, that explain some of how they act. One trait is how easily distracted they are. Babies that are easily distracted by a noise or sight can stop eating, even though they're still hungry. So when you think you're done feeding, they want to eat again. Feed these babies in a boring place. Fortunately, these same babies can be soothed more easily than others with a rattle or rocking.

Babies with easy temperaments can be both over-fed (because they'll eat even when they're not hungry) and under-fed (because they won't cry much when they're hungry). Children with fussy temperaments are more likely to be abused if parents don't know how to cope. Please see the advice on temperaments in chapter 14.

START SUCCESS EARLY: Give you and your baby or toddler a great start

Sensitively respond to your little ones

- **Talk to them warmly and touch them gently** many times every day. Ask little questions and say good things about them. Be cheerful, smile and laugh even when you don't feel like it. Repeat their noises and words.
- Don't pick up infants every time they cry. Do hold them whenever you can once they're old enough to reach up to you wanting to be held.
- Feed your infants under one year old when they seem hungry.
- **Respond to fussiness**—try to figure out what'll make them feel better.

Help them learn

- **Let them explore** what they want, for as long as they want, if it's possible, safe and appropriate. Repeatedly name and describe objects.
- Have a few brightly colored toys, **let them choose how to play** (if it's safe), and let them figure out how toys work- just give them little hints or show them once.
- Give toddlers many chances to **do things themselves.**
- **Praise** them when they do anything new (*"Good job!"*).
- Read **books** with them -- point and describe objects on the pages.
- Use **routines** for bedtime, meals, naps, activities, and bath time.
- Show them how to play and **interact with others**, but at age 3, interfere in play only for aggression or safety, or to teach sharing.
- **No TV** until age 2. At age 2, allow only occasional appropriate shows.

Early discipline

- **Before age 2**, limit what they do only for reasons of health or safety, protecting possessions, teaching basic manners, the good of other family members, following routines and giving yourself a break. If you decide your child shouldn't be doing something, do one of these and say why (but instead of, "No, put that down", say *"Scissors aren't for baby"*):
  Take him away from the situation (area or person) or
  Take away the object involved or
  Redirect his attention to something new
- **At age 2 and 3**, make sure they're capable of doing what you ask (see Appendix A). Action limits and time-out *may* work starting at age 2 ½. Expect them to resist doing what you ask-- it's normal. Avoid future problems by not using physical punishment. Praise every little good behavior. Don't say bad things about your child when he misbehaves, but gently say *what* he's doing wrong *("We don't... " "That's not for baby" "Oh, oh, that's messy" "We need to..." " That's only for...")*

Chapter 9

MORE ON SUCCESSFUL PARENTING OF TEENS: How to deal with the developing brain and other challenges

Life with a teenager can be wacky, confusing, and exhausting for parents. But it doesn't have to be that way. We are here to help. We thought it might be good to begin with a little humor. **You know your kids are teenagers when**:

- You think you may be slowly going insane.
- You just told your boss, "Dude, you're like totally, like, a loser."
- You're afraid that either your kids are seriously disturbed, or you are.
- The only way you can reach them is by text message.
- When they say "my space," it doesn't mean their bedrooms.
- Sometimes you don't understand a single word they say.
- Their rooms may get you in trouble with the health department.
- They tell you that you're stupid and don't know anything—and you're starting to believe them!
- You wonder who they are and what they've done with your kids.

Nevertheless, we have good news for our readers. The research clearly shows that what parents do with teens, and how they do it, matters—a lot. If you have learned the *7 Skills*, you already have most of the skills you need to raise a successful teen. Now we'll teach you other things you need to know to keep them safe while helping them become independent, responsible adults who still feel close to you.

Let's start with more good news. It's nobody's fault that it's tough to raise teenagers. The problem is all in their heads! Well, more specifically, the problem is in their brains that are still changing.

The Teenage Brain is Not Fully Developed Yet

Parents of teenagers may wonder if their kids have a brain at all! They do have a brain, but it's undergoing some major remodeling. First, let's go over some basics of our command center, the brain. The brain has different parts that help us do certain things. Movement, thinking, memory, emotions, sexual behavior, planning, motivation, and creativity are all done by different parts of the brain. While genes we're born with partly decide how our brains work, the experiences we have change how it works, too

The brain physically changes during childhood. At about age 11, there's a burst of growth in the number of brain cells called neurons. This continues into the early 20's. After new neurons are made, they need to be connected (or wired) together in order to work properly. That's because neurons carry signals to each other. The wiring process for certain parts of the brain starts in the early teen years, but it isn't finished until the early to mid 20's. This process of making new brain cells and wiring them together is what makes children able to do things better as they get older, like moving, talking, learning, and making decisions.

Brain development has recently been studied using some really cool machines that take brain pictures. Pictures of adult and teen brains have been compared, and there are some big differences.

Teenagers are big kids—NOT young adults

Since teens don't have fully functioning (or wired) brains yet, they aren't able to figure out life very well for themselves. This explains many of the things we notice in teenagers. They aren't able to make decisions and function as well as they will be able to when they're adults. For instance, teens can't connect what they do with what happens next very well. As a result, they will decide to take more risks than we would. Their emotions often aren't logical either. Teens also aren't good at figuring out how other people feel. The teenage brain is a work in progress.

A parent's job is to help kids wire their new brain cells

It's normal for teens to push away their parents when they still really need them. Teenagers still need parents to love and support them, to teach them, and to help them wire their new brain cells. Luckily, you don't need to be a brain surgeon to do this! It sounds more complicated than it is. The main thing to do is to affect their experiences in certain ways. We'll show you how to work on your rewiring project while keeping your relationship intact. Relax—most of what you need was already covered in the *7 Skills*.

Brain parts under construction in teenagers

While some brain wiring happens throughout our lives, most of the wiring in certain parts of the brain occurs during the teen years. If these parts aren't wired then, it's very hard to wire them later. In fact, brain cells that aren't used can die and can't be replaced. Ever heard of "use it or lose it"? That applies to the teen brain—it needs to learn how to do some things now, or it may never learn. Some people never have a chance to wire their brains in healthy ways as teens. So they continue to have problems with immaturity their whole lives. We all know people like this!

The fact that the brain is still immature explains "teen moments," when parents wonder what the heck their kids are thinking. Let's look at which brain areas grow and get wired as a teenager.

Decision and impulse control center

The most important teen brain remodeling goes on behind the forehead (in the area of the brain called the prefrontal cortex). This brain area has many very important jobs, and it has a lot to do with personality and ability to tell right from wrong. It's involved in reasoning, managing emotions and relationships, controlling impulses, weighing consequences for actions, planning ahead and making decisions. Ah-hah! No wonder parents struggle with getting their teens to do these things! Their teens' brains just aren't fully ready.

Teen brains are not wired yet to make good decisions. So don't think just because you tell your kids to "make good decisions" that they can actually do it. You can only trust a normal teen brain so far. Even if you think you have a good kid who usually makes good decisions, he or she can still make bad ones. Don't be fooled if you have one of those really "smart" kids. Parents often assume that because their child is smart, he or she will make good decisions. Hear the buzzer? Wrong!

Kids who are told they are very smart are just as likely as other kids (if not more likely) to make bad decisions. That's because they may think they're smarter than other people and know what to do better than anyone, including you. **Being smart has very little to do with making good decisions** in teens, because the part of the brain that does this isn't fully operational yet.

Teens **can't control their impulses well yet** either. An impulse is a sudden urge or desire to do or say something. It's not planned or thought out ahead of time. Common teen impulses are to do risky things. As we age, we learn to control impulses—we think before talking or acting. For example, controlling an impulse would be to calm down before busting out with anger or tears when we don't want to. On the other hand, over-control of impulses can lead to holding things in an unhealthy way. How we control impulses is a big part of our personality.

Short-term memory center

When something new happens, or is learned, it can be stored in this brain part. With all the remodeling going on here, your teens may have trouble remembering new things. This is a good time to help your children learn how to remember. Keep them organized with a planner. Write things like chores or house rules down. Use a family calendar of what's happening and when. Encourage them to do things now, when they're thinking of it, so they won't forget later. Teach them **memory tricks**: visualize things, write or say them over and over, make up funny sayings, and use acronyms. P.S. I'M HELPING is a parenting acronym, and Kind Hearted Dads Drink Chocolate Milk is a math acronym of the metric system units (kilo, hecto, deca, deci, centi, milli).

Motivation center

Your teens' brain remodeling is part of the reason for low motivation. They may seem lazier than when they were younger, but you can help. Unless there's a good reason for change, keep their activities and schedules going even when they don't want to. For example, it isn't good to let kids sleep in too long on the weekends. They should get up within a couple hours of when they usually do on weekdays. Have family activities regularly. Help them with homework if needed. Help them look into the future. *("It's important to do well in school so you can pick the career you want.")* Also keep your expectations realistic (use skill #6).

Sexuality center

Oh boy—so much to say, and so little room. This brain part launches and controls hormone and body changes that lead to more sexual thoughts in teenagers. (Thanks a lot, Mother Nature!) Sex drive starts to develop, and masturbation is normal for both boys and girls. **Hormones** are raging like a river. Higher testosterone levels in boys develop their bodies and brains so they're more aggressive, angry, afraid (yes, afraid), sexual, and protective of themselves and their stuff. They may be more violent when they think they've been hurt. In girls, estrogen and progesterone develop their bodies and stimulate their brains leading to moodiness (including symptoms of depression and anxiety) and sexual thoughts and behaviors.

Both boys' and girls' hormones lead them to follow their impulses and take risks. This is very bad, since the part of the brain that helps them make decisions and control impulses is under major reconstruction. Their hormones are telling them to take risks, and the brain part that should be saying no isn't working yet. Disaster! We have a whole exciting, yet scary, section on sex for you later on in this chapter.

Emotion centers

One of these might as well be called the, **"You just don't get it—you bug me. Oh, and can I have some money?" personality center.** Sound familiar? This is a time when kids show wild changes in emotions, for no earthly reason. They'll unexpectedly over-react with fear or tears. They'll misinterpret what you say. They may be more irresponsible or quieter than before. Even though it's hard to understand, this is a normal phase. Their behavior and whole personalities seem to change while their brains are remodeling.

Teens are often **cranky and moody**. They may not know or be able to explain why they're grouchy. This may be easier to understand when you think about everything that is happening to them. This is a time for moving up in school with new pressures. Teens worry a lot about what other kids think of them. They usually don't get enough sleep. Their bodies are changing and they worry about how they look. Parents may have high expectations for them in sports, school, religious life, and so on. They may get bummed out and lose self-esteem when they can't live up to these expectations. Of course their brains are also changing, and this, along with surging hormones, makes them just not feel good.

Part of the problem is that **teens don't read emotional cues as well as adults**. Sometimes, they'll think people are mad when they aren't. They may inaccurately think someone did something to hurt them, and feelings will get hurt more easily. Teens can be very sensitive when they have made mistakes, or even defensive. What you think is a simple, pleasant question may be seen as an attack. They may fall apart because friends hate them, even if there is no evidence that this is true.

How can you cope with all this? Remember that their wacky emotional spikes probably have nothing to do with you. It's all in their heads. And it's not their fault either, so cut them some slack for irritating **moodiness** they can't help, as long as they do not disrespect or defy you. Be calmer than they are. Be available and listen more than you talk. Now that you know which brain parts are getting remodeled, let's talk about other "pleasant" changes you'll probably see in your teen.

It's Normal for Teens to Pull Away from Their Parents

This is one of the first parts of gaining normal independence, so expect it. Teens do want close relationships with their parents. But they won't show you the same affection they did when they were little, and they won't want to be with you as much, or in the same way. This happens no matter who you are, or how close you used to be. Try not to let it hurt your feelings. But DO NOT allow them to talk you into relaxing safety rules just because they want to be independent. They are big kids, not adults. Helping them become more independent and giving them space doesn't include allowing your kids to do unsafe things.

If you're afraid you are losing touch, or they're obviously more quiet or distant, have a talk. Say, *"You seem more quiet than usual. What's* *going on? I'm worried that you're not OK"* or *"Are we Ok? You seem upset at me. What has happened between us?"* or *"You look sad, what are you feeling down about?"* Or you can try guessing what's wrong.

If they won't talk about it, give them some time and say you'd like to talk about it when they're ready. They may feel moody and not be able to tell you why. If so, let it go for a day or two and then check in again. If your child still won't talk later, and you think something is bothering her, it's time to insist she tell you at least some of what's on her mind. You could say, *"You know, if you were quiet and acted like you didn't want to be around your friends, they wouldn't like that. In relationships, it's best to keep talking, even when it's uncomfortable, just to get things out in the open. You need to keep talking to people you care about, to keep relationships going. It's the same with family as it is with friends."* We have also found that special time helps teens open up.

If all else fails, you can use an action limit. *"We need to talk about what's on your mind, or you can't (go out, watch TV, play your game) until you do. I need to know what is bothering you."* If that doesn't work, get your child an appointment with a school counselor or other professional. No matter what, stay involved in your teens' lives. They still need you, and you can give them some distance while staying available.

If they open up and say they're having a problem with YOU, try not to react negatively! They won't talk about problems again if you do! Thank them for telling you, listen carefully and try to make compromises as safety allows.

How they talk to you: from attitude to defiance

Most of us with teens have thought or said, "Don't give me that attitude!" So what is **attitude**, anyway? It simply means acting annoyed. Examples of giving you attitude are clicking the tongue, sarcasm, crankiness, whining, complaining, raising the voice, and saying "Yeh, right, geez Mom, I did!" or "Yeh—I said I would— whatever." It can mean "having a tone," or mumbling when you ask them something, or occasionally walking away without answering. We're sure all parents of teens have their own wonderful examples of attitude.

But as long as they actually do what you ask (the chore or whatever), you can let these attitude behaviors go uncorrected. As long as they do what you asked, who cares what attitude they do it with?! If you're expecting them to follow orders with an "Aye, aye captain" and a smile, you're expecting too much. You can continue to fight for a good attitude, but it will just cause more problems. Asking, "Did you have a tone with me?" is a slippery slope you don't need to be on. When you see them do something for you with a positive attitude (it could happen), be sure to jump all over it with praise. Say, *"Hey thanks for doing that quickly without complaining. That sure makes life easier!"*

So you can choose your battles and not deal with their annoying attitude. But, **if they refuse to answer your questions often** (not just every once in a while), this can be very annoying! Here are things to try. Answer your question for them. If they don't like your answer, they may pipe up with their own. If you said, *"Would you like to do your chore now or after dinner?"* and they don't answer, say, *"Well you can do it now then."*

If that doesn't work, say that if they want privileges (like TV or friend time), they need to answer you politely, and loud enough so you can hear. If they still won't answer, use an action limit: *"If you don't answer me politely so I can hear,* (or *if you choose not to talk to me right now), there will be no internet all weekend* (or other consequence)." Give the consequence if they refuse. If that doesn't get them to answer you, try the advice above under "losing touch."

It's normal for teens to feel annoyed at even the greatest, coolest parents. It's a normal part of wanting independence. They want to do what they want, even when it's not best for them. If you think they're annoyed at you, ask them and listen to the answer. Let's say they're annoyed at you for doing what you think is best for their safety. For instance, you won't let your 16 year old drive his friends around, or you won't let your daughter party without supervision. Say, *"I know that must feel annoying, but I'm just doing what good parents do to keep their kids safe. There are parents out there that don't care, and don't spend the energy keeping their kids safe, but I do."* If they're annoyed at something you could compromise on, then compromise. Remember that their annoyance won't always make sense, because their little brains are remodeling! Plus, they may not really be annoyed at you, but at something else.

Disrespect is different than attitude. It's acting like you are worthless, or not honoring your wishes, needs, thoughts, and actions as a parent. Examples are cussing, calling you names like *stupid* or *bitch,* yelling, throwing things, or threatening to hurt you or your things. These behaviors need to be disciplined. Calmly explain, *"That is disrespectful. I deserve to be respected and so do you."* Tell them specifically what they did that was disrespectful. Tell them what will happen if they remain disrespectful (*"You will not be able to go to the football game unless you apologize and be respectful."*) Spend more relationship building time and, for a while, take away access to friends you think may be part of the problem.

Arguing and debate was covered in skill # 4. You MUST learn how to deal with debate, to avoid **one of the worst outcomes of parenting**. What is one of the worst things that can happen? Feeling so frustrated that you throw up your hands and say something like this: "I give up, you just go and do what you think is best" or, "Whatever—I don't care anymore." Doing this teaches your kids that they can do whatever they want, not because you have no control over them, but because you don't care anymore. This is the step that often happens before children are lost to crime, drugs, or death.

Are you feeling like giving up on your kids? Perhaps fear, embarrassment, pride, fatigue or denial is keeping you from action. Maybe you figure you shouldn't bother anymore, since things aren't that bad, and nothing seems to work anyway. Maybe you don't think you have any more energy to deal with your child, or the money to get help. Well, if you don't think you have the energy or money now, think about how much it will take to raise a grandchild when your teenager becomes a parent. How much will legal fees cost if your child gets into legal trouble? How much does residential drug treatment cost? How would you feel burying your child, or growing old alone? If your child had appendicitis, would you get medical care? Ask yourself why you won't you take action to save you and your child from bad things that happen when a child is out of control. Learn and use your powerful *7 Skills*. If they don't work for you, seek help from a professional now.

Defiance (or opposition) is when kids outright refuse to obey, and tell you that they won't. If this happens to you, remaining calm and loving while using your seven skills can still bring your child around. Start by making and enforcing only one limit, like curfew. Write it down. Try to have your child say the limit out loud and the consequence for not following it. It can be a reward if the limit is obeyed, or a punishment consequence if not. When you first start working on enforcing a limit, give consequences soon (maybe every day). Then gradually move consequences like rewards out to one week (for instance, your child would get a reward if he or she follows the limit all week long). Once that limit is being obeyed regularly, add other limits you want to enforce.

If you're still having trouble, and consequences don't work, enlist help from teachers, relatives, clergy, juvenile centers and counselors. If your children won't comply with curfew, you can either go out, find them, and haul them home, or ask a relative or trusted friend to do it. If you are having trouble getting them to do homework, try asking teachers to keep them after class to do it.

If that still doesn't work to turn behavior around, have a school counselor, relative or clergy member meet with your child to see if one of them can make a connection and help your child figure out what he or she is so angry or troubled about. You can have an **intervention** meeting with you, other adults and your child to explain your concern and your plan of action. Use adults that agree to help support your plan and enforce the limits you set. Take action now—it's never too late as long as your child is still alive.

Teens will question your values

That's a normal part of becoming independent from you. They may also criticize your traditions, likes and dislikes. Listen without judging or fighting. Their opinions may not make sense to you, and will usually change as they grow up. Share your opinions calmly and respectfully, so they'll listen. Say, *"Well, I think..."* or *"I feel..."* They'll have opinions you won't agree with, and that's okay unless they act on them in dangerous ways. For example, if your kids think that smoking pot is fine, that opinion is not acceptable to act on, because it endangers them.

Physical, Social, and Emotional Issues for Teens

Teens are tired

Teens are in a tough spot. They have new pressures, their brains are changing and they don't get enough sleep. Teenagers actually need nine hours to feel well and perform their best. Most get only about seven hours. So try to get them close to nine hours when  you can. Don't allow a huge shift in sleeping schedules during the weekend. They'll do best if they go to sleep around the same time on the weekends when possible. If they stay up late, let them sleep in to get nine or ten hours, but no more. More sleep than that can make them more irritable—we sure don't need that!

Depression

Even though hormones can cause depression symptoms, never assume that being depressed is due just to hormones. Changing some things at home can usually help teens a lot. If your child loses interest in the things he or she used to like, sleeps too much or can't sleep, loses weight, tells you he or she doesn't care about anything anymore, or withdraws from the family—get professional help.

Suicide is the second most common cause of death in teens

One out of every five teens thinks seriously about killing him or herself. Kids who use drugs or alcohol, are sexually abused, or have problems with depression or anxiety are more likely to commit suicide than other kids. When do they usually do it? After they feel rejected by friends, family or people in school. Most kids who kill themselves do so under the influence of alcohol or drugs—just another reason they shouldn't be using these.

Just being aware can prevent suicide. Ask your teens if they have ever thought of hurting themselves. If they say yes, ask if they have a plan for how to do it. The more specific the plan, the more concern you should have. Most kids give a warning (a comment, note, or other sign like giving away valued possessions) just before they do it. Take it seriously— call your health provider immediately, or take your child to the emergency room. Make sure they don't have access to objects they could use to kill themselves, and keep them away from drugs or alcohol. When kids hurt themselves (like cutting their skin), they are asking for help, and they must get it.

Your teen's body image

The physical changes of puberty can be embarrassing for your kids— even when adults think the changes are good (like growing taller). How they look is very important to teens, and they compare themselves to other kids a lot. Kids are assaulted by unnatural and unusually attractive bodies in media. So, they're more unsatisfied with their own bodies than ever before. When kids become teens, their self-esteem is more linked to their body image (how good they think their bodies are) than when they were younger.

Teens care more about what other kids think of their bodies, too. Other kids often make insensitive comments, and hurt children's feelings. You can help by occasionally pointing out nice things about your child's body. Comment on shiny hair, shapely legs, pretty smile, nice hands, or whatever. Help them recognize that their bodies are a lot like other people's, and don't have anything to do with their most important parts—heart, soul, mind and personality. Tell them that even the best bodies wrinkle, sag, and fall apart, so body type doesn't matter as much when people grow up. Address obesity from a medical standpoint only.

Help build your children's self-esteem based on things other than their bodies. Give them the tools they need to succeed in school and in relationships (like social skills). Point out their internal beauty and strengths, and help them learn that they are capable of doing things. Tell your teens how lucky you are to have them.

How they dress, and how about that hair!

Another normal way for kids to pull away from parents is to dress, talk and act differently. It's important for most teens to fit in with other kids' styles. But some teens want to stand out. There's a tendency for parents to criticize the clothes teens wear, the music they listen to, etc. But teen brains have trouble separating criticism of things they like from criticism of themselves. So try not to criticize or tease about their tastes.

Try not to make a big deal out of dressing like most of the other kids (even if you wouldn't wear that stuff!). Just tell them you noticed they decided to change their look. If you feel your daughter's style is overly sexual, tell her you are concerned and suggest a compromise. You could say, *"Your style may attract guys who want to use you for sex or hurt you. It can make you look like you don't have confidence or self-esteem. I'd like to see you cover a little more."*

A warning sign that children aren't doing well is when they dress *much* differently than most kids. Parents should be concerned when their children's "look" is shocking to others or gets negative attention. Examples can include "goth" and punk styles, or excessive tattoos and piercings. Children may say they're just being individuals or expressing their uniqueness. But they often end up isolating themselves from other kids and adults, or identifying only with a small fringe group of kids. Neither of these is good for children.

Small strange changes can start a slippery slope to extreme styles. If you aren't sure their look is extreme, pretend it was your neighbor's kid. What would you think? Paying for strange clothes and praising their unique look can speed up the process. And helping your children isolate themselves with extreme styles doesn't support them, but hurts them. That's because in addition to dressing differently, these kids **often start to think differently**—and usually not in a good way. They may say, "It's my right to look this way. People better accept me for who I am." Then when they get people's natural negative reactions, they start thinking people just don't understand them. They ostracize themselves and yet blame others for it.

Extreme styles can be used as an excuse for not succeeding—for not getting a job or getting along with others, or for failing to do well in school. Instead of seeing their role in their own failures, teens with extreme styles may blame others. Dressing much differently sets kids up to be rejected and be victims. It gets hard to keep good friends who don't dress the same way. These extreme looks and thoughts make it hard for kids to be respected. Their style may seem to say, "Stay away—I have issues."

What do you do if your child starts dressing way out there? It's alright to limit extreme styles, since it's part of P.S. I'M HELPING. That's because extreme styles may make your teen a target for bullies, make adults upset or embarrassed, or cause long-term problems due to isolation and limited friendships and job options.

Tell your teen why you are concerned and what he or she needs to do. Say he needs to dress more mainstream for now. Don't allow a debate. This will give him time to develop the decision making part of his brain and grow up. Don't do it out of anger, but because you care. Be clear about where your limits are, but give a little. (*"You can wear your hair spiked if you keep it shorter and don't color it." "You can wear those pants if you take the chains off."*) Don't let them use guilt or anything else to make you back down. Build up your child by praising other things about her and give her more good attention. Get her involved and interested in other things and people.

When your children are young, point out other kids' extreme styles. *"See that kid with the purple hair and pierced face? I wonder if he's alright and why he needs attention."* Everything about extreme styles can apply to extreme behaviors too, like frequent swearing or joining hate groups.

Tattoos and body piercing

Some teens also use these to try to stand out and get attention. We've already talked about why teens can't always make good decisions. Many parents want advice about how to keep their kids from changing their bodies permanently, as a tattoo does. Just say you won't allow it because they may change their minds and regret it. Maybe they could choose to do it when they're 21 (when they'll pay for it, too). Tell them what consequence they'll get if they do it before then (losing their cars, allowances, or another big privilege for a long time). Your kids may be glad they have an excuse to tell their friends (*"I can't because my parents will throw a fit and I'll lose...."*)

Teenage Sexuality

And now...the whole sex thing. Don't be afraid and skulk off now! We discussed how you can tell your younger kids about sex in chapter 6. But teenagers need the gritty details. First of all, parents often think about sex differently in their sons versus their daughters. Some may think it's normal and healthy for teenage boys, but not girls, to think about sex. But normal, healthy teenage girls have sexual thoughts and desires too. It doesn't make any sense to expect teen girls not to be interested in sex, and then all of a sudden expect them to have healthy, active sex lives as adults. This thinking can lead to decreased sex drive in women. And even though it's normal for both teenage boys and girls to have desires, it's a dangerous time to let them act on them.

Teens think that sex is only having intercourse

Most adults consider any genital activity between people as sex. But teens think that oral sex, and other touching of another person's genital areas, is NOT really having sex. Most sexually active teens have had oral sex before they have intercourse. So, when teenagers say they aren't having sex ("I am **abstaining**"), it **may mean they've done everything sexual besides intercourse**. Almost half of all high school kids have had intercourse, and 14 percent of those have already had four or more partners!

The risks of teenage sex

Just as many kids in America have sex as in other developed countries, but our kids are much more likely to get a disease or get pregnant. Experts believe this has to do with inadequate education and protection, and having a higher number of partners. A teenager's risk of getting a **sexually transmitted disease** (STD) is higher than an adult's risk. Many of these diseases can be caught by just touching genitals, or from sexual activities besides intercourse, like oral sex.

Four million new cases of STDs are diagnosed every year in teenage children. The most common is called **HPV** (human papilloma virus), which usually has no symptoms (except for those teenagers who get warts). Condoms only partly protect against getting HPV, which can be transmitted just by sexual touching. It is estimated that half of sexually active teens will get infected. In females, this virus causes abnormal pap smears, and cancer of the cervix and vulva. I find that most of the teens and young women that I see for abnormal pap smears aren't aware of how easy it is to get infected. These patients often have to come in for repeat pap smears, biopsies, freezing or other treatments of the cervix. HPV is also linked to other cancers, including, in males, anal, penile, mouth and throat cancers. There is no cure, but vaccination can partially prevent infection in girls, especially if given before their first sexual encounter.

Chlamydia and gonorrhea can cause infertility and chronic pelvic pain in girls. **Herpes** causes recurrent painful genital blisters in both boys and girls, which can be treated but not cured. Early treatment of a first outbreak is important, as it may prevent future outbreaks. Herpes is often transmitted through oral sex.

The rate of **teenage pregnancy is still 10 times higher in America** than in other developed countries! Every year, 800,000 American teens get pregnant. In some families, having children as a single teen seems almost expected. This is hard to understand, since becoming a parent doesn't help the teen brain develop faster. Children raised by teenagers have more behavior problems, do worse in school, and more often live in poverty than other children. It's sad for me to have seen single teens cry when their pregnancy tests are negative. They're often afraid their boyfriends won't stay, or they just want to create someone who loves them. You can prevent these unhealthy attitudes just by talking about them.

About sex education

A recent national poll of parents showed that the vast majority of Americans support giving their teenagers information on all birth control methods. Only 15 percent support abstinence-only education. Abstinence-only programs present only the option of abstinence, and no information on other birth control methods. There is no evidence that this type of program actually works to decrease sexual activity in teens. A study of kids who pledged to stay virgins until they were married showed that 90 percent ended up having pre-marital sex anyway, but these teens used birth control less often than children who had not pledged abstinence.

Abstinence-only education also has failed to decrease STD rates. Since kids often don't think that touching or kissing genitals is sex, they think they're abstaining while touching or kissing, which can spread STDs. Abstinence-only programs don't appear to decrease sexual activity in teens, but because the teens who have been in these programs have learned only about abstinence, when they do have sex, they do it without proper knowledge of birth control. They may end up getting inaccurate or even dangerous information on birth control from friends or media instead of medically accurate information.

But there is evidence that programs that give information on birth control methods *including* abstinence *do* delay the age at which teens have intercourse. These programs also decrease the incidence of STDs. Parents who responded to the same poll indicated that they do not think that stressing abstinence while also giving information on other forms of contraception is a mixed message. So, most parents think you can tell children you expect them to abstain, while still giving them other information. The fact is that few Americans are abstinent (no sexual activity) till marriage. Were you? Studies show that teens who decide to become sexually active will most likely use birth control if it is available. Your kids should also know that abstinence and condoms are the only birth control forms that can protect against STDs as well as pregnancy.

How to reduce the chance your teen will have sex

Studies show it helps to **tell your kids you expect them not to be sexually active until adulthood**. We recommend focusing on *delaying* sexual activity, instead of disapproving of sex. How do you do that? Emphasize that you want them to abstain only *for now*. Let your kids know how much you would disapprove if they became sexually active. Tell them that it's not good for them because of all the risks: being used or hurt, infections and pregnancy. Have discussions about when you think sex becomes a normal, healthy part of life. Share your thoughts. Tell them that touching oneself is normal and doesn't cause problems. Stress that adult relationships are going to mean much more, and there's nothing wrong with not having a boy/girlfriend until they are adults. They can have a lot more fun not messing with that right now!

Talk about how **sex in teens is usually not connected with long**

lasting love. There are often different reasons behind sex drive for boys and girls. But both can be excited about the idea of being touched by someone they think is attractive. For boys, sex drive may be mostly due to changing bodies and raging hormones. It is usually "just physical," and not about having a relationship. For girls, it's often more driven by the need to feel attractive, approved of, and close to someone. It can be about wanting a close emotional relationship. This often doesn't work out, since teens can't judge relationships very well yet. Girls with poor self-esteem, and little support and attention of parents and friends, may do anything for the approval of boys, including having sex.

Try to limit the sexual content they see in media, since it's linked with earlier sexual activity. Most teens say that the media is their leading source of sex information. But media messages usually say to teens that sex is frequent and risk-free, and that almost everyone is doing it.

Try to be the best source of accurate information, so they don't get bad information elsewhere. Tell your kids that if they have questions about sex, you want them to ask you, because you want them to know the truth. Watch media together as much as possible, and talk about what you're seeing. Challenge unhealthy and unrealistic scenes so your kids can learn from your experience. Give them information, even if they say they already know, or don't want to know. Go ahead and bug them!

Be physically affectionate to your kids (hug, kiss, hold, and give backrubs). This nonsexual contact is nurturing and an important part of feeling loved. Have as much fun as possible together! Make them feel worthy so they don't need as much attention from other kids. Keep non-critical talks going so they feel free to share things. You can challenge their unhealthy thoughts and actions without being critical by saying, "*I think...*" or "*I feel...*" instead of, "That's crazy."

Be aware of peer pressure. Your boys may feel pressured to have sex "to be a man." Tell your boys that being a man means taking responsibility and being caring and strong for himself and his family. Girls may feel pressured because they think they need to show that they are desired and attractive by having sex. Tell your girls they are special and beautiful, and that boys using them for sex won't make them feel any more so. Kids who have sex under pressure often abstain afterwards since they don't feel pressured anymore. Come up with cool ways your children can say they're not interested. If they do have sex, or get pregnant, don't let it ruin your relationship.

It's also important to **monitor their activities.** Have dating rules written down (that you want to meet their dates, time and place limits, etc). The only way to ensure abstinence is to always be with your teen, which would drive you both crazy. But limiting opportunities for teens to be alone really helps. Research shows that teens are more likely to have sex when they ask for time alone with other kids without supervision. Increased drug use is also found.

So **don't compromise on unsupervised time with other kids.** For example, you may not want to let them stay out longer just because they call, or have friends over when adults aren't home just because they ask, or let them have friends over when you can't directly check on them. Unsupervised time right after school is a high risk time for sex and drug use. Also, studies show that boys often have sex even though their parents trust them not to. Daughters are less likely to have sex when their parents trust them. Teen sex can happen anywhere there isn't enough supervision, even in your home. And so can sexual assault.

Homosexuality

It can take many years for teens to tell their families they are gay. In a society where there are such negative consequences for telling people, it's not hard to see why. Many gay children and adults are rejected when their parents can't accept something that's uncomfortable for them. Gay children need their parent's unconditional love, just like straight children do. By the way, it's considered normal for all kids to temporarily feel attracted to kids of the same sex, and it doesn't mean they're gay. It's not uncommon for young children of the same sex to touch each other in a sexual way.

Infatuation—the big fake out

Like adults, kids can have crazy, strong feelings when they first fall in love. People describe it like being high, and thinking there's no one else on earth as good for them. These intense feelings of attraction can happen fast and last only a short time (three to six months in teens). This is the all powerful infatuation period.

 When kids are infatuated, it's harder for them to tell if someone is bad for them, or using them. If you think this is happening, explain what infatuation is. Explain that they can only tell what someone's really like when infatuation has worn off for a while. Say that people change a lot when they grow up. So adults can tell much better whether they're going to be happy together for a long time. This may help them avoid pregnancy, STDs, or heartbreak because of an infatuation. When the infatuation is over for one teen, most relationships end, which can be painful. But it's like a bad cold he or she can definitely get over.

Friends

Friends play a big role in how your children think, feel and behave. Please review the friend section in skill #7 for important info. Your teens will talk differently to you than they talk to their friends. Parents often get the short end of the stick on cheerfulness. They know you'll always be there for them, so they won't be afraid to show you how they're really feeling. On the other hand they'll feel pressured to be cool around friends and not emotional, and will try to fit in. How they act can depend on whom they're talking to. Try not to take grouchiness personally.

Friendship troubles

Because they're so important to our kids, friendships will often cause worry and conflict. Kids are funny. They'll stick up for friends, even when they don't like what these friends are doing. There can be a lot of **drama**, especially with girls. You know—who's best friends with whom, who's popular and who isn't, who said what, and who is mad at whom. Oh, the drama of it all!

Encourage your children to share some of the drama with you, so you can see how they're handling things. Act interested, listen carefully, and say you understand their feelings. Be careful not to sound critical of their friends, because that can keep your child from trusting you. Also, try not to criticize what your children have done or their feelings.

Kids need to feel like they can figure out what to do themselves. It helps them gain confidence and independence. But what you *can* do to help is say what you would think in that situation as an adult. For example, a friend named Stacey said something bad about your daughter to another girl named Rita. Your daughter says, "I can't believe Stacey backstabbed me. I didn't even do what she told Rita." You could say, *"That would have hurt my feelings (or made me mad) too."* (You showed understanding and support.) *"Have you asked Stacey about it? Maybe there's an explanation. What do you think you'll do about it?"*

Let your child come up with a plan, and then listen to it. If it seems reasonable (even if it isn't exactly what you'd do), tell her you're proud she's taking steps to make it feel better. Tell her you'd love to know how it goes. If she has no plan, or you think her idea would make things worse, gently make suggestions. *"Maybe you could think about... I'm just wondering if you..."* In the above example, you might say, "Maybe *you could think about telling Rita politely that what she heard from Stacey isn't true. I'm just thinking if you stop talking to Stacey, it won't solve anything and might make things worse."* Say that she doesn't need to fix everything in friendships, since that's exhausting and just not possible! Tell her that saying *"I think..."* and *"I feel..."* to friends helps them feel less defensive.

When friends go too far

Sometimes kids get stuck in roller coaster relationships that are up, down and all around. They may worry almost every day about hurt feelings and backstabbing. Kids can even be manipulated into staying friends (by being told "I can't live without you" or "You'll be sorry"). That could mean your child is stuck in a dependent relationship. Watch for these signs of unhealthy relationships, and help your kids get out.

You can help your kids with friend problems without being intrusive. Tell them that you think teen drama and worrying about being popular are wastes of time. *"In a few years you probably won't even know these people."* Suggest ways to get involved with other kids. Suggest things to say to end unhealthy friendships, like *"It seems like we've grown apart. I need a break anyway. I think we can still be friends, but just hang out less." "My Dad says I need to study more." "My Mom said I need to take a break from hanging out for now."*

Look for **signs that your child is in an abusive relationship:** withdrawing from the family, being very quiet and secretive, having unexplained bruises, acting afraid you'll get to know a boy/girlfriend, and being afraid that a friend will be mad. Kids in abusive relationships are often pressured to do things, like sex, drugs or crime.

Having constant **computer and text message access** to friends can hurt parenting as well as friendships. Kids can write things in e-mails or on websites like MySpace that they regret. They can attack other kids with words or pictures for everyone to see, without learning how to deal with conflict in good ways. This type of contact can make relationships seem so much more important and dramatic. It can take too much time away from family and responsibilities. It seems best to limit the time they spend this way with friends, by limiting time on the computer and phone. Take away their phone, or their computer power cord as necessary. Consider using cell phone plans without texting.

Friends can drastically change what kids do, feel and believe. When their little brains are remodeling, teens can come up with some strange thoughts, kind of like their own alien reality that is different from that of mature adults. **Unhealthy teen thoughts** can include that they know best and that parents don't know much. Yah, that'll be true when pigs fly! You may remember how your great teenage ideas worked out. You obviously know much more as a parent, since you've got adult experiences and knowledge.

Sometimes their beliefs include that **they have "rights"** and should be allowed to do what they want, even if it isn't good for them. These unhealthy thoughts can include having "the right" to use drugs, drink, see who they want when they want, drop out of school, buy anything they want, commit crimes, disrespect you or move out of the house (be emancipated). Kids don't have the right to do any of these things.

What kids *do* have the right to, however, is a parent who tries to stop them from getting into trouble by doing stupid things. They have a right to adults who will support and do what is best for them until their brains are developed enough to make good decisions. Supporting children doesn't mean letting them do unhealthy things that are dangerous or that limit their opportunities. Kids have a right to parents who will challenge unhealthy thoughts out of concern, without putting them down. You may not be able to change their minds, but telling them what you think still matters. Your children really need you to keep them from acting on unhealthy thoughts.

Also please know this: **if you ignore unhealthy thoughts or actions,** or don't challenge them, it's the same as saying, "Go ahead and do what you think." Then kids will do just that! For example, if your daughter tells you she thinks that smoking is fine, and you don't say why you think it's not, and enforce a rule of "no smoking," you will be more likely to have a daughter that smokes.

Teens will often try to stop parents from challenging them. They may say, "You don't love me (like me, trust me, support me, or whatever)." This is just a way to try to shut you down in order to get what they want. They may even try to manipulate you away from taking action, by saying that people think you're mean or wrong. They may even pull out the big guns, like the old classic, "I hate you!" Just say something like, *"I'll just have to live with that. I still love you and will do whatever it takes to keep you on the safe track to becoming an adult."*

No matter what they say, your kids are counting on you to do the right thing for their sakes. They'll be grateful later. Don't allow debates about what is or isn't their right. Be in control using your debate skills from this book (see page 95). As always, if you can't set limits or enforce them, and you're worried about what is happening, it's time to get professional help.

Teen parties—we're not in Kansas anymore

There are new risks to teen parties these days. Girls can more easily be assaulted because of the date rape drug. If there's not enough supervision, drugs may be used. Make-out rooms are common, and your kids may feel pressured to participate (including with kids of the same sex). You could be prosecuted if underage drinking happens on your property, or kids are supplied with your alcohol, even if you don't know it happened. Our advice is not to allow kids to attend parties unless you know that there will be close supervision by adults who you know and trust (actually checking on all the kids often). Try making your house a place they want to bring friends. Provide teen's basic food groups—chips, candy, pizza and soda. Try to supply a game table, music, or movies. The kids can get used to you being around.

How to Lower the Risks of Teenage Driving

Remember how exciting it was to drive for the first time? But motor vehicle accidents are the number one cause of death from age 1 to 19. No matter how smart, responsible, or cautious a teen is, he or she just doesn't have the brain development and experience to be as safe as an adult. Remember, teens don't make great decisions and are risk takers—not a great combo behind the wheel! Also, many **substances** used by teens cause accidents. Alcohol is the most common, but marijuana has now been shown to be just as dangerous, or even more so. Studies are showing fewer accidents with new laws, where teens need to be older to drive.

Cell phones are the newest toy for kids and are proving to be quite expensive for families. Phones can be a safety device and a way to keep track of your kids (but only IF they remember to carry them, actually answer them, don't lose them and keep them charged!) Phones are also good things to take away as a consequence. Please don't allow teens to talk or text while driving—they really need to concentrate.

We advise waiting as long as you can to let teens drive alone. Drive with them as much as possible. Allowing only one passenger when you aren't with them makes it safest. It's best for you to own the car, and let the child use it. Then taking it or the keys away can be a good consequence. We also recommend making them pay for gas (and repairs and the increased cost of insurance if they have an accident). This teaches them responsibility. We'd also take away driving privileges for a while if they have more than one accident (even for just backing into the garage door), or make them take driving classes again. Teens think their car is their private space. So they may hide drugs, alcohol, tobacco, weapons or porn there.

Developing Brains Are Very Sensitive to Substances

Drugs, alcohol and tobacco are being used by more teens at younger ages than ever before! This is partly because these substances are more available, and kids have more money and don't see the dangers. Over half of American teens have been drunk or used an illegal drug in high school. Over one fourth have tried a drug other than marijuana. When the teen brain is growing and getting wired, it's more sensitive. Substances can permanently affect the brain during remodeling. So, teens are more easily addicted and affected long term than adult users are.

Alcohol use is very common in college (one out of three students actually has an alcohol problem), but even young teenagers become alcoholics. People who start drinking at a young age increase their chances of having learning and memory problems later on. Also, the younger a drinker starts, the more likely he or she is to become addicted. Younger drinkers often don't know they're drunk until they have high enough blood alcohol levels to die. Alcohol is often involved in murder, suicides and accidents that kill teens. These are all important reasons to keep your kids away from it.

Cigarettes are a major cause of disease and early death. Teens are more likely than adults to get addicted to tobacco, and they get addicted more quickly. Smokers eventually don't even get a buzz anymore when they light up, but need the cigarettes to "relax." What they call relaxing is just relieving the uncomfortable withdrawal between cigarettes. Also, teen smokers are more likely to drink and use other drugs, and to be addicted to things like gambling. Chewing tobacco can be deadly too. We think one of the greatest gifts you can give kids is to keep them away from tobacco until they can make the decision as adults.

Most drug addicts start with **marijuana**. Pot now has five times more active ingredient than it used to. This means pot smokers, especially those with teenage brains, are more likely to get addicted. Pot smokers are now much more likely to have prolonged problems with memory, motivation, concentration and coordination than they were when you were a teen. Pot has even been linked to getting anxiety disorders, depression, and schizophrenia. See skill #7 for more info.

Our space is limited. There are many more drugs that ruin lives, or even kill our kids. Methamphetamine (meth) highs are followed by devastating, unbearable lows, which may be partly why meth is so addictive. It causes heart attack, stroke, impotence, and long-term mental illness symptoms. Ecstasy, narcotics like oxycontin, cough/cold meds, glue, and medications for attention deficit hyperactivity disorder are all substances that kids misuse to get high. Feeling dizzy to the point of almost passing out is also used by kids to get a buzz. This is often done in dangerous ways like slowly choking a child or putting weight on his or her chest.

Ways to decrease the chance your kids will use substances

Gee, I wonder what we'll say first! That's right, you're all over it—have a strong relationship with your kids. This helps them take your advice, and decreases drug use. Other ways include discussing the dangers from an early age. Be well informed about your children's lives—monitor what they're doing and with whom. Tell them it's not OK to use because you care, and you'll find out if they do.

Preoccupy your child with other responsibilities and activities. This will help you avoid **one of the biggest reasons for trouble with teens**, which **is boredom**. Kids who have too much time (and or money) on their hands tend to get in trouble with weird thinking, alcohol or drugs.

Also, limit time for teens to be alone with others without supervision, and don't compromise on this. Have a curfew and enforce it. Show them other ways to feel "high," like hiking, watching sunsets, star gazing, laughing your heads off, having great family time, being with good friends, faith and spiritual activities, performing music, helping others, playing sports, and sharing moving music or movies. Get them what they need to do well in school, deal with problems like depression and build up their self-esteem. Keep your child away from kids that use. Ask your kids, *"How would you handle it if you went someplace where there was pot?"* If you are using substances or drinking heavily, it really helps your kids if you quit.

Watch for signs of substance use: change in dressing style, drop in grades, missing cash or not knowing where their money is going, lying, change in friends, being very withdrawn or secretive, more than usual moodiness or strange behavior. These could also be signs of a serious emotional problem. Other signs are smell of alcohol or smoke, strange phone calls, weight loss, eye changes (redness or pupil size), and saying things that indicate they approve of drug or alcohol use. Assume that if your teens' friends are using, your teens are also. Worry if your child comes home from being out and doesn't want to see you. Insist that they spend a few minutes with you talking after they've been out.

If you're suspicious, do whatever it takes to find out if they're using. Go ahead and show up where they hang out with friends. It's a parent's right to know what's in their kids' cars and rooms. It's your responsibility to **search** these things or other belongings if you suspect drug use or other illegal activities! It doesn't matter if they get upset— it's your duty. Although you don't need to warn them ahead of time, it's best to search in their presence, so they know you're doing it. That way you won't destroy their trust.

Families do best when parents have zero tolerance. That means if you suspect or catch your child using substances, or find drugs or drug items, you take immediate action. Early action is the key. See a doctor, start a rehab program and counseling, and take away all that they need to access the substance, including friends who are using. Say something like, *"I'm doing this because I love you, and won't let bad things happen to you."* Don't let fear, anger or guilt stop you. Their anger is nothing compared to what you'll have to deal with if they keep using! They may not understand now, but will be thankful when they grow up. Gradually give back privileges when you're sure they are clean for a few weeks. Do whatever it takes to make sure they don't use again—it will save you a lot of money and heartache, and it may save their lives.

You Can Survive the Wacky Years with a Teenager

Remember, it's nobody's fault that it's tough to parent teenagers. Their little remodeling teen brains can cause a lot of trouble. And don't forget to laugh! Their goofy behavior can be pretty funny. Never fear—they are full of great potential. One day they will blossom into adults with their own interests and achievements. Until then, don't let them loose to explore the world without enough supervision. They need just as much guidance from you as they ever did, but just in a different way.

Expect them to put a little distance between themselves and you for now, but keep your relationship intact, so you can be close throughout the rest of your lives. Focus on the good things about being together. These years aren't easy! But now you've got the skills you need to make it through just fine.

PUT IT ALL TOGETHER: Help your teenagers wire their new brain cells and keep them on the road to success

1. **Be armed with the knowledge you need.** Learn the *7 Skills* and the info in this chapter to get the job done well enough. You now know what brain parts aren't working well and how to help, about strange emotions and attitudes, and how to deal with disrespect and defiance. Please review how to stop debate and arguing in skill #4. (It's a must for success!) Remember that friends can cause problems. Teach them about drugs, tobacco, alcohol, driving, teen sex, guns and other dangers.

2. **Keep your relationship as close as possible.** Then they'll listen and care about what you say. A strong relationship is the number one way you can prevent problems (use skill #2). Try to accept that normal, short distance from you that prepares them for independence. Be silly and laugh with them often! Eat together whenever you can.

3. **Find interests that you can share**, even if it means bending your tastes. Find activities you can do together that they enjoy. That will give you time together so they can learn from you. One example is sharing music. Try not to criticize their tastes. Try to find something you like about what they're into—even if you have to fake it. So if you're a Mozart lover, try to find something good to say about rap music they like (like the beat, or how the group doesn't disrespect women or use drug lyrics). Shop for music or check the group out online together. Go to concerts— whatever it takes to make a connection.

4. **Continue to show them affection and approval** to help you stay close. Even if you don't have good feelings for them at the moment, they need to think you do. Just acting like you care about them can work. You can love them, but not have to like them right now! Acting affectionate will help them be affectionate to you and vice versa. Avoid using psychological control (see page 151).

5. **Set limits on their behavior and enforce them.** The teen brain is not wired to control impulses or make decisions well yet. Use P.S. I'M HELPING to set limits, and follow through on consequences (see skills #4, #5, and #6). Think safety first—this is a good reason to limit their activities. Secondly, set limits that affect achievement and character. Choose your battles. Expect teens to still be a part of the family and to follow house rules. Use trust exercises to teach responsibility (skill #5). Allow them to make safe personal choices. Have zero tolerance of substance use.

6. **Control your emotions when they can't control theirs.** This helps them hear what you say and follow limits. Controlling your emotions helps them learn to control theirs. Review skills #1 and #3 for ways to stay calm.

7. **Limit media in their lives, especially sexual and violent content** (skill #7). Don't let movies, television, games and computers wire your child's morals and behaviors. You, rather than other kids and media, must be their major source of information on sex, drugs, and alcohol. **Watch and listen to media with them and talk about things** you see or hear.

8. **Monitor where they are, who they're with, and generally what they're doing.** Even good teens can't always make good decisions. Ask questions of your children, their friends and their friends' parents, and supervise activities. Increase the chance that your teens will talk to you by using open communication and relationship activities. Don't allow unsupervised time that your children ask for with other kids. Review what intrusive parenting is so you can avoid it (see page 182).

9. **Keep them busy.** That helps them avoid boredom that can cause trouble. Routines help teens be successful, feel secure, and develop good habits and responsibility. Having jobs is also important, first around the home and later outside the home. It's best if you aren't their boss at an outside job, so they learn what it's like to work for someone else. Allow enough time for sleep, schoolwork, extracurricular activities and chores.

10. **Help them develop emotional intelligence and resilience** (see pages 40 and 159). Talk about feelings without judging by saying *"I think"* and *"I feel."* Teach them how to resolve conflict and solve problems. Encourage them to show negative emotions to you. Challenge unhealthy thoughts respectfully, by telling them what you think.

Chapter 10

SIBLINGS: How to turn foes into friends

Having a brother or sister to grow up with is a big part of childhood happiness for many. It can also be frustrating and disappointing for others. Here we simply state how to help your kids happily grow up together, while protecting your peace and sanity.

How to tell your children about your pregnancy

You can influence how your kids will react to a new little brother or sister while you're still expecting. First of all, you may not want to tell kids that you're pregnant until you're about thirteen weeks along (three months). It can be very difficult for younger kids to understand the loss of a pregnancy, and miscarriages usually happen before then.

After this time, especially when you're starting to show, talk about the baby in a good way. *"It's time to have another baby. It may be a boy or a girl, and we'll love it so much, just like we love you. Your little brother or sister will be so wonderful, just like you are."* *"We will be a happy family and have so much fun together."* *"You're so lucky that you'll be a big brother/sister now. You will have someone to play with."* If you know the sex of your baby, talk about the little brother/sister in your tummy. Let your children touch your belly to feel your baby kick. Have them open the presents at baby showers and give them big brother/sister gifts also.

Bringing a new baby home

Don't expect your children to be happy about it for a while. They may even ask you to take the little creature back! It's normal for older siblings to get cranky when they lose the attention they used to get. They'll be jealous at first, but you can soften the blow.

First, **don't overreact to their**

moodiness. So don't yell, scold, or try to make them feel guilty. That'll just make things worse.

Second, **pay attention to your baby's siblings as much as possible**. Give them a big brother/sister present when the baby gets home. Say, *"You're so lucky to be a big brother/sister now. You get a special present."* Have *more* special time, talk time, or play time. Remember, these only take a few minutes, but they are worth much more. Also give them the kind of attention that baby gets—feeding, rocking, and holding. When you're trying to feed or otherwise care for baby, let the kids stay with you and talk to them. Don't send them away! Give them *helper jobs* that they like to do, like getting into things they normally aren't allowed to (the refrigerator, baby wipes or a cupboard). Let them play with the baby's things.

The third thing to do is to **point out the advantages of being older** than the baby. When your kids get to do something fun or get treats to eat, tell them that the baby can't have treats or do things like they can. *"You are so lucky you're a big sister now, because you get special treats. Let's have some ice cream. But the baby can't have ice cream—he's too little."* Or say, *"Let's stay up later after the baby goes to bed, just the two of us. Babies can't play yet, but we can."* Find any little thing to praise about being a good big sister or brother, and do it often.

How to build relationships between your children

Talk about how important family is. Say, *"You know, friends will come and go, but family is forever. We'll always have each other for support and love. We'll laugh and have good times together all our lives."* But also point out that they need to respect and care for each other, if they want to have family friendship and help.

Teach your kids to be polite and help each other as they get older. (We know—it may not happen that often, but it still helps to encourage it.) Have one child do something nice for another, and then praise him for it. *"That was so nice of you to get your sister's coat—you are such a good brother."* Encourage the other child to appreciate it. *"Your brother got your coat for you—you have a sweet brother. Say thank you."* Then have her do something nice in return soon.

Find fun things siblings can do together. Do what you can to make playing as fair as possible, like watching that they take turns, that no one is beating on anyone, etc. Watching them play is a great time to show how to have **empathy** for each other. For example, when something bad happens to your daughter, say something compassionate and praise her sister for doing the same. *"That must have felt bad to be left out. Are you OK?"*

How to Avoid Competition

It's natural for children to compete for our attention and approval. It is also natural—and this is the key, folks—for parents not to recognize when they favor one child over the others. Well, a child who gets the impression that you have another favorite will think less of him- or herself and may act out more. Your relationship with that child will suffer. Whether it is true or not isn't the point—the impression this child has is the point.

When friends or relatives are asked who someone's favorite child is, they often have an answer. Parents often say things that give the impression that they have a favorite. They may mention one child in a good way much more often than the others. Or, they may say more negative things about one and mostly positive things about another. If you do have a favorite child (and many parents do), your other children need your attention and love just as much.

Ask yourself right now—who would your friends and relatives say is your favorite child? The bravest readers will do this. Go for it! Hopefully, they won't be able to tell you. If they do say you have a favorite, thank them and look at what you are thinking and doing with each child that gives that impression. Then try to improve your relationship with the children that didn't get rated as your favorites.

It's also alright to say something to other people who seem to have a favorite child. Say something like, *"Does Billy get jealous when you talk about his brother so much?"* Or, *"I haven't heard about Maria yet. What has she been doing lately?"*

Show your kids that you love them the same

Ok, you may think it's impossible to treat or love your kids exactly equally. Luckily, you don't need to. All you need to do is try to give them that impression. Just *acting like* you want and try to treat them equally is good enough to prevent problems.

It's normal for kids to ask which child you love the best. Say, *"I love you all just as much, but just differently."* Your child may tell you that he's afraid you love another child more. If so, ask why. Pay attention to what you're doing that may give this impression. If you mostly criticize one child, but talk about the cute and wonderful things another child does, that shows you have a favorite. Then kids who think they aren't your favorite may misbehave to get attention. It can also ruin your relationship with the apparently less favorite child.

On the other hand, sometimes children accuse parents of playing favorites on purpose to try to get what they want. Kids figure parents will feel guilty and give in. Feeling guilty isn't a good reason to give children gifts or to let them do things you don't think are good for them.

How to show that you *try* to treat them the same

Praise each child every day, even when you have to think hard to find something to praise! Think of the little things. Try to give all your kids attention and approval every day, so they won't need to compete. There are lots of times when we need to decide between our children's needs and wants (like who gets what). You can't be exactly fair, but just try to be as fair as possible. Try rotating who decides things (one child decides the restaurant and the other decides the movie on a night out).

Here are other ideas. Rotate chores, so kids about the same age have to do the same things. Try to give comparable gifts to all children (comparable or equal numbers of gifts, gifts of roughly equal price, or gifts that each child wants equally badly). Doing that doesn't mean you need to listen to arguments about who got what. Just say you tried to be fair. Then expect your children to say thank you.

Watch that you're **not putting labels on your children**. A label is anything you say a lot about your child—sort of like a name. Loving labels like "my sweetheart," "a good boy," or "my wonderful girl" are general, and a good thing. But labels about abilities or bad qualities can really hurt. If you have a good label about one child ("my talented one") and a bad one for another ("he's trouble"), then the one labeled "trouble" can get jealous and mad. "Trouble" may become even more trouble!

But here's what is weird. Even putting a good label on a child can backfire. If your son keeps hearing, "He's my easy one. He always does what I say," he might start being naughty so that you stop expecting so dang much. He might notice you don't ask the other kids to help because they complain. Praise this good boy for helping and make the other kids help without complaining too.

Try not to compare your children in front of them

Comparing your kids by talking about their different strengths can backfire, too. Saying that Susie is best at math tells the others that they aren't good at math. (That's what they'll think, even if it isn't true.) Then the others may not be motivated to try in math class. So, compliment a child in front of others about her math grade, but rave about her math skill only privately.

It's especially important not to compare character in front of your kids. If you say, "Your brother is so responsible, why can't you be that way," your child may hear, "You are a loser—I love your brother more." This won't encourage trying to be better, but will just cause anger at you and brother! Instead, say, *"I would like you to work on being more responsible for doing what I ask."* (Skip saying anything about brother.)

Keep in mind that as they grow older, what your kids are good at changes. Maybe one child just likes and spends more time on something, and that makes him look better at it. Perhaps another child will take up that same interest later and be brilliant. Remember kids are more motivated when you praise their effort more than how well they do.

What to Do About Sibling Fights

It's normal for siblings to fight, no matter how good they are. (We all just have to get over it.) The first chance children get to try to resolve conflict is with siblings. Kids who don't learn how to do this in healthy ways are more likely to be violent when angry or hurt. As a parent, you can teach the important life skill of resolving conflict peacefully. This will help them in all their relationships. Your job is also to limit the severity of fights so your kids grow up close and don't hurt each other.

If you always let your children work out conflicts themselves, then the biggest or smartest child will often win. You may even be allowing a child to abuse another without knowing it. That's why it can be a dangerous cop-out to tell kids they need to figure out things themselves before you teach them how to fight fair. Children don't know how to be fair, compromise or settle conflicts. But once you teach them how, *then* you can let them work many things out alone. Yes, we know life isn't always fair (your children will learn that soon enough). But at least you can make it fair enough in the only place you can control—your home—so they learn healthy ways to handle conflict and grow up close.

To ignore (or not to ignore) a fight

These suggestions apply only to children age 4 and up. For younger children, see chapter 8 instead. Ignore little squabbles about nothing that seems very important. Don't get involved and let them continue to "discuss" it themselves when no one seems very upset.

But if your child is doing something to a sibling that a bully would do (threatening, making fun of, calling names, physically hurting, saying or doing mean things in order to upset someone), or if your child is being rude (calling a sibling "stupid"), or doing something unsafe, use an action limit to stop it. Never allow your kids to physically hurt a sibling. These behaviors need to be disciplined in order for kids to like each other. The other child may need to be disciplined also for whatever sparked the anger.

Kids who are physically aggressive (shoving, hitting, kicking, biting) with their siblings are likely to be the same with other children. That's one good reason to forbid physical fighting between your children. Also, if you don't allow physical anger, your kids will have to figure out other things to do when they're mad, like talking, compromising, or walking away. This will prevent sibling fights and help them grow up close. It also teaches your kids how to behave and solve conflicts with other people.

Here are ways to handle arguments between your children so that they learn how to do it themselves. These methods also teach kids why it often doesn't pay to fight.

Things to try when they keep arguing about something silly
(like who plays with what, what's for dinner, who goes first, who won, or a childish comment). Try them one at a time.

1. **Point out how they're wasting time and energy.** *"I can't believe the energy you're spending trying to win. It won't even matter tomorrow. It's silly to waste time when you could be playing."*
2. **Laugh at what they're arguing about.** Tell them how ridiculous it sounds and you're glad none of their friends can hear. Say it sounds like they're fighting for world peace or something. *"I can't believe you're fighting about that."*
3. Say, **"I'm going to decide if you don't settle this in sixty seconds."** Start counting out loud, and if they keep fighting after 60 seconds, go ahead with your decision.
4. Or **just make the decision yourself.** Alternate who gets what they want. *"Suzie decided what we did last time. It's Maria's turn this time."*
5. Say, **"I'll be really proud of whoever can say she doesn't care about it anymore."** If one says something like, "Fine, whatever," praise her for letting it go. Tell her how grown up that was, thank her and give her lots of attention. That'll make the other child wish she had done it first, and she may try it next time.
6. Say, **"You'll both lose something if you haven't stopped fighting in one minute."** In other words, set an action limit to stop the fight. *"If you don't stop fighting, I'll take ____ away (or you'll both go to bed when we get home)."* You could take away the toy, activity, or privilege they were fighting over (even if an object belongs to one of them).

7. **Just go ahead and take away any object they're fighting over**. Then say, *"You must stop talking for now. The one who talks first after I count to three gives up a turn with the toy (or gets a consequence). The one who stays quiet the longest will get the toy back first."*

For bigger or longer lasting conflicts, use the following guidelines.

How to teach kids to settle conflicts—have "fight meetings"

1. Sit in a quiet place with no distractions. Everyone must use a **quiet voice** when talking. If kids continue to yell, put them in separate rooms until they're ready to talk quietly.
2. **Avoid the blame game**. It doesn't help for you to ask who started the fight, or who did what to whom. They'll tell you anyway!
3. **Ask each child one at a time, *"Tell me quietly what happened."*** Each child should get the same amount of time to quickly tell his or her side of the story (maybe a minute or two). No interrupting unless they're out of time. Nobody's allowed to make fun of or call people names. You can say, *"Tell me what you are thinking (or feeling)."* When your child's finished, repeat what was said. Correct stinking thinking (using words like always or never, and exaggerating or making something the worst case scenario). For example, if Carlos says, "She never lets me use her...," say, *"Actually, she has let you use it before, hasn't she? Do you mean that you'd like to use it more?"*
4. **Show empathy for each child**. Show you understand both sides. Let's say they're fighting because your daughter took your son's bike and rode it without permission. Try to say something good and bad about everyone's behavior. To your daughter, you could say, *"You really like his new bike. I can understand why you want to ride it. But how would you feel if your friend took your bike away? You need to get permission."* To your son, you could say, *"You didn't need to scream like that— it scares people and hurts my ears! I understand why you were feeling upset, but you may not break her things when you're mad. Nobody's allowed to do that to you, and I won't allow you to do it to anyone else, either."*
5. **Ask each, *"What do you think should happen next?"*** When you first start having fight meetings, listen to their ideas about how to

settle a conflict. Then help them decide what should happen. Encourage them to find solutions that give each person a little of what he or she wants (**compromise**). If they come up with a solution that is pretty reasonable (even if it isn't as good as yours), go with theirs. It'll give them confidence to solve problems again. Maybe they would decide that your son needs to pay for what he broke, and your daughter could agree to wash his bike and never take it without permission.

6. **If you don't think their solution is reasonable, or they can't find one, say what you think is fair and why.** Then carry out your own solution. Try to go with their ideas more often than yours, as long as it isn't really unfair to one child.

7. Once you've had a few meetings like this together, and you think they have a handle on how to do things, let them discuss and carry out a solution without you and see how it goes.

Chapter 11

SUCCESSFUL PARENTING IN THE STORM: Pearls for handling divorce

A sadly common event in children's lives today is the separation of their parents. Even if the parents are not married, when they split up it can feel the same as a divorce to children. Fortunately, parents can do certain things to help their kids stay emotionally healthy through the process. Here are some tips.

How to tell children about the separation

Include these things:
- The general reasons why the split is happening.
- It isn't your children's fault at all—it has nothing to do with who they are or how they act. They could not have prevented it.
- Both parents love them very much.
- This happens in a lot of families. Even though it hurts at first, usually kids end up doing just fine.

Also tell your kids these things, if they seem true:
- They will still see both parents on a regular basis, but not together.
- You feel you'll be a better parent and a happier person if you split up.
- You did try to find a way to stay together, but you just couldn't.

If the reason for the split is domestic violence or abuse, then say so. *"Daddy (or Mommy) hurts me (or you), and that's not OK. We need this change to be healthier and happier."* Otherwise, **don't criticize the other parent**, no matter how hard it is not to, and even if you've been criticized yourself.

If your children ask why you aren't staying together for their sake, say that sometimes it's not best for children to have unhappy parents staying together. In fact, children often do better when a bad relationship ends. Staying in a bad relationship makes it hard for parents to give kids the good attention they need. It also makes the home a stressful place, and puts pressure on kids to make their parents get along. Plus, it can increase behavior problems in kids. Say that you want life to be better for them.

What if your partner decides to leave you? Tell your children that it makes you sad, but you'll be fine because you have them. Say that people are free to make choices and you can't help your partner's choice.

Talk about how the breakup will affect your lives

Be honest and sensitive when you tell your kids what to expect. Explain what will change and what will stay the same in their lives. If you don't know some things yet, just say so. Sometimes kids have funny thoughts about what will happen to them after divorce. They may think that you or your ex-spouse won't be able to see them anymore. They may think they won't have a home, or that the siblings will be split up too. They may think you're mad at them, or don't love them anymore. Never assume that you know what your kids think—they need to be told that these things aren't true. Say, *"I guess some kids think that a breakup means their parents don't love them anymore, or are mad at them. I was wondering if you're thinking that."* Reassure them that these things aren't true.

Children of divorced parents can have more **behavior and depression problems** than other children (especially during the first year after the divorce). However, many times behavior problems will ease after a divorce. This may mean that the kids were acting out because of stress related to their parents not getting along at home. Research has now shown that parent-child relationships, parenting style and discipline all suffer when there is conflict between parents that live together.

Boys need just as much good attention from their parents as girls do in order to help them adjust to divorce. Boys often act out with anger and bad behavior earlier and for a longer time than girls do. Overtime, girls tend to develop more depression and anxiety than boys do. Both boys and girls tend to have trouble with their grades when a divorce happens during their middle or high school years. It's important to help teens focus on their school work and to get them help as needed to keep their grades up.

Frequent talks about a breakup will avoid some of the misbehavior that will normally happen. Allow your children to be angry and sad, and encourage them to tell you about it. Try not to criticize or brush off their concerns, even about little things. Listen carefully, and reassure them that you love them and that they'll be just fine. Make sure your kids are able to be with friends and other adults that they feel close to, so they get plenty of healthy attention and support. Teens may think about moving out early. Convince them that you still want them at home, and want to take care of them because you love them. If your child withdraws, is hard to talk to, or you are just worried, get a counseling appointment for him or her.

Also please remember that your children (even teens) aren't old enough to be your friends. It's really best if you don't ask them for advice or to listen to your problems, especially about your ex. It can put them in a terrible bind of feeling like they need to take sides. If you need to talk, do so with a licensed therapist or adult friend.

Tell them till you're blue in the face that it's NOT their fault

Say, *"It isn't your fault. In fact, the breakup has nothing to do with you. It only has to do with me, and your Mom/Dad (my partner). I still love you and will be a part of your life, no matter what."* Tell your children that the breakup didn't happen because they were bad, or not good enough, or not loved. It happened because something wasn't right between you and your ex-spouse. It is critical to your children's well being that they believe these things. Your kids may try to get you back together. Just say, *"There's nothing you can do, since it has nothing to do with you."*

Keep routines going as much as possible

When a major change in life like this happens, it's natural to go into crisis mode and not pay as much attention to your parenting. But your children need everything else in their lives to be the same as much as possible. In fact, they need *more* structure instead of less. Using the *7 Skills* will help your children get the attention, discipline and consistency they need to feel secure.

Children going through the separation of their parents **need consistent**

limits more than ever so the rest of their lives are predictable. Continue home routines like chores, homework, family meetings and sitting together for meals. Keep having talk time, special time, play time and outside activities. Don't allow children to miss school because they're sad or have tummy aches. Resist buying gifts to soften the blow. Gifts will only distract them for a short time and won't help like good attention will.

Your Relationship With Your Ex-spouse

Here's a key fact you need to know: **The most common reason children have problems after divorce** is that a bad relationship continues between their parents. Talk to your ex about this fact, and commit not to fight when you make arrangements for sharing the children and responsibilities. If you still fight, your kids may wonder why you broke up, since things don't seem any better. Also, if you keep fighting, you won't have as much energy to give your kids good attention and consistent limits and discipline.

Try not to trash your ex in front of the kids

If you say bad things about your ex-partner, your children may also feel criticized. It may not make sense to you, but that's just the way it is. This is especially true when your ex is their biological parent. Your child is part of that adult, and so they are connected forever. Saying things to try to get your kids to lose respect or affection for your ex makes them worry that you'll reject them also someday. It also increases the chance that your children could reject you, since you're criticizing someone they love.

Domestic violence is common in America. If your ex-spouse was abusive, or threatened to hurt you or your kids, be honest about it. But keep it general, without giving them details. Say that abuse and violence is never OK, and wasn't your fault or your child's fault. Say that your ex has problems (or is sick), and that you are taking steps so that he or she can't hurt the family anymore. Then make sure the abusive mate isn't around without supervision. Otherwise your kids may not trust you.

Try for a good enough working relationship with your ex

Treat **conversations with your former partner** like a business call, focusing on what's best for the kids. If you disagree on an issue, see where you agree first. Try not to interrupt, or criticize his or her opinions or feelings. Act like you have concern for your ex-partner (everyone has *some* acting talent*)*. Say, *"It may be hard for you to do that—would you like me to...?"* Don't waste energy trying to change little things that don't really matter. (He may let your daughter stay up later, but if she still does her homework, and stays healthy, forget about it.)

When you need something from your ex, make specific, polite requests. Say, *"I feel..."* and *"I think..."* when you talk. For example, say, *"When you drop him off an hour late* (**what happened**), *I feel worried that he won't get to bed on time and will have trouble with school the next day* (**why you are concerned**). *I was hoping you would be open to bringing him on time next week* (**a specific polite request**). *"* This gets much better results than, "Why can't you just..." or "You always..." which sounds critical and makes people defensive.

If your ex is frequently late to get the kids or bring them back, or cancels plans, say what you plan on doing next time it happens. You and your children will feel in control by having a backup plan. Decide what to do with your kids.

If you still argue, don't do it in front of the kids (or tell them about it)! Just stop the conversation and agree when you will continue it. (*"I have to run- let's talk again tonight. I will call you at seven if that's OK."*) That gives you both time to calm down and think before the next time you talk, when it may be easier to solve a problem.

If you still can't talk and solve problems, use someone else to mediate for you—another adult or attorneys. Under no circumstances should you put your kids in the position of a go-between to solve your fights. It's hard on the kids to ask them to keep secrets from your ex—or to take sides on issues. Work them out yourself with your ex. But, you can have your children ask permission from your ex to do something. For example, if your kids want to go on a trip with you when they're supposed to be with your ex-spouse, have them ask your ex to decide.

Guidelines for when there are two households for kids

Make sure that your children see the other parent regularly, unless he or she has been abusive. This gives kids security and the feeling that they are still loved by both parents.

Children will often live part of the time at each parent's home. This creates common problems. The rules for your child will probably be different in each home. Just as you would resent it if your ex made the rules for your home, your ex would not like you saying how to run his or her household. Tell your children they need to follow the rules for the home they're in. Use P.S. I'M HELPING to tell if you need to talk about something happening at your ex-spouse's home. Otherwise, think of the Great Wall of China. What happens on your side of the wall is your concern, and what happens at your ex's place is his or her thing. Explain to your kids that *"at your dad's house you may be able to _____, but at my house you are expected to _____."*

Also help them stay organized so they don't forget things going between homes. Don't blame them if they do—it would be hard for you to keep moving your stuff back and forth. Give your child a place to store things at each home.

Stepfamilies

How to introduce children to new love interests is covered in the next chapter on single parenting. Here we'll talk about when two families unite. Having people in the family that aren't related by blood makes it a stepfamily (except for adoption of children that aren't related to either parent). It takes years for newly joined families to adjust, and it's normally tough on everyone for a while. And, sorry to say, most people think it will be better than it actually turns out to be. But stepfamilies can work just as well or better than a first family. Just try to have realistic expectations—it's not going to be the Brady Bunch.

Children aren't usually happy to have new people in the household

They don't like losing control and your attention. When new kids join the family, your own children need to feel like they're still the most important children in your life—so tell them so. But this doesn't mean you can't be fair and show affection to your new partner's kids.

Listen carefully to your children

Bring up what you think they may be thinking or feeling when you're alone together. *"A lot of kids feel jealous when new kids move in. I was wondering if you are feeling this way."* Never disagree with their feelings, or say they're making too much out of something. Feelings are what they are, not right or wrong. Try to understand what is making them feel that way. Remember that kids' feelings may not seem to make sense to adults. If your kids can't say what is making them feel angry or jealous, ask them, *"What do you want me to do to help you feel better?"* Kids often know what they want before they know why they want it. You may not be able to do what they want, but it helps you see what they are thinking.

Expect more acting out when families first join together. Expect anxiety and anger. What can you do about it? Make time to talk it out and reassure your children that you'll try to make things all right. Use talk time, play time and special time to soften the blow, not gifts. Make sure all children in the house follow the same rules and do similar chores. Have regular family meetings, especially at first.

Also watch out for attraction between teen stepsiblings, and have open discussions about it. Just say that attraction between them isn't acceptable when they live with you.

Relationships with a new stepparent

It's best if you and your new partner have a close, working relationship. Although your kids may be jealous, this provides the stability they need. But don't expect a close relationship between your kids and their new stepparent, at least not for a long time. Tell your kids that the new adult will never replace their other parent, but will just be another, different parent who will care for them also. Say that you know they'll always love your ex-spouse and you hope they'll always be close. That doesn't have to change just because they have a new relationship with a stepparent. There is room for many close people in their lives.

Moreover, don't expect your children to call a stepparent Mom or Dad. They can use a first name or whatever respectable name they want. For teens, stepparents are often seen as friends instead of parents. This can work just fine. But make sure the child understands that he or she needs to cooperate with and treat the stepparent with respect.

Talk thoroughly about parenting before moving in with a new partner

It's very important for children to have consistent limits and discipline, even when the family changes. It's best if both partners are prepared to parent all the children in the home. It's also best for your kids if you pick a partner that uses similar parenting methods. If not, try to agree on compromises before forming the new family. Otherwise, parenting will be an immediate problem, causing conflict and stress for both of you, as well as your children. That's all you need, huh? Go over the *7 Skills* together and see where you can agree or compromise. You could leave the discipline to a child's own parent at first, until you unite your methods.

When going through separation and divorce, make your children's world as consistent as possible. Stay connected with your children, no matter what happens to your future adult relationships.

Chapter 12

GOING SOLO: Pearls for successful single parenting

We really admire and respect people that are able to raise good kids single handedly. There may be no job as difficult as being a single parent! If you live without another adult who also parents your children, life is tougher for you and your kids. Single parents have less money (one out of three live under the poverty line), less time, and more stress. Just making decisions alone is harder. Usually there isn't someone to take over when dealing with the kids has just been too much. Even though it's really difficult, you can do well enough for your kids. Here are some suggestions for success.

Simplify your life

Kids don't need all your free time, fancy toys or a lot of outside activities to be happy. They just need life to be as stress free and predictable as possible, and to have a loving parent who values them, no matter what. Keep the number of activities outside the home to a minimum, especially during the school year. Maybe only have one per child if it meets multiple times a week. Make homework, chores, meals, talk time and play time your top priorities for you and your kids.

Organize

Clean out all the unused things from your house, car and workplace, so you can find things easily. Otherwise, don't waste energy trying to keep your home neat as a pin. It only needs to be neat enough to be user friendly. By this we mean the home is clean enough to be healthy, you are able to find things and don't waste time and money buying things that you have but can't find. Make sure your children are doing regular chores to help out. Get ready for the next day the night before. Use bins with labels on them to organize your stuff. Make your kids use them too—you can set action limits if they don't.

You also might keep a schedule notebook with you all the time to help you remember appointments and make notes for school, work and other events. Make "to do" lists and shopping lists in the same notebook to stay organized and cut down on the trips you make.

Taking care of your needs is very important

We think simple pleasures are necessary for a single parent's mental health. These will often need to be scheduled to actually happen. A few minutes of alone time every day, getting counseling, occasionally going out with friends, and working out (even with an exercise video at home) can keep you on top of your game. It'll make you a happier parent.

Deal with depression, anxiety, anger, or substance use—right away

If you learned skill #1, you know how these problems make it difficult to be a good enough parent, and you are prepared to take action. Everything is harder for you and your kids when you allow these problems to continue. Get counseling and treatment—you and your kids deserve it.

Find the support you need and deserve

Getting help and support from other people is critical. Friends and family are important sources of emergency help, but try not to rely only on them. Look for people in the same boat, either individually or in a group. Ask community or religious organizations, schools, social service agencies, and workplaces if they have single parent groups or services. Or form your own club! Connecting with other single parents can help with ideas, emotional support, babysitting, carpooling and errand running. But never leave your children with someone until you know the person well and know that he or she is trustworthy.

Keep in mind that other parents will be more likely to help when you return favors, so the relationship isn't one sided. You'll get the best responses from people when it appears to them that you really do need help. People will also be most helpful when you seem very efficient. (In other words, they don't think you waste time or money on unnecessary things.)

Find parenting buddies

One of the hardest things about parenting alone is not having someone to test things out on. There's no one to ask, "Am I overreacting?" "Should I allow this?" and "What do you think about what my child is doing?" And there's no one to back you up on decisions you make.

If you don't have an ex-partner who will help you, find parenting buddies. You can find these in relatives, good friends or in the single parenting groups we just talked about. They don't need to be single parents. Parenting buddies are other parents you trust and know well, who agree to hear your ideas, and tell you what they would do. They may even agree to meet with you and your child after you've decided how to deal with a problem, but think it's too hard to do yourself. But you'll have to do the parenting, not your buddy.

A buddy is just for advice and support, and not someone to watch your children or to discipline for you. Your buddy may need a break at some point, or may not be that helpful. Then look for someone else. Be someone else's buddy. If you're still struggling, get help from a mental health professional.

Learn and use the parenting skills in this book

Using your *7 Skills* will help you stay in control, even when you're dead tired and stressed out. Using them over and over will help you know what to do automatically, like a reflex. They will keep stress, discipline and work with your kids to a minimum.

When older children help care for younger ones

This is often necessary in the one parent family. Make sure your older kids get rewards for helping, and lots of time to themselves when they don't have to help. Older kids who are asked many times every day often resent their younger sibs and parents. It feels unfair. After all, they didn't choose to have more kids!

Ask for help very nicely, and let younger children know that they need to cooperate with your older children. Expect all of them to grumble— that's normal. You can have your younger child thank and do nice things for big brother or sister in return. Remember that older siblings sometimes abuse younger ones—stay aware to keep them safe.

Dating and finding a new mate

Kids normally don't like it when their parents date. They don't want to share your time and attention! Reassure them that they're still the most important people in your life. Explain that adults need companionship but you will always respect their feelings about someone new. Say that you'll take great care when you pick a new partner.

It may be tempting to rush into a new relationship just so you aren't alone, or just to get help with the kids. Ask yourself if that's a big reason you're interested in someone. Relationships made for these reasons often don't last. Moreover, it isn't good for you or your kids to have adults come and go in your lives.

Also be aware that some men seek out relationships with single mothers who have children, just so they can abuse those children. Please don't close your eyes to what might happen. It's hard to tell who will be abusive when you've only been with a person for a few months. Unless you have known and trusted a partner for a long time, he or she probably shouldn't be watching your kids for you.

When should you introduce a new love interest to your children? Generally, we recommend waiting until you've been in a relationship for at least six months. If you're going to sleep with partners at your place, we advise not to until after that, and until a long-term commitment has been made. It's too confusing for kids to be introduced to a series of new partners in a short time period, and it makes them anxious.

In addition, don't forget to take care of yourself and make protecting yourself from pregnancy and disease top priorities. Many single women find themselves having another child alone when new partners abandon them. Some of those women even thought that the pregnancy would make their partner stay.

When another mate without children will be moving in

Don't expect your children to welcome someone new with open arms. This is a scary time when they'll feel rejected. They won't understand why they're not enough for you. It's crucial for you to show your kids that they are still the most important people in your life. Tell them that adults need adult companionship, but that they are still number one in your book. If you spend more time with your new mate than with your children, your children may act out to get your attention.

Your children will do best if they can get to know a new mate before he or she moves in. Do fun activities for months first. Talk many times with your kids about what to expect before it happens. It's also critical to tell your children that you'll make sure the new partner parents the way you want. Say that you'll always be their parent, and will always love them. Your new partner may become someone they love also. It's very important that you and your new mate follow the same parenting methods as much as possible, to keep life consistent and predictable for your children.

If your new partner has children, read about stepfamilies in the divorce chapter, and be consistent with all children in the household.

Children can't be your friends until they're adults

Your child needs you to be a parent, not a friend. We know it's tempting, but don't confide in your kids or expect them to help you solve your problems. That's not your child's job, and is overwhelming and bad for him or her. It's also confusing for your children when you act like they're friends and then you discipline them. Use other people for support instead.

Single parenting success

Many single parent families are happy and thrive. Focus on your relationship with your kids, while taking care of yourself. If you need help, keep trying to find it. If you think your children love you and are doing all right, you should be very proud of yourself for a job well done.

Chapter 13

HOW TO HANDLE COMMON PARENTING ISSUES

Here are suggestions for handling specific parenting issues or problems, listed in alphabetical order. These are things that parents often ask for advice on. Some issues are covered elsewhere in the book, so check the index to find more information.

Many common problems are bad behaviors that you want to stop. We'll tell you to **start by naming the behavior.** That simply means to tell your kids the name for what they're doing wrong. *"Marie, that is... (lying, cheating, etc)."* This helps your kids recognize when and how they are misbehaving.

ADHD—attention deficit/hyperactivity disorder (or ADD—attention deficit disorder)

This is a popular diagnosis lately. Some children who are diagnosed with ADHD may not really have the disorder. This is partly because guidelines for diagnosis are a little fuzzy. But generally, children with ADHD move a lot without any purpose (they fidget), and don't pay attention. They're impulsive (jump into things without thinking, have trouble waiting, and interrupt people). A child needs to have significant problems functioning in two different places (like school, home or job) to have the disorder. What is confusing is that even people with other disorders like anxiety and depression can have these symptoms, and when they take medications for ADHD, they pay more attention and do better. So it's easy to wrongly assume that they have ADHD if they do better on ADHD meds.

We recommend not allowing your child to be diagnosed based only on a behavior checklist that you fill out. Counselors may suggest a diagnosis of ADHD to try to explain behavior, school or relationship problems. If they're wrong, it can delay dealing with those issues appropriately. If you think your child may have ADHD, have him or her tested by a licensed psychologist. There may be a learning disability instead, and testing can find that also. If your child does have ADHD, manage the temperament traits like high activity, high distractibility and low persistence that go along with it (see chapter 14).

Adoption

Even though most adoptions are successful, there are common issues to know about. The first is that there are almost always transition problems in the years following the adoption. Parents often find themselves disappointed by some of the child's qualities or how the child acts. Adopted kids are a little more likely than other kids to have emotional, mental or physical problems. This can make adjustments harder for everyone. Adoptions are most successful when children are young and of the same race as the adoptive family. If your adopted child is of a different race, help her find out about her heritage, and make those traditions part of your family's life.

When should you tell a child about being adopted? **It's best if the child always remembers knowing that he or she was adopted.** That means telling the child by about age 3. You can say things like, *"Your birth mother and father made you but weren't able to take care of you (too young, sick, not enough money or skills)." " I really wanted a child and am so happy that you joined the family. I love you so much. You are my son/daughter. When your birth mother decided to place you for adoption, it had nothing to do with who you are as a person. You couldn't have done anything different to keep it from happening. The fact that you are adopted doesn't make you any less important a person. Lots of famous people were adopted."* First ladies like Eleanor Roosevelt, presidents like Gerald Ford, actors like Lee Majors, authors like James Michener, musicians like John Lennon and Nat King Cole, and even the philosopher Aristotle were adopted.

No matter what you do or say, adopted kids will probably feel abandoned by their birth parents, and struggle with this. Don't bring it up unless they do. There may be nothing you can say that will help, and it will set up hard feelings if you just tell them to forget it, or try to make them feel good about being adopted. Tell your adopted child you would like to talk to him about it any time he wants. Don't disagree with his feelings. They are his, and he just needs you to listen and support him. Get him counseling if he talks about abandonment often. Tell him how glad you are that he is part of your family, and how lucky you feel. Use other methods in this book to build up his self-esteem.

Give adopted children information on their birth parents as they ask for it. It's best to talk positively about birth parents, so the children will think they came from good people. Even when drugs or abuse led to the adoption, talk about birth parents having a problem, instead of being bad. Less than half of adopted children want to look for their birth parents. If they do, support it. But have them wait until they are adults so they can do it more on their own, and deal with it better. Don't worry—if they do find a birth parent, they will usually have a better relationship with you afterwards. Open adoptions also can work well. Adoption agencies often have helpful advice and training also.

Anger

Teach your children to tell someone when they're angry, instead of doing something physical about it (like yelling, hitting, breaking things, and having lovely fits). When you notice them starting to get upset, say, *"Are you feeling mad? Tell me about it."* For young children, say, *"Use your big boy/girl words."* For older kids, you could say something like, *"What's up? Lay it on me"* or *"What are you thinking about?"* Repeat back what they said, so they know you heard.

Don't get upset at what they're saying; otherwise they won't talk about anger again. **Praise them for talking** about being mad, even if they're mad at you. For younger kids, say, *"You are getting so much older. Being able to talk about being mad is great. Do you feel better? And you didn't get in trouble because you talked it out. I am so proud of you!"* Give them a hug and a few seconds of quiet attention. This encourages them to share anger in healthy ways instead of acting out. Then offer suggestions for what they're mad about.

For older kids, encourage them to tell you why they're mad. Say, *"You seem pretty upset. What's up? Give it to me straight."* Then listen quietly until they seem to be done talking (use open communication and talk time skills found in this book). If he swears or yells at you, or threatens to hurt you or an object, calmly say you won't listen until he gets in control and lowers his voice. If yelling, swearing, hitting, or throwing continues, then walk away saying that you'll be back once he calms down and is ready to talk. For repeat outbursts, use action limits with consequences just as you would for any bad behavior.

Anxiety and worry (also see "Fears")

More and more adults and children are having problems being anxious. Anxiety is actually the most common psychological problem in children. Causes include feeling pressure to perform, worries about crime and the world, seeing violence (real or imagined) and the stress parents show. The more stressed you are, the more stressed your kids can be. Using the controlling parenting style also leads to anxiety in children, so avoid using it (see page 164).

The American Academy of Pediatrics has expressed concern over increased stress in children. One way to help is to **stop over-scheduling your children**. Start by cutting back on activities that *you* want more than your kids want, and ones that won't add to their long-term success or happiness. Another way to help is to **decrease exposure to** nearly perfect bodies, unrealistic relationships, and violence in **media**. You can help just by turning off the television and video games.

Build up your kids' resilience. Say, *"I'd really like it if you tell me when you're feeling scared or worried or stressed out about anything."* When they do, listen without making fun. If they're afraid of crime, tell them they shouldn't get hurt as long as they follow what you say to stay safe. Say that you won't let anything bad happen to them.

You can teach them other ways to cope with feeling anxious. *"Close your eyes and see a wonderful place you'd like to go to. Count to 10 and let all your muscles go loose. Breathe in and out slowly until you feel better."* Show them how you deal with things without being anxious. *"I was kind of worried about work today, but I just did my best, and everything was fine!"*

Get professional help if worry or anxiety keeps your kids from doing normal things like going to school. Also seek help if your child has physical symptoms for more than a few weeks, like trouble sleeping, stomach or bowel problems, fatigue or not being able to concentrate.

Biting

Well whatever you do, don't bite back! That just makes it worse. Biting is normal in kids up to 3 years old. It helps comfort babies when they first get their teeth. If your infant older than six months bites when breastfeeding, or bites someone else, put her in her playpen for a short time and quietly say, *"We don't bite—biting hurts."* Calmly separate her from the person she bit. Do this enough times and she'll learn that she doesn't want to bite (because when she does, she loses attention). Give her things she *can* bite on, like a wet washcloth or teething ring.

Toddlers often bite when they're frustrated, because they don't know what else to do. Remove them from the area, and point to your own mouth and teeth. Say, *"We don't bite when we're upset. You need to use your big girl words instead. Tell somebody when you're mad. When you want something, say so. But no biting or you will go to time-out."* Don't show anger or give them any other attention after they bite, or they may do it more. Remember, many bad behaviors are encouraged by the attention kids get afterwards. But *do* give lots of attention to whoever got bit.

Cheating

Starting at age 4 or 5, if your child cheats on a game, name the behavior. *"That is cheating. It's kind of like lying. People won't believe what you say if you do that. We don't cheat. Games are no fun if someone cheats."* For older kids, emphasize that cheating will keep them from learning how to do things. If they rely on cheating to do well, they will fall behind when they can't cheat. *"As you get older, cheating can become a habit that can cause friendship trouble, get you thrown out of school, or get you in trouble with the law (such as cheating on taxes)."* Use action limits if cheating continues.

Counseling help

Many parents find that they need professional help dealing with their children. Moreover, many parents need help dealing with their own depression, domestic violence, anger management, alcohol/substance abuse, or anxiety. There are many kinds of professionals who can help.

Mental health professionals with the highest levels of education are those with doctoral degrees (PhD/PsyD or MD/DO). Doctors who have earned the PhD or PsyD degrees are non-medical doctors. All psychologists, some counselors and some social workers have one of these degrees. These mental health professionals focus on evaluating and treating problems with behavior, emotions and personality and usually don't prescribe medications.

A **child psychologist** is an expert in helping children and in helping parents deal with their children or their parenting (one of your authors is a child psychologist). Psychiatrists are medical doctors (MD or DO) who are trained to assess and treat behavioral, emotional and personality problems, often by prescribing medications. A child psychiatrist is a medical doctor who focuses on treating childhood behavior problems and mental disorders. Many families work with both a psychologist and a psychiatrist. The next-highest level of training for a mental health professional is the master's degree (MA/MS/MSW). Then there are others who provide counseling with only college degrees (BS or BA).

There are many different names that these professionals use. A psychotherapist is anyone who provides psychological therapy, and can have any level of training. (Even people with no specialized training can call themselves psychotherapists!) Social workers may provide psychotherapy and often have master's degrees. A counselor is anyone who provides counseling, and should have at least a master's degree. Then there are therapists who do specialized work like play therapy (usually they have at least a master's degree). Check what degree a provider has. For your safety, see only people who are licensed by your state.

It can be difficult to find professional help. One reason is that most insurance companies don't pay as much as these services are worth. That makes it hard to find professionals who are willing to take insurance payments. It's especially hard to find providers who will take Medicaid, because of the very low reimbursement, and all its regulations. It's often best to pay for care yourself if you can (without using insurance) with cash or a credit card, because this will give you the best options. Many counseling centers work on a sliding scale, where you pay less if you earn less. Universities often have lower-cost training clinics you can use. Ask your health care provider, friends, relatives, social service agency, or school counselor for recommendations. If your child needed surgery, you would do anything to get it done. Your child's emotional and mental health is just as important. Congratulate yourself for getting yourself or your child needed help.

If your child refuses to see a professional, and you think he or she really needs help, you can insist on going to an appointment. Kids will often be glad later, because they'll have someone to hear about their complaints and problems. You could also go by yourself at first, to get advice, and find out how serious your child's problems may be. Once your child is in therapy, if he or she doesn't seem to click with the therapist after about five sessions, or you have an uneasy feeling, try someone else. Sometimes the best treatment for a child involves treating the whole family. In family therapy, family members are seen together.

Day care

Ask a day care facility questions like these (including home day cares): How many other children will be in the same class? How many children does each teacher take care of (the adult-to-child ratio)? How much education do the teachers have? (It's best if some have college degrees.) Do they do criminal background checks on their employees? Are they accredited by an organization? Are they licensed? Talk to other parents who have used a center for a while. Visit a few times with your children before leaving them there. Then visit often without notice that you're coming. You should be able to see your child anytime.

Fears (also see "Anxiety")

Normal children have many fears that they outgrow. They may be afraid of insects, thunder, boogey men, elevators or anything. Avoid making fun of them (telling them they're dumb or a baby), threatening them with whatever they're afraid of as a punishment, punishing them for being afraid, and acting like you don't care (ignoring their fears). Doing these things can make their fears even worse.

Here's how to help. Talk about it, including why they are afraid and why you aren't. Read stories about their fear, and gradually expose them to it while you're with them. If you can't convince them that their fear doesn't make sense, reassure them. For example, if they're afraid of monsters at night, leave a small light on, and check for monsters in closets and under the bed with them.

Fears aren't healthy if they keep your child from doing what he or she needs to do several times a day. If that happens, or when your kids are afraid of things that are a real threat, see a professional. Make sure your children aren't getting exposed to things that can cause long lasting fear, like violence in the media or real life. Please be aware of the bad effects of long lasting fear on children (see page 193).

Foster parenting

Foster parents provide temporary homes for children who need them. These unfortunate children have often been neglected or abused, and may need to be rescued from their parents or other caregivers. But removing them from what they know, even if what they know isn't good for them, can add to their trauma. These children are in special need of consistent limits and good attention. They will often need special health services, especially counseling, to help them cope with what has happened to them.

Help them adjust to their new home with you. Good attention and frequent talks are important. Give them private space for sleep, as well as toiletry and other household items and toys that they can call their own. After a short time, ask what they like about living with you. Also ask if there's one thing they would like to change—then change that if possible. That gives them a little sense of needed control. Don't make any promises about the future, as placement changes for many foster children. You're goal is not to try to form a long-term relationship, but to show affection and caring while building self-esteem, resilience and healthy behaviors in your foster child.

Here is some advice on **talking about the parents who lost custody**. Don't say negative things about them unless the child does, and you want to show you understand. It helps to tell foster children that their parents do love them, but can't take care of them, and that's why you are. Tell the children it was never their fault, and it was never OK for them to be mistreated (or not taken care of). Sometimes parents do bad things to kids even though they love them, often because they're overwhelmed or mentally ill. Avoid criticizing or disagreeing with a child's feelings, but do encourage talking about it. These kids will often still have strong, good feelings for their parents. When they grow up, they can decide how involved they'll be with them.

Help them prepare for visits with their parents. Tell them where and how long the meeting will be. Say it might be hard for the parent to see them. The parent may even say things that are hard to hear. If you know about difficult things that might happen, talk about them beforehand, so they can think about how they might respond.

Foster parents aren't allowed to use any physical punishment for discipline. This is a very good rule since these children may have been severely punished when it wasn't called for. Besides, if you learned skill #5, you know this doesn't work anyway, and creates a lot more problems.

Since foster children have often been abused, possibly even sexually, keep a close eye on how they interact with your other kids. Make sure all your children understand and follow your house rules. The National Foster Parent Association (nfpainc.org), foster care agencies and other websites can give you great ideas and support.

Gifted and talented children

Children are most commonly called "gifted" if they have either very high IQ (intelligence quotient) scores or special abilities. Let's start with some good news for those of us whose children are probably not gifted, or for those who haven't tried to find out. First of all, it turns out that a very high IQ can be linked with social problems for kids. Being gifted also has no long-term link to success in life, relationships or career. These things may have more to do with persistence, creativity and emotional intelligence (and those are hard to test for). It also can cause problems between siblings, if one is labeled as gifted, and others aren't. Your other children may see the gifted one as your favorite. You may ignore your other children's qualities and talents that are just as (or even more) wonderful.

Other problems happen when parents would *like* to have their child called gifted, so they try to make it happen. This is often done by pressuring the child to learn at a faster pace than other children learn. In the toddler chapter, we talked about how this lowers a parent's ability to sensitively respond, which little kids need to succeed, including in school. Sometimes parents feel better about themselves when their child is called gifted. This puts children in an unhealthy, stressful position of supporting their parent's self-esteem.

The worst problems come when children who have been called gifted no longer qualify for programs for gifted children. These kids may feel humiliated, thinking they did something wrong, or failed. They may actually feel bad about being normal, good students. Worse yet, they may think that their parents are disappointed in them. If this happens to your child, tell him he or she is the same bright, wonderful child you love, and that'll never change.

Parents or teachers often want certain children placed in gifted and talented classes so they stay challenged and don't get bored. This is one of the better reasons to do so, *IF* your child really needs to be challenged. But we recommend not making a big deal out of this to your child. Don't brag about it. Give her good attention, and stress more important qualities, like kindness, persistence, effort, love of learning, and a good work ethic.

Hitting or kicking

Sometimes kids hit or kick when they're frustrated. They learn to do this by seeing other people do it—in real life and on TV. Moreover, kids who are hit by parents (including spanking) are more likely to hit others. Talk to your kids about why you think hitting is bad: It doesn't fix anything, it hurts people, and it makes the hitter look bad and get into trouble. Help them find other ways to handle anger. *"Next time you're mad and feel like hitting, say 'I'm upset—really upset.' Tell people why you're mad, and what you want."* Give them something else to do, like turning around with their arms crossed, and letting out a big huff, or walking away while humming a song. Practice, and be silly and laugh while you act it out, to help keep them calm when they do it for real. Praise them if they try it! If they still need to hit, have them hit something safe like a pillow or punching bag.

If you still have trouble, set an action limit. *"If you hit, then you will...(lose a privilege or thing, or go to time out)."* When your child hits, take the child away from the area. Say, *"We don't hit,"* or *"Hitting hurts."* Saying the same thing every time helps him learn more quickly. Don't let him see you hit anyone. When he's frustrated and doesn't hit or kick, reward him (even if he yells instead—you can work on that later). Ask him if there was a time he was mad today when he didn't hit, and what he did instead. Then reward him.

Lying

Small children normally lie sometimes, and they don't understand what lying means. They can start understanding when they are about six years old. Say, *"Lying is when you say something you know isn't true."* When kids feel pressured to do things really well, or are afraid to admit they made a mistake, they lie more. They may feel that a punishment is so bad, or fear your reaction so much, that they can't admit doing something wrong. Also, kids lie more when they hear their parents lie (such as when the parents make up excuses to a friend on the phone when they don't want to do something).

Everyone lies at times, but explaining why honesty is best helps kids be honest. *"If you lie, then people (I) can't trust what you say. Then if you say you didn't do something bad, they (I) might not believe you. That would be scary and unfair."* *"How would you feel if your best friend lied to you? How about if I lied to you?"* *"Some people lie so much it becomes a habit—those people are hard to be around."* If your child lies after you've talked about this, first name the behavior. *"That is lying. I said next time you lie (a consequence) will happen."*

If your child lies to cover up misbehavior, focus on the bad behavior and not the lying. When your kids openly admit doing something bad, reward them by explaining how you'll be softer on their consequence. Also say, *"I'm sure glad you told me. Now I can trust you—way to go."* If you suspect they are lying, give them a way out. *"That sounds made up. Are you sure that happened? If it didn't, I hope you'll tell me—that would be really good."* Reward your kids for admitting when they made something up. If your children are lying a lot, they may need more good attention, or lower expectations from you. Lying also can be a sign of drug use, addiction or criminal activity in a teenager.

Nightmares and night terrors

A nightmare is a bad dream that scares a person. Don't make fun of your children for being scared of a dream. Reassure them that it's only a dream and that you'll never let anything hurt them. If they're afraid to go to bed, search their room with them until they know nothing scary is there. Make sure they have comfortable objects like blankets or stuffed animals to sleep with, and don't leave until they feel safe. Leave lights on and doors open if it helps. It's best not to let your child sleep with you (it can become a habit), but occasionally lying on the floor by you is fine.

A **night terror** is when the child suddenly sits up and cries for several minutes, while still asleep, with eyes open and staring. It might freak you out at first! But don't worry—nothing is wrong with your child. He or she won't even remember it happening. Night terrors will go away by themselves. If they happen around the same time of night, you can try temporarily waking kids up before that time to prevent them.

Pacifiers

Pacifiers can soothe a baby. But some children continue to suck on them as a habit, when they no longer need soothing. If a child continues to use a pacifier throughout the day when he is 2 years old, it will keep him from trying to talk, and he needs to talk at this age. So first of all, we suggest that pacifiers not be used automatically when a baby fusses. It's normal for babies to cry sometimes, so try to soothe them some other way first. Try not to use pacifiers after they turn 1 year old. If you want to stop pacifier use, never use punishment, criticism or teasing. It doesn't work, and can make things worse. But do reward them when they don't suck on it! Kids outgrow these things by themselves, especially when they start caring what other kids say. Luckily, this is an object you can just take away.

Potty training

 Most children are toilet trained (urinate and have bowel movements only in the toilet) by age four. But children can only be trained when their bodies are ready, and that happens at different times in different kids. Some learn to control urine before bowels—others do it the other way around. Only one out of

four children can stay dry during the day by 24 months of age. Most can stay dry in the daytime by 36 months. Nighttime dryness comes a few months to years after daytime dryness.

If you push children to potty-train before they want to, or before they're able to, it sets up problems between you that can last a long time. It can also decrease their self-esteem, cause long term bowel problems, create power struggles and frustrate you. So, DO NOT FORCE THEM to train, or punish them for not staying dry. Just gently encourage them to practice.

You can start training when they are age 2, but if your child resists (or doesn't have success), wait a few months before you try again. It's normal to go backwards before there is more success. It takes a few months to train them, and girls are easier. Use a child potty chair and let them watch you use your toilet. Say, *"Tell me when you think you might go pee-pee or pooh-pooh."* Then take them to the potty chair to practice sitting there, but only for a few minutes (longer is NOT better, but worse). He may tell you after he already soiled his diaper. Praise him for letting you know, and say, *"Now try telling me before it happens next time."* Make sitting on the potty chair part of their routine (after waking up, before bed, etc.). When they do anything in the potty chair (any little trickle), praise and hug them. When they've had a few successes on the potty chair, use training pants next.

Children will learn to want dry pants when you mention how icky their skin feels with a dirty diaper or soiled clothing on. But don't use negative words, like *dirty,* about the potty chair or toilet. It helps to offer treats along with praise for going on the big boy/big girl potty, or for staying dry. Never act disgusted or tell children they are bad when they aren't successful. Don't punish or scold—doing those things can make training take longer and really damage your kids. If they aren't trained by age 4, you can try making them change their own diapers or training pants, and carry soiled clothes to the laundry.

Still being wet at 5 years of age during the day, or during the night at 7 years of age, is called **enuresis**. This should be evaluated by a doctor, but usually no medical disease will be found. We now know that this is usually NOT caused by any emotional or psychological problem. A common cause is the genes we're born with. Bedwetting will usually resolve on its own by the time a child is age 10. Never tell children it's their fault, that they are bad, or anything else negative. That can be very damaging to your child's mental health. Reassure him or her that kids grow out of it. Get advice from your doctor on how to deal with it, such as using a bed alarm.

I once worked with a parent who was disciplining his 9 year old for pooping in his pants at school. The child had been toilet trained years before, so the parent knew he was capable of holding in his bowel movements. Because the parents had a very good relationship with their child, I suggested that their son may not be able to control his stools due to a medical condition. A physician did diagnose their son with **encopresis**, where constipation causes uncontrollable leaking around hard stool. With medical treatment, what they thought was a behavior problem went away.

Selfishness

Young children are naturally selfish—they can't help it. The way parents treat them has a lot to do with their ability to grow into less self-centered people who care about others. Let's look at ways you can teach your children to grow up caring about other people as much as themselves.

Teach them empathy by giving it yourself. Notice people in need and say, *"That would be awful to have to look through trash for food and clothes." "She fell—ouch! Let's see if she's all right."* Suggest that your child make a new child feel more welcome. *"That's scary to be new. Why don't you eat lunch by her today, and ask where she's from."*

Insist that your kids do things for others, in your family and outside of it. You can even set limits on it. *"Billy, if you don't help your Dad carry his things, you will lose game time."* Notice when they're acting selfish and label the behavior so they learn to recognize it. *"That's acting selfish, not letting the other kids play your game."* Expect to be thanked when you give them things. Don't give them too many gifts, or they won't appreciate them. Make presents count, by giving them for special occasions or good behavior. Review the section on how to prevent materialistic values (see page 107). Make sure you notice and praise them like mad when they do things or show concern for others.

The style that parents use influences how selfish children are (see chapter 6). Parents who use the controlling style frequently criticize and expect a lot from their kids. Those children often feel that their parents care more about obedience and order rather than their relationships, and then often act selfishly to get what they need and want. They learn to stick up for themselves. Kids raised by parents using the permissive style learn to be self-centered because they're used to getting what they want and aren't expected to do much. Using the controlling style at times and the permissive style at other times also encourages kids to be self-centered. The best style to use to raise kids that care about themselves as well as other people is called the balanced style. Check it out on page 171.

Separation anxiety

When you leave your children somewhere, we recommend telling them that you're leaving, and kissing them goodbye, instead of sneaking off. Say that you'll be back and will see them soon. If you sneak off and leave, they may get anxious that you'll do it again. Have practice sessions: Leave your child in a safe place for a couple of minutes and tell them you'll be right back. Greet them when you return. Have them play with a new babysitter in your presence for the first night or two.

No matter how much your children cry when you leave, they are all right. Kids usually grow out of this. When separation anxiety is severe (for example, if children refuse to go to school), it may be a sign of a more serious problem. Seek professional help in that case.

Sleep problems

When kids don't sleep enough, it's hard on the whole family! Parents often ask how to get their kids to sleep, stay asleep or sleep long enough. (Normal sleep hours for kids are on page 48.) It's best for children to gradually learn to fall asleep alone. If your child is used to going to sleep with a certain routine that you need to change, gradually change it by taking parts of the routine away (or shortening the time). The goal is to get him to fall asleep alone in his own bed. Give him something to hold that he has only at bedtime (stuffed animal, or blanket). Or give him something to listen to, like a non-scary story tape (not TV).

If your child wakes up at night and comes to you, put him back in bed, kiss him and leave him there. Don't cave in to what he wants (like sleeping with you, or another snack). It will take some time for your child to learn this routine, but it usually will work within a week's time.

If your little child (infant, toddler or preschooler) cries when you put her in bed, here's what to do. Give her a kiss, tell her you love her, and leave. If she's still crying in one or two minutes, come back, give her a pat and a smile and go away again. If she still cries, this time wait two or three more minutes before you go back to reassure her. Repeat with longer and longer wait times until she's asleep or not crying. If she isn't crying, don't go back in the room. While trying this routine, be affectionate and calm. She will cry louder at first, but it will work if you stick with it. This is hard to do, and it may make you cry, too! But do it because it's best for both of you. She's not crying because she is hurting. She's crying because she wants it the way she wants it.

If your older children won't go to bed, set a consistent bedtime that you enforce. Use action limits with consequences if necessary, especially rewards. Set an alarm to alert your kids that it's time to go to bed. Have them read at bedtime to get them sleepy. Avoid active play and caffeine in early evening. Get stuff done for the next day before bedtime. Use nightlights (don't keep bright lights on), and don't allow television before bed (they may lie awake thinking about what they saw) or naps late in the day. And remember, no TV in their rooms! Have the house quiet. Evening snacks and listening to calm music or a story tape may help. Kids will try to distract you from bedtime, but don't pay any attention.

The **family bed** (where kids and parents sleep together) has many pitfalls. We recommend avoiding it because everyone will sleep better, and good sleep is important to performance and health. When your child sleeps alone, it helps her be independent, and gives you private time with your partner. That's a good thing for you, which is good for your kids. Besides, you'll have a heck of a time getting your kids to give it up once they get used to it. As a compromise to the family bed, your children could lie on the floor by your bed sometimes.

Stealing

Children can't understand what stealing really means until they're in grade school. Say, *"If you take something without the owner's permission, or take it from a store without paying, it is stealing. Stealing is against the law and is mean."*

If you think your child stole something, calmly ask about it first. Don't accuse him or her of stealing if you aren't sure, since this can destroy trust. If you're sure something was stolen, how you react is important. Strongly say that you disapprove. *"Stealing is wrong. How would you feel if another kid stole your bike?"* *"Older kids go to jail for that. The store would have called the police if you were caught."* Give them a punishment like taking away their favorite things for a few days. Make sure they make it right by apologizing and returning the item. (Don't let them keep it, even if they pay for it.) Before you return something to a store, you may want to find out if the store owner has to or will call the police when you return it, so you know what to expect.

If stealing is a recurring problem, explain, *"We have a house rule of no stealing. Unless we bought you something, or saw you buy it, we will assume something was stolen. If you steal, you will (get a consequence)."*

Swearing

Our society is unfortunately getting more vulgar. Just look at the number of times the "f word" is said in movies, or bleeped out on TV these days. Obscenities aren't used just when people are upset anymore, and some people say them out of habit, maybe because they don't know many other words!

The first way to decrease the chance that your kids will swear is to limit their time with media and other people who use foul language. Also, avoid saying words you don't want your kids using. Make a comment when they hear or say a word that you find unacceptable. *"That is swearing—we don't swear."* Go over which words you think are fine to say when upset.

Tell your kids why you don't want them to swear. *"It makes you look uneducated (mad, bratty, rude, insecure, mean)."* *"It makes it sound like you only care about yourself (you don't care about offending people), and have no manners."* If all this doesn't work, set an action limit with a consequence.

Tattling

This is when one child tells an adult about what another child did, just to get the first child in trouble. Telling an adult to keep people safe, or to keep someone from getting hurt or upset, isn't tattling. Tattling can hurt relationships, so don't allow it. Name the behavior, and set an action limit. *"That is tattling. If you do that again, (a consequence) will happen."*

Temper tantrums

More than half of normal toddlers have regular tantrums—you know, when they're loud, wriggling and angry. Oh, yeah—good times! A tantrum usually lasts five minutes or less. Little kids use tantrums to express their frustration, because they aren't old enough to talk about it like older kids can. Some use tantrums to try to get what they want.

The following things all increase tantrums, so avoid doing them:

1. Giving negative attention (scolding, punishing, getting upset) during tantrums.
2. Giving positive attention (or things they want) during tantrums.
3. Using controlling or permitting parenting styles.
4. Being inconsistent.
5. Not using routines.
6. Setting unnecessary limits.
7. Frequently telling them "no".
8. Not giving your child choices.
9. Letting your child see violence (real or imagined).

Here's what to do when your child has a tantrum. **Ignore** what she's doing. Stand or sit a few feet away and don't talk to her. Calmly say, *"I won't talk to (your child's name) or pay any attention until she stops yelling and squirming."* Do something else and wait a few minutes to see if it stops. Never allow kids having a tantrum to hit, bite or hurt anyone, including themselves. Just calmly move them away from you and danger. Don't ever let your child see you get upset about a tantrum.

If your child is old enough to talk, you can try saying, *"I hope Moe will use his big boy words to tell me how upset he is. But I can't talk to him until he does."* If he won't calm down and talk, ignore him until he stops the tantrum. When he does stop (he'll wear down eventually), praise him for sitting quietly, and then ask what he was so upset about.

Act sympathetic even if you don't feel like it. *"It's upsetting when your brother takes his toy back, isn't it? Maybe he'll let you play with it again later if you don't yell or fuss anymore."* If he talks about being upset, say, *"Good job using your words!"* When you ignore tantrums, they will often get worse for a few days, but then they'll get better. So hang in there!

For children 3 years old and up, you can try looking at something else while smiling or quietly chuckling. Your child may stop screaming, shocked at your behavior. He may act hurt, saying, "Don't laugh at me!" Then say, *"I'm not laughing at you, but just at what you're doing. I can't believe that's my big boy in there. What are you so upset about anyway?"* Hopefully then he'll talk about what set the tantrum off, instead of screaming.

If that doesn't work, and the tantrum continues, just let him or her alone until it does stop. (Your child will eventually run out of gas or even fall asleep.) After a tantrum's over, talk in a quiet place when you are both well rested. Ask what frustrated your child, or what she was thinking. Say that tantrums are not an OK way to show frustration, and that it embarrasses you both. Give her other ways to deal with feeling mad and overwhelmed. *"You can ask for a little attention, or just tell me your feelings. You can shout, 'I'm just so frustrated!' or you can march like a soldier (or something else you both come up with)."* Then say, *"But if you have another tantrum, you will lose (a privilege or thing), or get an extra chore."*

If your child is working into a tantrum, remind her of the consequence and give one chance to avoid it. If she can't stop, she gets the consequence afterwards—no question.

Spirited kids may have more tantrums because their temperament traits cause frustration. Traits they were born with can make them feel overwhelmed and out of control. Follow these same tantrum suggestions. To prevent tantrums, try to figure out what makes them feel overwhelmed. Also, if there are certain times of the day that tantrums happen, change your schedule to try to avoid activity and stimulation then. See chapter 14 for ways to manage spirited children.

Thumb sucking

 It's normal for small children to suck their thumbs for comfort, but if they are still sucking a thumb at age 4 or 5, it can cause problems. That's when it can cause dental problems like changing the jaw shape or forming buck teeth. This can make speaking and chewing harder. The thumb can also become chapped or callused, and the nail can get infected. These older children may get teased about sucking their thumbs, damaging their self-esteem. Most kids will decide to stop doing it before age four on their own. Good thing—since you can't *make* them stop doing it. But you can encourage them to stop.

Here's what to do. Don't say anything to children younger than 4 when they suck their thumbs, or they might do it more for attention. But, do praise them when they don't suck their thumbs. *"I like how you don't have your thumb in your mouth. Now I can see your pretty lips (or now you can talk to me)."* When your child has a thumb in his mouth, you can also try to distract him with something else he wants to touch. At all ages, threatening or punishing kids will backfire into more thumb sucking and behavior problems.

After age 4, make a plan for quitting with your child. Tell him that his habit may give him funny looking teeth, or that other kids may tease him. *"We're going to help you stop sucking your thumb so those things don't happen. The first thing I will do is remind you when you're sucking to take your thumb out and put it in your other hand or your pocket. Now let's pick what else to do."* You could give a reward when he has gone a few hours without sucking. Or you can *make* him suck his thumb for fifteen minutes at a certain time every day (he might not like being told to do it and lose interest in it). Or, put a liquid on it from the drugstore twice a day that makes it taste yucky (no prescription needed). He can also wear a glove, hand wrap (ace bandage) or thumb splint, especially at night.

Whining

All kids (and we dare say adults) whine sometimes. Kids do it when they want something, including attention, or when they feel irritated. But whining can be very irritating to parents! When your child whines, first name the behavior, *"That is whining."* Then calmly say, *"I'm not listening until you say it nicely, in your big girl voice."* That tells her what to do instead to get your attention and get you to listen. This works better than just telling her to quit whining. *"When you want something, you need to say, 'Mommy, may I ask you something?'"* Never give in to what your kids want when they whine, or they'll whine more often. After age 3, if they continue whining, set an action limit. *"Next time you whine, (a consequence) will happen."*

Yelling and screaming (also see "Anger")

This is normal for small children 3 and under, because they often communicate with their emotions. As they get older, they'll learn to use words instead when they're frustrated. Kids learn how to behave from what they see other people do, including family. So, don't allow anyone else to yell at home.

First of all, when kids yell, don't yell back—they'll just yell more. Just calmly name the behavior. *"That is yelling. We don't yell."* Teach them to use their words to say why they're upset. *"Tell me when you're upset instead of yelling. Then you won't get in trouble, and I can help."* If your child keeps yelling, say, *"I won't listen until you talk in your inside voice (your quiet voice, or your whisper voice)."* Be sure not to pay any attention until he lowers his voice. Just ignore him and repeat what you said until he's quiet. Then reward the quietness by talking about what upset him. For teens, see "disrespect" in the index also.

Chapter 14

TEMPERAMENT SKILLS: How to manage the traits that children are born with

For centuries, parents have noticed that every child reacts to things a little differently, even at a few months of age. Naturally reacting in certain ways toward people and things is known as **temperament**. It affects how we behave and do things without thinking or deciding. We all had a certain temperament growing up, and still do. It makes up much of our personalities. Because temperament is seen so early, it's probably at least half inherited in the genes we're born with.

Understanding temperament can help parents with their kids. First of all, temperament can change over time as your children get more control over how they react. What you do affects this a lot. Even though temperament is partly inherited, the genes kids are born with don't make up their destiny. Identical twins with the same genes can have different temperaments. Experiences and parenting make a big difference in how a child's temperament gets expressed.

Secondly, understanding temperament can help you avoid disciplining the reactions your child has little control over. This helps your child behave better and keeps your relationship strong. Thirdly, knowing how to manage temperament can relieve stress for both of you.

There are three main temperament styles that describe how children react to things. Researchers sometimes call them by different names, but we call them *spirited, cautious* and *easy*. Not all kids will react in only one style, but most will behave mainly in one style over time. Two children that have the same style won't react exactly alike, however. That's partly because parents manage their children's styles differently.

This table list reactions usually seen in children with each style. See which styles you think your children have. Then guess what yours is.

| Spirited style | • energetic with a high activity level |
| | • can be very emotional and sensitive (often fussy, easily upset) |

	• fearful of new people or places • irregular in eating and sleeping habits • not very adaptable • easily distracted from doing things • can be very persistent trying to get what they want
Cautious style	• often shy • tend to be inactive, fussy, sensitive, and withdrawn • react negatively to new situations and people • moods aren't very intense • reactions gradually become more positive with experience
Easy style	• have positive moods • adapt fairly easily to change • aren't easily upset or very intense • are regular in eating and sleeping habits

Spirited temperaments

No matter what temperament you and your kids have, your relationship is crucial for successful parenting. But a spirited temperament in a child may make it harder to form a close relationship. The child's high-strung ways can lead parents to feel frustrated, annoyed, or angry. Parents can end up spending less time with (or more time criticizing) their spirited child, which also makes it hard to form a close connection. Parents may think that their spirited children are disobeying on purpose (even when they're not), since these children are often fussy and upset just be nature.

Remembering that your children's genes lead them to behave this way can help you be more patient and forgiving, and relieve your stress. Keep in mind that these children are more likely than others to be abused when their parents can't control their own anger. If both you and your child have spirited temperaments, you can clash, making it even harder to get along. Making the effort to form a close tie will make parenting your spirited child easier.

Kids with spirit are more likely to have social problems, and be aggressive when they're little. But this usually goes away or gets much better by the teen years. Research has clearly shown that a child's environment can make this aggression turn into criminal or other bad behavior. So, how parents manage aggression really matters! It's very important not to withhold affection or give in to the intense demands of these children.

Spirited children *can* be taught to react more calmly and behave well enough. The most important thing you can do is to be calm around them yourself. If you let *their* high activity level or intense mood make *you* louder and more upset, it makes things worse. Staying calm and quiet helps your children act that way too. Also, be on the lookout for any good, calm, quiet moment they have, and reward it.

There is good news! Their energy may be driving you nuts now, but these kids often channel it into high achievements in areas like business, sports, or entertainment when they grow up. Their activity, intensity and energy can lead to very successful careers!

Cautious temperaments

These children's sensitive, withdrawn natures may also be frustrating to parents who are more outgoing and energetic, especially if they want their kids to be the same. You'll get the best results by being patient and giving them plenty of time to adjust to new surroundings and people. They'll gradually feel more comfortable with more experience.

You can help by calmly encouraging them to try new things and by not criticizing their fears. Avoid showing disappointment when they don't try new things—that will make them anxious and lose confidence. Not pushing or rushing them works best. For example, throwing them in the water if they're afraid will make them more terrified of water. Instead, make a game of dipping toes in and gradually wading in to get them ready to swim.

There is good news! There are clear advantages to a cautious style, such as being more wary of strangers and less willing to take dangerous risks. Their sensitivity can make them more emotionally intelligent, an important part of adult success. Their lower activity level can make them easier to keep track of, and their less intense moods can be easier to handle.

Easy temperaments

Don't be fooled—just because their temperament is easy doesn't mean these kids are easy to raise. It takes a lot of work to raise any child, but these kids are easier to teach and form close relationships with, especially when parents also have this style. But we can't all be that lucky!

These kids tend not to be as fussy as other kids, and adapt pretty easily to change. But that's not always good. Parents often pay more attention to their kids with spirited or cautious styles. Since they need just as much attention, easy temperament children may get harder to handle in order to get more of your attention. Yikes! If you're lucky enough to have a child with an easy style, praise and reinforce it. By the way, please don't tell your kids what their temperaments may be, or compare them in front of each other. That can lead to anger and bad behavior.

The 9 Temperament Traits

The styles that we just described are made up of nine temperament parts, called **traits**. Think of them as personality parts that children are born with. They reflect how 1) active, 2) adaptable, 3) bold (as opposed to shy), 4) distractible, 5) intense, 6) moody, 7) persistent, 8) regular, and 9) sensitive a child is. Everyone has more or less of each trait, from high to low levels. It is the combination of these trait levels that makes up a whole temperament style.

Note that temperament traits do NOT include being mean, violent, selfish or otherwise bad. Most experts believe that people aren't born this way, but that other people and experiences make them act this way.

Your kids may have mostly medium trait levels, meaning they don't usually react very strongly or weakly to people and things. All trait levels are considered normal, but frequent strong (high level) or weak (low level) reactions can cause problems and frustrate parents. The good news is that all these reactions can be managed. First, see if you think your children have any high or low traits by reading the descriptions in the chart below. This is especially important to do if you feel frustrated by how your child reacts. If a description seems to match your child, look in the next section for ways to manage this trait.

1.	High activity	Low activity
How kids act	Move quickly with high energy most of the time. Move a lot in most activities like eating, sleeping and playing.	Move slowly, and not very often during most activities like eating, sleeping and playing. Have low energy.
Pros	Have energy to entertain themselves, may do physical things more easily.	Stay calmer and easier to manage around a lot of stimulation or people.
Cons	May have trouble getting along with others and finishing things.	Slower pace may make it take longer to do things.
2.	**High adaptability**	**Low adaptability**
How kids act	Flexible and able to adjust to new things. Make decisions more quickly and accept limits and rules well. May also be bold in first reactions.	Resist and slowly adjust to new things. Make decisions slowly and fight limits. Fussy when things change. May have cautious first reactions.
Pros	More easily influenced by good people and things, and get used to changes easily.	Less likely to be affected by peer pressure and bad influences.
Cons	Can be influenced by peer pressure and bad influences.	Have trouble adjusting to new things or people.
3.	**Bold first reactions**	**Cautious first reactions**
How kids act	Comfortable in new situations, jump right in, and aren't afraid to try new things.	Hesitate in new situations. Don't like to try new things. Shy or withdrawn with new people—slow to warm up.
Pros	Outgoing, have easier time with new things and people.	Less likely to take dangerous risks.
Cons	May not be cautious enough with new things and people—so may be in more danger.	Less likely to take advantage of new things and situations that could be good for them.
4.	**High distractibility**	**Low distractibility**
How kids act	Easily interrupted by noise, people etc. Don't seem to pay attention, listen, or focus well. Can also be persistent (forget what *you* say, but not what *they* want!)	Hard to interrupt—don't seem to notice noise, movement, people or other things while doing something.

Pros	More easily distracted away from things you don't want them doing. While an infant, they can be soothed by distraction with food or a toy.	Can get things done easily when around other people, noise or other distractions.
Cons	Easily interrupted when they're supposed to be doing something, so have trouble finishing tasks.	May miss signals of danger.
5.	**High intensity**	**Low intensity**
How kids act	React strongly with high energy. Move and talk loudly. Have dramatic strong feelings—things are often either really good or really bad (not in between).	React mildly, with little movement and soft voices. Don't show much emotion (low-key, mellow and calm).
Pros	Can get attention and get needs met. You don't have to guess how happy or unhappy they are with something, because they show how they feel.	Their calmness makes it easier for adults to be around.
Cons	Adults usually like things calmer, so it can be annoying.	You may miss when they need something or are hurt.
6.	**Positive mood**	**Negative mood**
How kids act	Pleasant, cheerful, and friendly.	Fussy, unfriendly, serious, whiny or grumpy. (We're all like this at times, but we're talking about kids who usually act this way.)
Pros	Likable, easy to be around.	Hmmm… well, it may make you pay more attention to their needs.
Cons	May be hard to tell if they have a problem that needs to be dealt with. They may seem to ignore other people's feelings or problems, or may seem insensitive.	Sees the bad more than the good in things. May not show joy when you do something nice for them. May be harder to be around, especially if your mood is positive.

7.	High persistence	Low persistence
How kids act	Tend to stick with things until finished. Keep trying to do things or get what they want. Have longer attention spans.	Tend not to try a second time after initial failure—easily discouraged, give up easily. Attention span stays shorter as they age (it's naturally short in young kids).
Pros	Easier for them to finish things and perform well.	Easier to get them away from bad influences, and redirect to better things. They often take "no" for an answer.
Cons	Hard to interrupt them while they're doing something. Hard to change their mind—they may seem stubborn and like to argue (oh-oh).	Harder for them to finish things. May have trouble doing well in school or activities. (This can change when they're really interested in something.)
8.	High regularity	Low regularity
How kids act	Very consistent and predictable. Eating, sleeping and bowel habits tend to be on schedules. Are organized, neat, and use routines when older.	Very unpredictable in how they respond to things. Eating, sleeping and bowel habits change often.
Pros	You know what to expect from your child.	Adapt more easily to unexpected schedule or routine changes.
Cons	Uncomfortable for them when schedules or routines change.	Hard to know how they'll react. May have trouble falling or staying asleep.
9.	High sensitivity	Low sensitivity
How kids act	Easily notice sounds, smells, sights, tastes, touches and temperatures (notice some more than others). React to small changes. Things may not interrupt or distract them though. As older kids, they can sense other people's thoughts and feelings.	Don't notice sounds, smells, sights, tastes etc. very much (notice some less than others). It takes a big change to get them to react. (Don't expect little kids to be sensitive to the needs of others— they normally aren't.)

Pros	More sensitive to people's needs and feelings as they grow up. Noticing changes around them can keep them safe.	Less likely to be bothered by changes in surroundings, or to get over-stimulated.
Cons	May be a more colicky baby. Surroundings may bother or interrupt them. May have trouble sleeping, or get overwhelmed easily. May be picky or overreact.	May not pick up on important changes in surroundings or signals from people. As they grow older, they may not notice that someone is upset or hurting.

How to Manage Temperament Traits

First of all, **how you feel about your child's traits** affects how you can manage them. Some traits may be frustrating or embarrassing, and you may think people blame you, or you may blame yourself. If you let a trait upset you, you won't be able to manage it as well and your relationship can suffer. If you find traits disappointing, you may show your child less affection.

Trouble can also come when a trait is different than your own. For example, if you'd like your child to be adaptable and flexible like you, and he isn't, it can cause you to resent something that neither of you chose. Being upset with a child because of the way his temperament leads him to behave is like being upset at him for having poor eyesight. Just as there are ways to make up for poor eyesight, there are ways you can help him manage his traits. You both can learn to make them work for you, your child and your family.

Manage traits one at a time, instead of trying to deal with a whole style. If your child has high or low traits like those in the table, how *you* react can help her learn to react a little differently. Your child will behave best when you do things that fit with her temperament. Below, you'll find suggestions for managing traits. There will be an adjustment period, so give both of you time for things to work. Praise the reactions you like so they'll keep happening.

And—this is important—don't discipline your kids for having traits they were born with. Instead, limit the bad behaviors that happen because of the traits. Use P.S. I'M HELPING to decide if a behavior needs to be limited. For example, say your daughter with high intensity hauls off and hits her brother when she's mad. (Nice!) Try our suggestions here for managing her high intensity, *and* use an action limit to prevent her from hitting in the future.

How to manage high activity

Children with this trait are born *needing* to move—just like adults *need* enough sleep. So try not to criticize or call them names like "hyper," "bad" or "hard to handle." Instead, say, *"You're energetic, and fast, but Dad needs you to freeze (be still, sit on this chair) for a couple minutes."* Plan many times each day when they can move around as much as they want. Make home and yard areas where they can play and move a lot without causing trouble. Take breaks from active kids every day—use babysitters, or have them play in their rooms or playpen alone for a while. Minimize stimulation like TV and computer games.

Save yourself frustration by not planning to do many things that require them to sit still very long until they're older. But, when you need them to sit still for an activity, such as a religious service or a meal at Grandma's, take them to the park first or let them run around the yard before you go. Then bring along things they can play with while sitting (but don't expect them to stay seated for long). Give them time to cool down after being active and don't expect them to stop immediately.

Don't limit their movement unless you really need to, and don't punish them just for moving (they can't help it). But do reward less movement. *"If you stay sitting in the chair at... you can have... afterwards."* Be on the lookout for any calm, inactive time and praise it. *"I love when you sit and look at your books."* Make sure they get enough sleep and good food to keep up with their movement to avoid more crankiness.

Stay calm and quiet with your child. Have you ever seen a moving, loud little child whose parent is also moving and talking loudly, trying to get the child to settle down? The parent may be yanking at the child, saying, "Knock it off!" That child may have inherited this trait from that parent! But a parent's motion and loudness feeds a child's, making it worse. Instead, act like you're in a slow motion movie scene. Use a soft voice, or even whisper exactly what you want your child to do.

Many active children have symptoms of hyperactivity. **Hyperactivity means** moving without any purpose (fidgeting) so that it keeps children from doing what they need to do (see page 286).

How to manage low activity

If you have high energy, you might be frustrated by your child's slower mode. Please understand that this is NOT the same as laziness (not wanting to do any work). These kids can end up being very good workers, if they aren't criticized or called lazy. Give them extra time to do things, praise them for finishing, and don't mention how long it took. Make a big deal out of when you see them hurrying to do something. *"Wow—that was fast!"* Praise their other good qualities.

How to manage high adaptability

Teach your kids about peer pressure so they won't be as likely to pick up bad habits from other kids. Plus, don't expect them to always give in to you. These easy going kids may start to feel irritated if they think you don't compromise very often on your desires in order to meet theirs. And if other siblings get what they want by resisting you, your adaptable child may start resisting to try to get what he wants for once.

How to manage low adaptability

Use routines whenever possible. If a big change is necessary (such as a move to a new house, school or daycare), spread it out over time if you can, instead of making the change all at once. Give plenty of warning before something new will happen. Expect adjustments to take a while, and praise your children when they get used to a change. Avoid criticizing or pushing new things on them. That will make them *less* adaptable.

How to manage bold first reactions

Praise your kids for being friendly, but teach them about stranger danger and peer pressure to keep them safe. Don't expect that they'll always be bold, and don't show disappointment when they aren't.

How to manage cautious first reactions

Talk about your children's worries without making fun or putting them down. Tell them lots of people are **shy** and that you understand. Instead of pushing, gently encourage them to try new things. Try new things together. Don't avoid new situations, so they can have new experiences.

Here are things to say about facing something new. *"Let's try it together a little, and then if you don't like it, we can leave it alone." "Let's watch those other kids do it, and then if you feel like trying it, you can." "I can see why that tastes weird to you and why you might not like new tastes. It sure is yummy to me though. I bet you'll like it when you're older." "I remember being afraid of trying new things when I was your age—that's OK. It sure is fun once you get used to it though." "I remember when you were afraid of elevators. And now, you aren't at all. I am so proud of you! You won't mind doing this someday, too."*

When something new is coming up, help them get used to the idea before it happens. For example, make visits to a new day care before you leave them there. Break down new experiences into short ones and do a little at a time together. Talk about how to meet new people. *"Talking to new people is just being nice, and makes them feel good."* Explain that people often have to think about what they're going to say before they talk to someone. Practice having conversations.

When they get over a fear or try something new, praise them. *"I know you were worried about the new babysitter, but you were so nice to talk to her."* Praise makes them more confident and courageous to try something new again. Reacting with disappointment or anger can make a shy child even more cautious. Also don't assume that your children will always dislike or never try something they reacted negatively to. They'll gradually be bolder, but you can't force them to be. They may naturally decide they like something or someone later unless they feel pushed or have a bad experience the first time.

How to manage high distractibility (being easily distracted)

Give them gentle reminders for things they need to do. When they need to study or do a chore, make the area quiet and free of TV, people and noises. Try running a fan, or playing soft classical music to keep outside noises out. Really praise them when they finish things. You can even use rewards. When you tell them to do something, lay your hand on their shoulder and have them look at you while you talk. Have them repeat back what you said to help them understand and remember. Don't give them too many things to do at once. Follow our other talk to teach guidelines to help them listen. Don't allow them to interrupt your request by claiming they can't do it, or they don't understand. They need to listen to all the directions—*then* they can ask questions.

How to manage low distractibility (being hard to distract)

You may need to try harder to get their attention, but do it gently. Encourage them to take breaks during tasks like homework. Minimize media like TV, games and the internet, since they may spend hours wasting their time and tuning you out.

How to manage high intensity

Whatever you do, **don't overreact to their overreactions!** Adults are more able to stay calm than kids are. The more upset you get, the more intense *they* get. Reaching for them and yelling, "Stop it!" is an intense reaction, not a calm one. Calmly looking at them and quietly saying what you want works better.

If your intense child is upset and screaming, slowly and quietly say, *"I won't listen to you until you use a quiet voice."* Then ignore what she says until she quiets down. Say it again if needed. If her voice doesn't get quiet enough, say, *"I can't listen to you until you whisper quietly in my ear."* You can even whisper in her ear to get her attention. If she's moving a lot at the time, it may be asking too much for her to sit still also. Manage one thing at a time. Ignore things you don't need to react to. Pick your battles and stick to the important ones.

Try to identify when your children are getting too excited or over-stimulated and catch them before they act out. When you notice a raised voice, or rough motions, ask them to sit alone for 10 seconds. You can say, *"Use your inside voice."* They'll need reminders! Or ask them to do something else to distract them. Or, quietly say, *"Look in my eyes. You need to cool down. Let's count to 10 together."*

Teach your children what to do when they're frustrated instead of acting out. Ask your son how his body was feeling before things got out of hand. *"Use your words to tell me what you were feeling when you were frustrated. Tell me when it happens next time and then you won't get in trouble."* Or, when he starts getting intensely upset, teach him to cover his face with his hands and sit by himself while he counts to ten. He could also come to you for a little attention (hug and hold for a minute, quiet talk). Praise him for saying that he's upset instead of acting out. Be on the lookout for any calm reaction he has, and praise it. *"That was cool how you just let it go instead of getting upset. You're really growing up. (That made it more fun; Uncle Joe noticed it too.)"*

Don't give in to their intense demands just to get them to quiet down. Then they'll use intensity again to get what they want, by being loud and obnoxious. Also, sometimes their intense concerns will sound more serious than they really are. Judge their complaints by the facts, and not by how they express them.

How to manage low intensity

These kids may be hurting or have a serious problem, even when they don't act like it. When they do complain, take it seriously. Intense parents may find themselves frustrated by their children's calmness about good surprises and upsetting things. Don't forget that this is their natural way—they don't decide but just naturally react that way.

How to manage positive mood

Teach your children empathy. If they don't seem concerned about someone's distress, ask them how they think that person feels. Encourage giving that person attention and help. If you think something may be bothering your child, encourage him or her to talk about it and share feelings.

How to manage negative mood

Remember that this isn't anyone's fault, and that moodiness can come from things that happen because of their other traits too. Plus, this trait can change with time, especially if you do certain things. Remember that children with this trait need their parents just as much as children with more positive moods do. Separate your child's mood from yours. Try to stay calm and logical. Show them your pleasant mood often, even if you have to fake it.

To help them modify their mood, don't mention it that much—that can reinforce it. Instead, occasionally help them recognize their mood gently. *"Aren't you a grumpy guy today? That's no fun."* *"How about saying good morning?"* Give him a hug and smile if he does. You can ask him, *"Are you OK?"* when he seems grumpy. That can help him recognize how he's acting. Look for any pleasant or cheerful behavior and praise it. *"I just love it when you... (laugh, smile, are excited)."*

Kids with a negative mood often **complain or whine**. You can set action limits: *"If you whine or complain about anything this afternoon, we won't go to the movie."* Then don't let her go to the movie if she does. Praise her for not complaining. *"It is so nice for me when you don't complain—thanks."* Praise your kids when they let things go. Also, just because they complain doesn't mean their needs are more important than your other kids' needs.

How to manage high persistence

Don't try too hard to change this trait, or criticize it, since it can be a big asset in adulthood. For a toddler that keeps trying to get what she shouldn't have, remove it so she can't get it. For a child 4 years old or older who keeps asking for something, or who keeps getting into something she shouldn't, set an action limit. Don't give in to what your kids want just because they keep asking! When they can't have or do something, give them something else sometimes. *"I know you want to do that, but you can't. Would you like to ... instead?"*

If you know they'll need to stop doing something soon, give them a warning ahead of time. Don't let them start something when they'll have to quit soon. Get them into many different kinds of activities, and avoid screen games and the internet. (They may get addicted more easily than other kids.) Praise when they leave something fun without finishing. Tell them it's OK to finish some things later, or not at all. *"Hey, you put away the game without fussing—I sure appreciate that."*

How to manage low persistence

Allow these children more time to finish things than you think they ought to need. Help them learn to break jobs down into parts. They need to finish one part before taking a break. Make them responsible for coming back and finishing. You may need to remind them, or use an action limit. Reward finishing any little thing. *"Way to go, you did it! When you finish the next part, let's play catch."* Teach them to ask for help if they start to get frustrated, but don't do something for them when they could be doing it themselves. Do part of it, or give hints for what needs to be done. Then let them work alone and help as needed.

Provide a place for homework that is free of noise and other distractions, and have them do all their homework there. Break study time up, so your child works on one thing for a while, and then does more after a break. Use a schedule, and watch to make sure they follow it. Help with homework so that they don't lose interest because they can't figure it out by themselves.

How to manage high regularity

Your child will do best with routines and schedules. She'll be more comfortable, and you may avoid crankiness by providing them. For instance, don't leave the house without snacks if she always gets one at the time you'll be out. Let her know ahead of time when a routine will be interrupted or changed.

How to manage low regularity

While it's hard to know what to expect as far as eating, sleeping, or reactions, try not to be frustrated by something you have no control over. Let infants eat and sleep when they want. Gradually introduce schedules at 1 year of age. Children who are of preschool age and older should live by the family's schedule, including mealtimes, but with some flexibility. (If they aren't hungry at dinner, they could also have a snack later.) When they are of grade school age, teach them how to get snacks themselves, and then expect them to do it.

Have children follow a regular sleep schedule, even if they don't actually sleep regularly. They can lie in bed and look at books for a while if they aren't tired. Don't encourage irregular sleep by letting them get out of bed or be with you if they wake up or can't fall asleep.

Try to get them enough rest, even if it's on a strange schedule.

How to manage high sensitivity

Keep noise in your house to a minimum. Remove things that seem to bother your children. Have your children do all their homework in the same quiet area. If they keep mentioning a sound (like a ticking clock), take it away if possible. For sleeping problems, try running a fan to cover background noise. If they complain of itchy clothing, cut out clothing tags and use only clothing made from soft fabrics. Limit how much they watch media—TV, video games, and internet. Sensitive children may be overwhelmed by what they see. Don't overreact to their overreactions—stay calm and quiet when you respond to complaints. Encourage talking about how they feel, instead of acting out. When they do talk, give them attention and praise.

How to manage low sensitivity

First, this trait doesn't apply to small children, since they are NOT normally sensitive to the feelings and needs of other people. For older children (maybe mid elementary school and on), when you notice changes in things, bring it to their attention. This will help increase their sensitivity. *"It has really gotten hot today."* Help them notice feelings and senses. *"Oh, that lady lost her dog. She must be so sad."* *"Oh, that would really hurt." "What is that—it stinks!"* Watch closely to catch on when they're sick or hurting. When something seems to be bothering them, ask if they're feeling or thinking about something.

Every child has a unique temperament

Use this chapter to understand your children better by learning about the temperament traits that they were born with. Remember not to discipline your children for their natural traits, but only for the behaviors that violate P.S. I'M HELPING. Manage those traits that seem frustrating or worrisome to you in order to make them work well enough for you, your child and your family.

Appendix A

WHAT KIDS CAN DO BY AGE: Communication, self-care, social skills, and chores

This chart shows at what age children can typically learn to do things. If you're wondering if you can expect your child to do something, look it up here. In each row a different task or skill is described. There is a vertical column for each age. Shaded boxes mean that a child can start doing that task at those ages. An X means a child should be able to do it before then. For example, row number one shows that babies should be able to turn their eyes toward sounds before they are 1 year old (because the shaded box is in the <1 column).

- **Don't expect your child to do a task if he or she is younger than the age columns that have shaded boxes.** You're expecting too much. You can harm children by trying too much. For example, look at row number seven. Since the box in the < 1 year old column isn't shaded, don't expect a 10 month old to be able to point to most of his or her body parts.

- **If there's a shaded box in your child's age column, your child *may* be able to do the skill described** in that row. But notice there is usually more than one normal age at which children can do something consistently. Your child may only learn to do the skill at the oldest age column containing a shaded box, and that's normal. For example, kids can learn to point to body parts at age 1 **or** 2. It's normal to not be able to do it until age 2.

- **Where there's a box containing an X,** look up to the top of the column to find the age. If your child can't do the task at that age, you're expecting too little, or there could be a problem. If you haven't tried to teach your child the skill, do so now. If your child still appears to be unable to learn it, ask for professional advice. For example, if your child can't point to most body parts by age 3, see a professional. **If there is no X in a row,** it means children may be able to do it, but can't be expected to do it consistently—it's really an adult skill. (Please note, this chart may not work for children with special needs or developmental delays.)

	Ages at which children usually can do the skill or task
X	Age at which to get professional advice if you can't teach your child to do it

Age in years

Communication	<1	1	2	3	4	5	6	7	8	9	10	11	12	13	14	15	16	17
1	Turns eyes toward sounds.		X																
2	Tries to imitate sounds made by others.		X																
3	Can say single words and be understood.			X															
4	Shows that he or she understands the word "no."			X															
5	Responds to simple commands like "Give me a kiss."			X															
6	Calls siblings or friends by the same name or nickname. (Pronunciation doesn't need to be great.)			X															
7	Accurately points to most body parts (nose, hands, legs, elbow, teeth, neck, stomach, hair).				X														
8	Will say one or two words together ("play outside" "my car"). Pronunciation doesn't need be perfect.				X														

	Communication (continued)	<1	1	2	3	4	5	6	7	8	9	10	11	12	13	14	15	16	17
9	Accurately describes events in detail ("We went to the park. I fell and cried. Daddy got ice and I ate candy.")						X												
10	Can retell a simple joke, describe a show or repeat a story.						X												
11	Can recite all the letters of the alphabet without singing the song.							X											
12	Legibly prints his/her first and last names (reversed letters are fine).								X										
13	Can tell when someone is angry without the other person saying anything.								X										
14	Answers the phone—says hello and then gets the person the caller asked for.								X										
15	Correctly says your phone number when asked.								X										
16	Expresses ideas in more than one way. (If you don't understand what the child is talking about, he/she may show you something to help you understand.)								X										
17	Can print at least 15 simple words from memory.									X									
18	Can alphabetize a simple list.									X									

Communication (continued)	<1	1	2	3	4	5	6	7	8	9	10	11	12	13	14	15	16	17
19	Is interested in books or magazines and reads without being asked.										X								
20	Can place local phone calls to friends or family.											X							
21	Will NOT give out personal information to a stranger (address, saying if parents are home, etc.).												X						
22	Uses a book or online dictionary to define words.												X						
23	Follows commands that have up to four steps—"Go outside and pick up your toys. Then pick up the trash and throw it away." (Commands with fewer steps are found later in this table.)												X						
24	Can log onto internet websites.														X				
25	Can write in cursive when asked to.														X				
26	Can look up and call a phone number (even long distance).														X				
27	Will speak to strangers on the phone when necessary (call in a pizza order, ask a store clerk if an item is in stock).																X		

	Communication (continued)	<1	1	2	3	4	5	6	7	8	9	10	11	12	13	14	15	16	17
28	Can give complex, step-by-step directions (how to get from home to a place miles away, how to make a recipe, or how to solve a math problem).																X		
29	Responsibly uses a cell phone- doesn't lose it, stays within plan minutes, knows when not to use it (in class, while driving). (Note that there isn't an age that all kids can do this!)																		
30	Will not give out private information to strangers on the internet. (Note that there is no age at which kids can always do this, even when you explain).																		

	Self-Care	<1	1	2	3	4	5	6	7	8	9	10	11	12	13	14	15	16	17
1	Opens mouth and removes food from a spoon.		X																
2	Eats solid food.			X															
3	Understands that hot things are dangerous.			X															
4	Indicates with words or actions when diaper is dirty.			X															
5	Feeds self with a spoon without spilling very much (all kids spill sometimes).				X														

328 |

Self-Care (continued)	<1	1	2	3	4	5	6	7	8	9	10	11	12	13	14	15	16	17
6	Poops and pees in a potty-chair or toilet (has few daytime accidents).					X												
7	Does not poop in underpants during the night.						X											
8	Does not pee in underpants at night. (See doctor if child is not dry at age 7, but usually this just takes time.)												X						
9	Wipes own bottom after bowel movements.							X											
10	Can fasten most buttons, snaps and zippers.							X											
11	Fastens own seat belt or booster seat belt in the car.								X										
12	Can tie shoelaces without help.									X									
13	Can shower/bathe, including washing/drying hair alone.										X								
14	Will dress for the weather if he/she knows about it (will wear a coat/hood etc. if knows that it will snow).											X							
15	Will finish homework with a reminder. (Child will need help with topics he/she doesn't understand).											X							

Self-Care (continued)	<1	1	2	3	4	5	6	7	8	9	10	11	12	13	14	15	16	17
16 Can tell time by five minute intervals without a digital clock (knows when it's five or ten minutes "after the hour").									░	░	░	X						
17 Can use a stove and microwave alone (turn on and off, set to the right temperature and time, clean up spills).												░	░	░	X			
18 Uses basic household cleaners properly (laundry soap, window and bathroom cleaners).												░	░	░	X			
19 Cares for own finger and toe nails without help.												░	░	░	X			
20 Can care for own minor health needs (puts a band-aid on small cuts, takes medicine as shown on the bottle, reads thermometer, knows how to contact doctor or ambulance).												░	░	░	X			
21 Completes homework without reminding (will still need help with topics he/she doesn't understand).													░	░	░	X		
22 Earns spending money regularly.																	░	░
23 Saves money for big future purchases (college, a car, etc.).																	░	░

Self-Care (continued)	<1	1	2	3	4	5	6	7	8	9	10	11	12	13	14	15	16	17
24 Can manage a checking account (doesn't lose checkbook or bounce checks).																▓	▓	▓
25 Responsibly holds a part-time job (goes to work on time, notifies employer when sick or delayed, gets clothes/uniforms ready).																	▓	▓
26 Can responsibly use a credit card. (Note that there is no age at which every child can do this!)																		▓

Social Skills	<1	1	2	3	4	5	6	7	8	9	10	11	12	13	14	15	16	17
1 Shows interest in caregivers (smiles, reaches up to and touches).	▓	X																
2 Shows affection for others (give kisses, cuddles, etc.).	▓	X																
3 Shows interest in what other people are doing or their toys.	▓	▓	X															
4 Laughs along with others even if he/she doesn't understand what was funny.	▓	▓	▓	X														
5 Seems to want to please caregivers.				▓	X													
6 Plays make-believe.					X													
7 Seems to like some playmates more than others.					X													

Social Skills (continued)	<1	1	2	3	4	5	6	7	8	9	10	11	12	13	14	15	16	17
8	Can say when he/she feels happy, sad, or scared.					X													
9	Sometimes shares toys and other things without being told.							X											
10	Will compliment or praise caregivers (says "good girl Mommy").							X											
11	Prefers to play with others, rather than play alone, when other kids are around.							X											
12	Takes turns and follows rules of simple games without being reminded.							X											
13	Apologizes for unplanned mishaps or accidents.							X											
14	Generally follows rules at day care or school.								X										
15	Responds nicely when introduced to strangers (says "hi," shakes hands, etc.)									X									
16	Says "please" and "thank you" without being reminded.									X									
17	Will unexpectedly tell parent "I love you."									X									
18	Brings up that he/she wants to buy small gifts for family/friends.										X								

Social Skills (continued)	<1	1	2	3	4	5	6	7	8	9	10	11	12	13	14	15	16	17
19	Keeps "good secrets" for longer than a day (won't tell sibling about a gift).										X								
20	Returns things he/she has borrowed without being reminded (a sibling's toy, library book, etc.).											X							
21	Doesn't say things that he/she knows will embarrass others (such as "Are you pregnant? You look fat").												X						
22	Can order from a restaurant menu and use table manners (doesn't chew with mouth open or talk too loud, uses utensils and napkins, stays seated).													X					
23	Recognizes when she or he is being manipulated (controlled unfairly by others for their own benefit) by another child. But your child probably won't know what to do about it.														X				
24	Understands that advertisements don't always tell the truth.															X			
25	Usually thinks about the consequences of his/her behaviors before acting (but still may not be able to make good decisions).															X			

Appendix A: What Kids Can Do by Age

	<1	1	2	3	4	5	6	7	8	9	10	11	12	13	14	15	16	17
Social Skills (Continued)																		
26	Will sometimes start conversations about things that he/she knows are interesting to another person ("How was work today Mom?")														X			
27	Has two or more friends with whom he/she often does things, both in and out of school.														X			
28	Recognizes when others need assistance and offers to help.														X			
29	Remembers people's birthdays without reminders.															X		
30	Begins to recognize his or her sexual identity.																	
31	Goes on a date with other people along. (Date should be of appropriate age).																	
32	Goes on a date alone (these dating items are just appropriate ages for dating-these aren't skills that kids need).																	
	<1	1	2	3	4	5	6	7	8	9	10	11	12	13	14	15	16	17
Chores																		
1	Can follow specific one-step commands ("Please give me the book.") He/she will do that and then follow your next command, like, "Now hold your cup."			X															

Chores (continued)	<1	1	2	3	4	5	6	7	8	9	10	11	12	13	14	15	16	17
2	Can follow two-step commands ("Pick up the book and put it on the table" or "Pick up the paper and throw it away.")				X														
3	Can do two totally different tasks when asked ("Please get your shoes on and get me my coat.")							X											
4	Can do three different tasks when asked ("Please finish your homework, set the table and feed the dog.")												X						
5	Can clear the dining table, and only rarely break something.							X											
6	Can dry dishes with a towel.								X										
7	Can empty trash cans in the house and take them to a garbage bin.									X									
8	Can make own bed when asked (but won't do it as well as an adult can).									X									
9	Can load dishwasher.										X								
10	Can tell if laundry is dirty or clean.										X								
11	Sweeps, mops, or vacuums the floor without help.											X							
12	Can feed and clean up after a family pet alone.												X						

Chores (continued)	<1	1	2	3	4	5	6	7	8	9	10	11	12	13	14	15	16	17
13 Can clean a bathroom alone (use cleaners to clean the sink, shower/tub, toilet, floor), but not as well as you can.													X					
14 Can clean the kitchen by him/herself (but probably not as well as you can).													X					
15 Can water plants without being reminded.														X				
16 Can straighten own room without being reminded.															X			
17 Can run the washing machine and dryer (separates clothes, uses correct amount of detergent, usually reads and follows clothing labels, folds clothing).																X		
18 Can watch a younger child for less than an hour while an adult at home is busy.																	X	
19 Can baby sit for at least two hours without adult supervision.																	X	
20 Can make a complete meal alone.																		
21 Can run simple errands for you by foot, bike or car (getting milk, going to the post office).																		
22 Can take proper care of a car (gets the oil changed, knows it has enough gas).																		

Appendix B

FEELING WORDS TO TEACH YOUR CHILDREN: Words to use when they are happy, sad, scared, confused, or angry

When kids learn to say how they're feeling, they'll act out and get in trouble a lot less. Using words about feelings helps build relationships and emotional intelligence. Here are words that describe common ways people feel. Some of the words are about *why* people feel that way. Some kid-friendly definitions are given.

Use these words with your kids by saying, *"I feel_____"* and you will teach your kids to say them when they feel the same way. Or, try to guess how they are feeling: *"I think you feel..." "It seems like you feel..." "You might feel..."* or *"I'm wondering if you feel..."* If you say, *"Sounds like you feel flustered,"* and they say, "Huh?" you can say, *"That means very confused and frustrated."* You don't have to get the definitions just right—the point is to talk about feelings so your children learn to do it.

Other words for HAPPY

		STRONG		
Excited	Ecstatic	Energized	Thrilled	Loved
Elated	Terrific	Enthusiastic	Uplifted	Marvelous
		MEDIUM		
Admired	Cheerful	Valued	Encouraged	Relieved
Joyful	Alive	Grateful	Accepted	Respected
Proud	Confident	Appreciated	Amused	Delighted
Assured: to feel certain or confident				
Gratified: to satisfy a desire and feel rewarded				
Justified: to feel that something is proven right, or there is a good reason for something				
		MILD		
Content	Glad	Peaceful	Fulfilled	Flattered
Relaxed	Satisfied	Hopeful	Pleased	Fortunate
Lucky				

Other words for SCARED

STRONG				
Fearful	Panicky	Terrified	Dread	Shocked
Alarmed	Desperate	Horrified	Tormented	Frantic

Appalled: to be struck with fear or dread
Dismayed: to feel sudden loss of courage because of trouble
Petrified: to feel paralyzed with fear, hard to move or act
Vulnerable: to feel open to attack, hurt, criticism, temptation

MEDIUM				
Tense	Threatened	Uneasy	Skeptical	Shaken
Overwhelmed	Startled	Insecure	Swamped	Afraid

Apprehensive: to feel uneasy that something bad may happen
Defensive: to protect against real or imaginary attacks to the ego, like criticism, even if it could be helpful feedback
Intimidated: to feel forced or threatened to do something

MILD				
Anxious	Shy	Timid	Doubtful	Unsure
Impatient	Nervous	Concerned	Suspicious	

Reluctant: to feel unwilling or resistant

Other words for CONFUSED

STRONG				
Trapped	Immobilized	Baffled	Flustered	Disoriented

Bewildered: to feel something is hard to figure out because of many conflicting things involved
Perplexed: to feel that things are very complicated and uncertain

MEDIUM				
Misunderstood	Awkward	Torn	Troubled	Foggy
In doubt	Puzzled	Disorganized	Hesitant	

Ambivalent: to feel both positive and negative about something or someone, making it hard to make a choice

MILD			
Surprised	Distracted	Uncomfortable	Undecided
Unsettled	Bothered	Uncertain	Unsure

Other words for SAD

STRONG				
Devastated	Helpless	Empty	Terrible	Disgraced
Hopeless	Crushed	Miserable	Unwanted	Rejected
Sorrowful	Worthless	Defeated	Unloved	Hurt
Wounded	Burdened	Abandoned	Mournful	

Anguished: to feel intense mental pain

Dejected: to feel lw spirits or downhearted

Condemned: to feel strongly disapproved of and judged unfit

Depressed: to feel pushed down or in a gray cloud, with physical symptoms like sleeping or eating changes or pain, feeling so sad that it's hard to function

Distraught: to feel very emotionally agitated, extremely worried or upset

Exploited: to feel used or taken advantage of for someone else's benefit

Humiliated: to feel that pride, self-respect or dignity is lowered; shamed or embarrassed

MEDIUM				
Lonely	Drained	Disappointed	Unappreciated	Distant
Neglected	Slighted	Inadequate	Discouraged	Lost
Isolated	Degraded	Disheartened	Ashamed	Dismal
Alienated	Humbled	Unhappy	Distressed	Upset

Deprived: to feel that something needed is taken away or withheld

Disillusioned: disappointed that something is false, or not reality

Regretful: to feel sad about something lost or done

Resigned: to give up on or accept something unwanted

MILD			
Sorry	Bad	Deflated	Disturbed

Apathetic: showing little or no emotion, interest or concern

Disenchanted: to be disappointed that something turned out to be not as good as you thought

Other words for ANGRY

STRONG				
Furious	Abused	Pissed off	Mad	Sabotaged
Seething	Hateful	Outraged	Used	Betrayed
Enraged	Ticked off	Fuming	Irate	

Hostile: feeling unfriendly or like an enemy
Incensed: to feel inflamed with extreme anger at something unjust
Patronized: to feel put down by someone who acts superior
Rebellious: resisting authority or control
Spiteful: wanting to be mean or hurt people for revenge, not forgiving
Vindictive: to feel (and act) like you want revenge

MEDIUM				
Resentful	Offended	Agitated	Perturbed	Grumpy
Disgusted	Controlled	Frustrated	Dominated	Upset
Smothered	Peeved	Irritated	Cheated	

Aggravated: to feel that something is making you angry
Coerced: to feel forced or threatened to do something
Exasperated: to feel extremely annoyed
Harassed: to feel persistently attacked or irritated by someone
Provoked: to feel that anger is stirred up by something or someone
Ridiculed: to feel made fun of or mocked

MILD			
Uptight	Displeased	Miffed	Annoyed

Dismayed: to lose enthusiasm for something
Tolerant: respecting something even though you don't agree with it

Other Good Sources of Information for Parents

American Academy of Family Physicians: Numerous articles at **www.familydoctor.org**

American Academy of Pediatrics: Numerous articles at **www.AAP.org/parents.html**

Baker, D. (2004). *What Happy People Know.* New York: St Martin's Griffin.

Cohen-Sandler, R., & Silver, M. (1999). *"I'm Not Mad, I Just Hate You!"* New York: Penguin Putnam.

Severe, S. (2000). *How to Behave so your Children Will, Too!* New York: Penguin Putnam.

Sheedy Kurchinka, M. (1998). *Raising your Spirited Child.* New York: Harper Collins Perennial.

Steinberg, L. (2004). *The Ten Basic Principles of Good Parenting.* New York: Simon and Schuster.

Walsh, D. (2004). *Why Do They Act That Way?* New York: Simon and Schuster Free Press.

References

Discipline

Arnold, D. S., O'Leary, S. G., Wolff, L. S., & Acker, M. M. (1993). "The Parenting Scale: A Measure of Dysfunctional Parenting in Discipline Situations." *Psychological Assessment, 5*(2), 137–144.

Dopke, C. A., Lundahl, B. W., Dunsterville, E., & Lovejoy, M. C. (2003). "Interpretations of Child Compliance in Individuals at High- And Low-Risk for Child Physical Abuse." *Child Abuse and Neglect, 27*(3), 285–302.

Gaffney, K. F., Barndt-Maglio, B., Myers, S., & Kollar, S. J. (2002). "Early Clinical Assessment for Harsh Child Discipline Strategies." *American Journal of Maternal/Child Nursing, 27*(1), 34-40.

Gordon, T. (1991). *Discipline That Works: Promoting Self-Discipline in Children.* New York: Penguin Putnam.

Heidgerken, A. D., Hughes, J. N., Cavell, T. A., & Willson, V. L. (2004). "Direct and Indirect Effects of Parenting and Children's Goals on Child Aggression." *Journal of Clinical Child and Adolescent Psychology, 33*(4), 684–693.

Herrenkohl, R. C., & Russo, M. J. (2001). "Abusive Early Child Rearing and Early Childhood Aggression." *Child Maltreatment, 6*(1), 3–16.

Kilgore, K., Snyder, J., & Lentz, C. (2000). "The Contribution of Parental Discipline, Parental Monitoring, and School Risk to Early-Onset Conduct Problems in African

American Boys and Girls." *Developmental Psychology, 36*(6), 835–845.

Knutson, J. F., DeGarmo, D., Koeppl, G., & Reid, J. B. (2005). "Care Neglect, Supervisory Neglect, and Harsh Parenting in the Development of Children's Aggression: A Replication and Extension." *Child Maltreatment, 10*(2), 92–107.

Lansford, J. E. et al. (2006). "Developmental Trajectories of Externalizing and Internalizing Behaviors: Factors Underlying Resilience in Physically Abused Children." *Development and Psychopathology, 18*(1), 35–55.

Lorber, M. F., & Slep, A. M. (2005). "Mothers' Emotion Dynamics and Their Relations with Harsh and Lax Discipline: Microsocial Time Series Analyses." *Journal of Clinical Child and Adolescent Psychology, 34*(3), 559–568.

Mandara, J. (2003). "The Typological Approach in Child and Family Psychology: A Review Of Theory, Methods, and Research." *Clinical Child and Family Psychology Review, 6*(2), 129–146.

Mann, D., Corell, A. P., Ludy-Dobson, C., & Perry, B. D. (2002). "Child Physical Abuse." In D. Levinson (Ed.), *Encyclopedia of Crime and Punishment* (Vol. 1, pp. 197–202). Thousand Oaks, CA: Sage.

Mulvaney, M. K., & Mebert, C. J. (2007). "Parental Corporal Punishment Predicts Behavior Problems in Early Childhood." *Journal of Family Psychology, 21*(3), 389–397.

National Center on Child Abuse and Neglect, National Child Abuse and Neglect Data System. Factsheets and publications. Washington DC: U.S. Department of Health and Human Services. Retrieved from http://www.acf.hhs.gov/programs/cb/stats_research/index.htm#cw

National Clearinghouse on Child Abuse and Neglect Information. (2003). *Children and Domestic Violence: A Bulletin for Professionals.* Retrieved from http://library.adoption.com/articles/children-and-domestic-violence-a-bulletin-for-professionals.html

Nix, R. L., Pinderhughes, E. E., Dodge, K. A., Bates, J. E., Pettit, G. S., & McFadyen-Ketchum, S. A. (1999). "The Relation Between Mothers' Hostile Attribution Tendencies and Children's Externalizing Behavior Problems: The Mediating Role of Mothers' Harsh Discipline Practices." *Child Development, 70*(4), 896–909.

Perry, B. D., Colwell, K., & Schick, S. (2002). "Child Neglect." In D. Levinson (Ed.), *Encyclopedia of Crime and Punishment* (Vol. 1., pp 192–196). Thousand Oaks, CA: Sage.

Pinderhughes, E. E., Dodge, K. A., Bates, J. E., Pettit, G. S., & Zelli, A. (2000). "Discipline Responses: Influences of Parents' Socioeconomic Status, Ethnicity, Beliefs About Parenting, Stress, and Cognitive-Emotional Processes." *Journal of Family Psychology, 14*(3), 380–400.

Romano, E., Tremblay, R. E., Boulerice, B., & Swisher, R. (2005). "Multilevel Correlates of Childhood Physical Aggression and Prosocial Behavior." *Journal of Abnormal Child Psychology, 33*(5), 565–578.

Sege, R. D., Hatmaker-Flanigan, E., DeVos, E., Levin-Goodman, R., & Spivak, H. (2006). "Anticipatory Guidance And Violence Prevention: Results From Family And Pediatrician Focus Groups". *Pediatrics, 117*(2), 455–463.

Smith, J. R., & Brooks-Gunn, J. (1997). "Correlates and Consequences of Harsh Discipline for Young Children." *Archives of Pediatric and Adolescent Medicine, 151*(8), 777–786.

Steinberg, L., Lamborn, S. D., Dornbusch, S. M., & Darling, N. (1992). "Impact of Parenting Practices on Adolescent Achievement: Authoritative Parenting, School Involvement and Encouragement to Succeed." *Child Development, 63*, 1266–1281.

Drug, Alcohol and Tobacco Use (also see Media Influence)

American Academy of Child and Adolescent Psychiatry. (2004). *Teens: Alcohol and Other Drugs.* http://www.aacap.org/cs/root/facts_for_families/teens_alcohol_and_other_drugs

American Academy of Pediatrics Committee on Substance Abuse. (1999). "Marijuana: A Continuing Concern for Pediatricians." *Pediatrics, 104*(4), 982–985.

Bahr, S. J., Hoffmann, J. P., & Yang, X. (2005). "Parental and Peer Influences on the Risk of Adolescent Drug Use." *The Journal of Primary Prevention, 26*(6), 529–551.

Bush, T., Curry, S. J., Hollis, J., Grothaus, I., Ludman, E., McAfee, T., et al. (2005). "Preteen Attitudes About Smoking and Parental Factors Associated with Favorable Attitudes." *American Journal of Health Promotion, 19*(6), 410–417.

Chen, C. Y., Storr, C. L., & Anthony, J. C. (2005). "Influences of Parenting Practices on the Risk of Having a Chance to Try Cannabis." *Pediatrics, 115*(6), 1631–1639.

Fergusson, D. M., Boden, J. M., & Horwood, L. J. (2006). "Cannabis Use and Other Illicit Drug Use: Testing the Cannabis Gateway Hypothesis." *Addiction, 101*(4), 556–569.

Hall, W. D. (2006). "Cannabis Use and the Mental Health of Young People." *Australian and New Zealand Journal of Psychiatry, 40*(2), 105–113.

Hall, W. D., & Lynskey, M. (2005). "Is Cannabis a Gateway Drug? Testing Hypotheses About the Relationship Between Cannabis Use and the Use of Other Illicit Drugs." *Drug and Alcohol Review, 24*(1), 39–48.

Hashibe, M., Straif, K., Tashkin, D. P., Morgenstern, H., Greenland, S., & Zhang, Z. F. (2005). "Epidemiologic Review of Marijuana Use and Cancer Risk." *Alcohol, 35*(3), 265–275.

Jacobsen, L. K., Pugh, K. R., Constable, R. T., Westerveld, M., & Mencl, W. E. (2007). "Functional Correlates of Verbal Memory Deficits Emerging During Nicotine Withdrawal in Abstinent Adolescent Cannabis Users." *Biological Psychiatry, 61*(1), 31–40.

Kelly, E., Darke, S., & Ross, J. (2004). "A Review of Drug Use and Driving: Epidemiology, Impairment, Risk Factors and Risk Perceptions." *Drug and Alcohol Review, 23*(3), 319–344.

Patock-Peckham, J. A., Cheong, J., Balhorn, M. E., & Nagoshi, C. T. (2001). "A Social Learning Perspective: A Model of Parenting Styles, Self-Regulation, Perceived Drinking Control, and Alcohol Use And Problems." *Alcoholism: Clinical Experimental Research, 25*(9), 1284–1292.

Plancherel, B., Bolognini, M., Stephan, P., Laget, J., Chinet, L, Bernard, M., et al. (2005). "Adolescents' Beliefs About Marijuana Use: A Comparison of Regular Users, Past Users and Never/Occasional Users." *Journal of Drug Education, 35*(2), 131–146.

Schepis, T. S., & Rao, U. (2005). "Epidemiology and Etiology of Adolescent Smoking." *Current Opinion in Pediatrics, 17*(5), 607–612.

Schwartz, R. H. (2002). "Marijuana: A Decade and a Half Later, Still a Crude Drug with Underappreciated Toxicity." *Pediatrics, 109*(2), 284–289.

Wadsworth, E. J., Moss, S. C., Simpson, S. A., & Smith, A. P. (2006). "Cannabis Use, Cognitive Performance and Mood in a Sample of Workers." *Journal of Psychopharmacology, 20*(1), 14–23.

Zvolensky, M. J., Bernstein, A., Sachs-Ericsson, N., Schmidt, N. B., Buckner, J. D., & Bonn-Miller, M. O. (2006). "Lifetime Associations Between Cannabis Use, Abuse, and Dependence and Panic Attacks in a Representative Sample." *Journal of Psychiatric Research*, 40(6), 477–486.

Early Childhood

American Academy of Pediatrics. (2004). *Caring for Your Baby and Young Child, Birth to Age 5* (Rev. ed.). New York: Bantam.

Bates, J. E., Olson, S. L., Pettit, G. S., & Bayles, K. (1982). "Dimensions of Individuality in the Mother-Infant Relationship at Six Months of Age." *Child Development, 53*, 446–461.

Belsky, J., & Fearon, R. M. (2002). "Early Attachment Security, Subsequent Maternal Sensitivity, and Later Child Development: Does Continuity in Development Depend upon Continuity of Caregiving?" *Attachment and Human Development,* 4(3), 361–387.

Bonstein, M. H. (1985). "How Infant and Mother Jointly Contribute to Developing Cognitive Competence in the Child." *Proceedings of the National Academy of Sciences, 82*, 7470–7473.

Brook, J. S., Zheng, L., Whiteman, M., & Brook, D. W. (2001). "Aggression in Toddlers: Associations with Parenting and Marital Relations." *The Journal of Genetic Psychology, 162*(2), 228–241.

Campbell, S. B. (1995). "Behavior Problems in Preschool Children: A Review of Recent Research." *The Journal of Child Psychology and Psychiatry, 36* (1), 113–149.

Coates, D. L., & Lewis, M. (1984). "Early Mother-Infant Interaction and Infant Cognitive Status as Predictors of School Performance and Cognitive Behavior in Six-Year-Olds." *Child Development, 55*, 1219–1230.

Deater-Deckard, K. (2000). "Parenting and Child Behavioral Adjustment in Early Childhood: A Quantitative Genetic Approach to Studying Family Processes." *Child Development, 71*(2), 468–484.

DeVito, C., & Hopkins, J. (2001). "Attachment, Parenting and Marital Dissatisfaction as Predictors of Disruptive Behavior in Preschoolers." *Development and*

Psychopathology, 13(2), 215–231.

Landry, S. H., Smith, K., Miller-Loncar, C. L., & Swank, P. R. (1998). "The Relation of Change in Maternal Interactive Styles to the Developing Social Competence of Full-Term and Preterm Children." *Child Development, 69*(1), 105–123.

Landry, S. H., Smith, K. E., & Swank, P. R. (2003). "The Importance of Parenting During Early Childhood for School-Age Development." *Developmental Neuropsychology, 24*(2-3), 559–591.

Landry, S. H., Smith, K. E., Swank, P. R., Assel, M. A., & Vellet, S. (2001). "Does Early Responsive Parenting Have a Special Importance for Children's Development or Is Consistency Across Early Childhood Necessary?" *Developmental Psychology, 37*(3), 387–403.

Landry, S. H., Smith, K. E., Swank, P. R., & Miller-Loncar, C. L. (2000). "Early Maternal and Child Influences on Children's Later Independent Cognitive and Social Functioning." *Child Development, 71*(2), 358–375.

Lewis, M. D. (1993). "Early Socioemotional Predictors of Cognitive Competency at 4 Years." *Developmental Psychology, 29*(6), 1036–1045.

Londerville, S., & Main, M. (1981). "Security of Attachment, Compliance, and Maternal Training Methods in the Second Year of Life." *Developmental Psychology, 17*(3), 289–299.

National Institute of Child Health and Human Development. (1996). "Characteristics of Infant Child Care: Factors Contributing to Positive Caregiving." *Early Childhood Research Quarterly, 11,* 269–306.

National Institute of Child Health and Human Development Early Child Care Research Network. (1997). "The Effects of Infant Child Care on Infant-Mother Attachment Security: Results of the NICHD Study of Early Child Care." *Child Development, 68*(5), 860–879.

National Institute of Child Health and Human Development Early Child Care Research Network. (1998). "Early Child Care and Self-Control, Compliance, and Problem Behavior at Twenty-Four And Thirty-Six Months." *Child Development, 69*(4), 1145–1170.

National Institute of Child Health and Human Development Early Child Care Research Network. (2000). "The Relation of Child Care to Cognitive and Language Development." *Child Development, 71*(4), 960–980.

National Institute of Child Health and Human Development Early Child Care Research Network. (2003). "Early Child Care and Mother-Child Interaction from 36 Months Through First Grade." *Infant Behavior and Development, 26,* 345–370.

National Institute of Child Health and Human Development. (2004). *The NICHD Study of Early Child Care and Youth Development.* Retrieved from http://www.nichd.nih.gov/publications/pubs/upload/seccyd_051206.pdf

Olson, S. L., Bates, J. E., & Bayles, K. (1984). "Mother-Infant Interaction and the Development of Individual Differences in Children's Cognitive Competence." *Developmental Psychology, 21*(1), 166–179.

Renfrew, M. J., Lang, S., Martin, L., & Woolridge, M. W. (2000). Feeding Schedules in Hospitals for Newborn Infants. *Cochrane Database of Systematic Reviews, 2000*

(2), CD000090.

Shaw, D. S., Keenan, K., Vondra, J. I., Delliquadri, E., & Giovannelli, J. (1997). "Antecedents of Preschool Children's Internalizing Problems: A Longitudinal Study of Low-Income Families." *Journal of the American Academy of Child and Adolescent Psychiatry, 36*(12), 1760–1767.

Skinner, E. A. (1986). "The Origins of Young Children's Perceived Control: Mother Contingent and Sensitive Behavior." *International Journal of Behavioral Development, 9*, 359–382.

Webster-Stratton, C. (1998). "Preventing Conduct Problems in Head Start Children: Strengthening Parenting Competencies." *Journal of Consulting and Clinical Psychology, 66*(5), 715–730.

General Parenting Topics

American Humane. (2007). *Fact Sheets on Child Sexual Abuse, Child Neglect, Emotional Abuse, Child Physical Abuse,* and *Child Abuse and Neglect in America. What The Data Say.* Retrieved from www.americanhumane.org.

Asbury, K., Dunn, J. F., Pike, A., & Plomin, R. (2003). "Nonshared Environmental Influences on Individual Differences in Early Behavioral Development: A Monozygotic Twin Differences Study." *Child Development, 74*(3), 933–943.

Bensley, L., Ruggles, D., Simmons, K. W., Harris, C., Williams, K., Putvin, T., et al. (2004). "General Population Norms About Child Abuse and Neglect and Associations with Childhood Experiences." *Child Abuse and Neglect, 28*(12), 1321–1337.

Bor, W., & Sanders, M. R. (2004). "Correlates of Self-Reported Coercive Parenting of Preschool-Aged Children at High Risk for the Development of Conduct Problems." *Australian and New Zealand Journal of Psychiatry, 38*(9), 738–745.

Bradley, R. H., & Corwyn, R. F. (2007). "Externalizing Problems in Fifth Grade: Relations with Productive Activity, Maternal Sensitivity, and Harsh Parenting from Infancy Through Middle Childhood." *Developmental Psychology, 43*(6), 1390–1401.

Briesmeister, J. M., & Schaefer, C. E. (Eds.). (1998). *Handbook of Parent Training: Parents as Co-Therapists for Children's Behavior Problems* (2nd ed.). New York: John Wiley & Sons.

Caissy, G.A., & Toepfer, C.F. (2002). Early Adolescence: Understanding the 10 to 15 Year Old. Cambridge, MA: Perseus Publishing.

Chung, H. L., & Steinberg, L. (2006). "Relations Between Neighborhood Factors, Parenting Behaviors, Peer Deviance, and Delinquency Among Serious Juvenile Offenders." *Developmental Psychology, 42*(2), 319–331.

Ciarrochi, J., Forgas, J. P., & Mayer, J. D. (Eds.). (2001). *Emotional Intelligence in Everyday Life: A Scientific Inquiry.* Philadelphia: Psychology Press.

Colder, C. R., Lochman, J. E., & Wells, K. C. (1997). "The Moderating Effects of Children's Fear and Activity Level on Relations Between Parenting Practices and Childhood Symptomatology." *Journal of Abnormal Child Psychology, 25*(3), 251–

346 |

263.

Deater-Deckard, K., Dodge, K. A., Bates, J. E., & Pettit, G. S. (1998). "Multiple Risk Factors in the Development of Externalizing Behavior Problems: Group and Individual Differences." *Development and Psychopathology, 10*, 469–493.

Dworkin, P. H. (2003). "Families Matter—Even for Kids in Child Care." *Journal of Developmental and Behavioral Pediatrics, 24*(1), 58–62.

Edwards, M. E. (2002). "Attachment, Mastery, and Interdependence: A Model of Parenting Processes." *Family Process, 41*(3), 389–404.

Feldman, S. S., & Weinberger, D. A. (1994). "Self-Restraint as a Mediator of Family Influences on Boys' Delinquent Behavior: A Longitudinal Study." *Child Development, 65*, 195–211.

Ferdinand, R. F., Bongers, I. L., van der Ende, J., van Gastrel, W., Tick, N., Utens, E., et al. (2006). "Distinctions Between Separation Anxiety and Social Anxiety in Children and Adolescents." *Behaviour Research and Therapy, 44*(11), 1523–1535.

Fiese, B. H., Tomcho, T. J., Douglas, M., Josephs, K., Poltrock, S., & Baker, T. (2002). "A Review of 50 Years of Research on Naturally Occurring Family Routines and Rituals: Cause for Celebration?" *Journal of Family Psychology, 16*(4), 445–446.

Forgatch, M. S., Degarmo, D. S., & Beldavs, Z. G. (2005). "An Efficacious Theory-Based Intervention for Stepfamilies." *Behavioral Therapy, 36*(4), 357–365.

Furnham, A., & Cheng, H. (2000). "Perceived Parental Behavior, Self-Esteem and Happiness." *Social Psychiatry and Psychiatric Epidemiology, 35*(10), 463–470.

Gaensbauer, T., & Wamboldt, M. (2000). *Proposal for CPS and CCAPS Statement Regarding Gun Violence.* American Academy of Child & Adolescent Psychiatry. Retrieved from http://www.aacap.org/

Gardner, F. E. (1989). "Inconsistent Parenting: Is There Evidence for a Link with Children's Conduct Problems?" *Journal of Abnormal Child Psychology, 17*(2), 223–233.

Goldstein, S., & Brooks, R. B. (Eds.). (2006). *Handbook of Resilience in Children.* New York: Springer.

Hembree-Kigin, T. L., & McNeil, C. B. (1995). *Parent-Child Interaction Therapy.* New York: Plenum Press.

Herz, L, & Gullone, E. (1999). "The Relationship Between Self-Esteem and Parenting Style: A Cross-Cultural Comparison of Australian and Vietnamese Australian Adolescents." *Journal of Cross-Cultural Psychology, 30*(6), 742–761.

Hibbs, E. D., & Jensen, P. S. (Eds.). (1996). *Psychosocial Treatments for Child and Adolescent Disorders: Empirically Based Strategies for Clinical Practice.* Washington, DC: American Psychological Association.

Kazdin, A. E., & Weisz, J. R. (2003). *Evidence-Based Psychotherapies for Children and Adolescents.* New York: Guilford Press.

Knafo, A., & Plomin, R. (2006). "Parental Discipline and Affection and Children's Prosocial Behavior: Genetic and Environmental Links." *Journal of Personality and Social Psychology, 90*(1), 147–164.

Knight, G. P., Tein, J. Y., Shell, R., & Roosa, M. (1992). "The Cross-Ethnic Equivalence of Parenting and Family Interaction Measures Among Hispanic and Anglo-

American Families." *Child Development, 63*(6), 1392–1403.

Knutson, J. F., DeGarmo, D. S., & Reid, J. B. (2004). "Social Disadvantage and Neglectful Parenting as Precursors to the Development of Antisocial and Aggressive Child Behavior: Testing a Theoretical Model." *Aggressive Behavior, 30*, 187–205.

Lansford, J.E., Malone, P.S., Castellino, D.R., Dodge, K.A., Pettit, G.S. & Bates, J.E. (2006). "Trajectories of Internalizing, Externalizing, and Grades for Children Who Have and Have Not Experienced Their Parents' Divorce or Separation." *Journal of Family Psychology, 20*(2), 292-301.

Lengua, L. J., Wolchik, S. A., Sandler, I. N., & West, S. G. (2000). "The Additive and Interactive Effects of Parenting and Temperament in Predicting Adjustment Problems of Children of Divorce." *Journal of Clinical Child Psychology, 29*(2), 232–244.

Lindsay, A. C., Sussner, K. M., Kim, J., & Gortmaker, S. (2006). "The Role of Parents in Preventing Childhood Obesity." *The Future of Children, 16*(1), 169–186.

Martinez, C. R., & Forgatch, M. S. (2001). "Preventing Problems with Boys' Noncompliance: Effects of a Parent Training Intervention for Divorcing Mothers." *Journal of Consulting and Clinical Psychology, 69*(3), 416–428.

McKee, T. E., Harvey, E., Danforth, J. S., Ulaszek, W. R., & Friedman, J. L. (2004). "The Relation Between Parental Coping Styles and Parent-Child Interactions Before and After Treatment for Children with ADHD and Oppositional Behavior." *Journal of Clinical Child Adolescent Psychology, 33*(1), 158–168.

Mrazek, D. A., Mrazek, P., & Klinnert, M. (1995). "Clinical Assessment of Parenting." *Journal of the American Academy of Child and Adolescent Psychiatry, 34*(3), 272–289.

National Institute of Child Health and Human Development. (2001). *Adventures in Parenting: How Responding, Preventing, Monitoring, Mentoring, and Modeling Can Help You Be a Successful Parent.* NIH Pub. No. 00-4842. Retrieved from http://www.nichd.nih.gov

National Rifle Association. (2006). *Parents' Guide to Gun Safety.* Retrieved from http://www.nrahq.org/safety/eddie/infoparents.asp

Petry, N. M., & Steinber, K. L. (2005). "Child Maltreatment in Male and Female Treatment-Seeking Pathological Gamblers." *Psychology of Addictive Behaviors, 19*(2), 226–229.

Pevalin, D. J., Wade, T. J., & Brannigan, A. (2003). "Precursors, Consequences and Implications for Stability and Change in Pre-Adolescent Antisocial Behaviors." *Prevention Science, 4*(2), 123–136.

Rorty, M., Yager, J., & Rossotto, E. (1995). "Aspects of Childhood Physical Punishment and Family Environment Correlates in Bulimia Nervosa." *Child Abuse and Neglect, 19*(6), 659–667.

Ruiz, S. Y., Roosa, M. W., & Gonzales, N. A. (2002). "Predictors of Self-Esteem for Mexican American and European American Youths: A Reexamination of the Influence of Parenting." *Journal of Family Pscyhology, 16*(1), 70–80.

Schneider, W. J., Cavell, T. A., & Hughes, J. N. (2003). "A Sense of Containment:

Potential Moderator of the Relation Between Parenting Practices and Children's Externalizing Behaviors." *Development and Psychopathology, 15*(1), 95–117.

Shelton, K. K., Frick, P. J., & Wootton, J. (1996). "Assessment of Parenting Practices in Families of Elementary School-Age Children." *Journal of Clinical Child Psychology, 25*(3), 317–329.

Shoebridge, P. J., & Gowers, S. G. (2000). "Parental High Concern and Adolescent Onset Anorexia Nervosa." *The British Journal of Psychiatry, 176*, 132–137.

Smetana, J. G., & Daddis, C. (2002). "Domain-Specific Antecedents of Parental Psychological Control and Monitoring: The Role of Parenting Beliefs and Practices." *Child Development, 73*(2), 563–580.

Stanger, C., Dumenci, L., Kamon, J., & Burstein, M. (2004). "Parenting and Children's Externalizing Problems in Substance-Abusing Families." *Journal of Clinical Child and Adolescent Psychology, 33*(3), 590–600.

Størksen, I., Røysamb, E., Holmen, T.L., & Tambs, K. (2006). Adolescent Adjustment and Well-being: Effects of parental divorce and distress. *Scandinavian Journal of Psychology, 47*, 75-84.

Stormshak, E. A., Bierman, K. L., McMahon, R. J., & Lengua, L. J. (2000). "Parenting Practices and Child Disruptive Behavior Problems in Early Elementary School. Conduct Problems Prevention Research Group." *Journal of Clinical Child Psychology, 29*(1), 17–29.

Totsika, V., & Sylva, K. (2004). "The HOME Observation for Measurement of the Environment Revisited." *Child and Adolescent Mental Health, 9*(1), 25–35.

Whiteside, M. F. (1998). "The Parental Alliance Following Divorce: An Overview." *Journal of Marital and Family Therapy, 24*(1), 3–24.

Media Influence on Children

American Academy of Pediatrics. Committee on Public Education. (2001). "Children, Adolescents and Television." *Pediatrics, 107*(2), 423–426.

American Academy of Pediatrics. Committee on Public Education. (2001). "Media Violence." *Pediatrics, 108*(5), 1222–1226.

Brown, J. D., L'Engle, K. L., Pardun, C. J., Guo, G., Kenneavy, K., & Jackson, C. (2006). "Sexy Media Matter: Exposure to Sexual Content in Music, Movies, Television, and Magazines Predicts Black and White Adolescents' Sexual Behavior." *Pediatrics, 117*(4), 1018–1027.

Browne, K. D., & Hamilton-Giachritsis, C. (2005). "The Influence of Violent Media on Children and Adolescents: A Public-Health Approach." *Lancet, 365*(9460), 702–710.

Bushman, B. J., & Cantor, J. (2003). "Media Ratings for Violence And Sex. Implications for Policymakers and Parents." *American Psychologist, 58*(2), 130–141.

Bushman, B. J., & Huesmann, L. R. (2006). "Short-Term and Long-Term Effects of Violent Media on Aggression in Children and Adults." *Archives of Pediatrics and Adolescent Medicine, 160*(4), 348–352.

Cantor, J. (2000). "Media Violence." *Journal of Adolescent Health, 27*(2 Supplement), 30–34.

Champion, H. L., & Durant, R. H. (2001). "Exposure to Violence and Victimization and the Use of Violence by Adolescents in the United States." *Minerva Pediatrica, 53*(3), 189–197.

Cheng, T. L., Brenner, R. A., Wright, J. L., Sachs, H. C., Moyer, P., & Rao, M. R. (2004). "Children's Violent Television Viewing: Are Parents Monitoring?" *Pediatrics, 114*(1), 94–99.

Coyne, S. M., Archer, J., & Eslea, M. (2004). "Cruel Intentions on Television and in Real Life: Can Viewing Indirect Aggression Increase Viewers' Subsequent Indirect Aggression?" *Journal of Experimental Child Psychology, 88*(3), 234–253.

Earles, K. A., Alexander, R., Johnson, M., Liverpool, J., & McGhee, M. (2002). "Media Influences on Children and Adolescents: Violence and Sex." *Journal of the National Medical Association, 94*(9), 797–801.

Escobar-Chaves, S. L., Tortolero, S. R., Markham, C. M., Low, B. J., Eitel, P, & Thickstun, P. (2005). "Impact of the Media on Adolescent Sexual Attitudes and Behaviors." *Pediatrics, 116*(1), 303–326.

Fremont, W. P. (2004). "Childhood Reactions to Terrorism-Induced Trauma: A Review of the Past 10 Years." *Journal of the American Academy of Child and Adolescent Psychiatry, 43*(4), 381–392.

Fremont, W. P., Pataki, C., & Beresin, E. V. (2005). "The Impact of Terrorism on Children and Adolescents: Terror in the Skies, Terror on Television." *Child and Adolescent Psychiatric Clinics of North America, 14*(3), 429–451.

Funk, J. B. (2005). "Children's Exposure to Violent Video Games and Desensitization to Violence." *Child and Adolescent Psychiatric Clinics of North America, 14*(3), 387–404.

Gentile, D. A., Lynch, P. J., Linder, J. R., & Walsh, D. A. (2004). "The Effects of Violent Video Game Habits on Adolescent Hostility, Aggressive Behaviors, and School Performance." *Journal of Adolescence, 27*(1), 5–22.

Gentile, D. A., & Stone, W. (2005). "Violent Video Game Effects on Children and Adolescents. A Review of the Literature." *Minerva Pediatrica, 57*(6), 337–358.

Haninger, K., Ryan, M. S., & Thompson, K. M. (2004). "Violence in Teen-Rated Video Games." *Medscape General Medicine, 6*(1), 1.

Haninger, K., & Thompson, K. M. (2004). "Content and Ratings of Teen-Rated Video Games." *Journal of the American Medical Association, 291*(7), 856–865.

Huesmann, L. R., Moise-Titus, J., Podolski, C. L., & Eron, L. D. (2003). "Longitudinal Relations Between Children's Exposure to TV Violence and Their Aggressive and Violent Behavior in Young Adulthood: 1977–1992." *Developmental Psychology, 39*(2), 201–221.

Lee, E., & Kim, M. (2004). "Exposure to Media Violence and Bullying at School: Mediating Influences of Anger and Contact with Delinquent Friends." *Psychological Reports, 95*(2), 659–672.

Strasburger, V. C. (2004). "Children, Adolescents, and the Media." *Current problems in Pediatrics and Adolescent Health Care, 34*, 54–113.

Strasburger, V. C. (2005). "Adolescents, Sex, and the Media: Ooooo, Baby, Baby—A Q & A." *Adolescent Medicine Clinics, 16*(2), 269–288.

Tamburro, R. F., Gordon, P. L., D'Apolito, J. P., & Howard, S. C. (2004). "Unsafe and Violent Behavior in Commercials Aired During Televised Major Sporting Events." *Pediatrics, 114*(6), e694–698.

Veenema, T. G., & Schroeder-Bruce, K. (2002). "The Aftermath of Violence: Children, Disaster, and Posttraumatic Stress Disorder." *Journal of Pediatric Health Care, 16*(5), 235–244.

Villani, S. (2001). "Impact of Media on Children and Adolescents: A 10-Year Review of the Research." *Journal of the American Academy of Child and Adolescent Psychiatry, 40*(4), 392–401.

Walma van der Molen, J. H. (2004). "Violence and Suffering in Television News: Toward a Broader Conception of Harmful Television Content for Children." *Pediatrics, 116*(6), 1771–1775.

Walsh, D. A., Gentile, D. A., & Van Brederode, T. M. (2002). "Parents Rate The Ratings: A Test Of The Validity Of The American Movie, Television, And Video Game Ratings." *Minerva Pediatrica, 54*(1), 1–11.

Wolak, J., Finkelhor, D., & Mitchell, K. (2004). "Internet-Initiated Sex Crimes Against Minors: Implications for Prevention Based on Findings from a National Study." *Journal of Adolescent Health, 35*(5), 424.e11–20.

Wooding, S., & Raphael, B. (2004). "Psychological Impact of Disasters and Terrorism on Children and Adolescents: Experiences from Australia." *Journal of Prehospital and Disaster Medicine, 19*(1), 10–20.

Mental Health

Biederman, J., Petty, C., Faraone, S. V., Hirshfeld-Becker, D. R., Henin, A., Rauf, A., et al. (2005). "Childhood Antecedents to Panic Disorder in Referred and Nonreferred Adults." *Journal of Child and Adolescent Psychopharmacology 15*(4), 549–561.

Brost, L., & Johnson, W. (1995). "Retrospective Appraisals of Fathers' Effectiveness and Psychological Health of Adults." *Psychological Reports, 77*(3, Pt. 1), 803–807.

Chorpita, B. F., & Barlow, D. H. (1998). "The Development of Anxiety: The Role of Control in the Early Environment." *Psychological Bulletin, 124*(1), 3–21.

Dwyer, S. B., Nicholson, J. M., & Battistutta, D. (2003). "Population Level Assessment of the Family Risk Factors Related to the Onset of or Persistence of Children's Mental Health Problems." *Journal of Child Psychology and Psychiatry, 44*(5), 699–711.

Hill, N. E., Bush, K. R., & Roosa, M. W. (2003). "Parenting and Family Socialization Strategies and Children's Mental Health: Low-Income Mexican-American and Euro-American Mothers and Children." *Child Development, 74*(1), 189–204.

Kavanaugh, M., Halterman, J. S., Montes, G., Epstein, M., Hightower, D., & Weitzman, M. (2006). "Maternal Depressive Symptoms Are Adversely Associated with Prevention Practices and Parenting Behaviors for Preschool Children."

Ambulatory Pediatrics, 6(1), 32–37.

Lesesne, C. A. & Kennedy, C. (2005). "Starting Early: Promoting the Mental Health of Women and Girls Throughout the Life Span." *Journal of Women's Health, 14*(9), 754–763.

Muris, P., Schmidt, H., Lambrichs, R., & Meesters, C. (2001). "Protective and Vulnerability Factors of Depression in Normal Adolescents." *Behaviour Research and Therapy, 39*(5), 555–565.

Waters, T. L., & Barrett, P. M. (2000). "The Role of the Family in Childhood Obsessive-Compulsive Disorder." *Clinical Child and Family Psychology Review, 3*(3), 173–184.

Parenting Style

Aunola, K., Stattin, H., & Nurmi, J. E. (2000). "Parenting Styles and Adolescents' Achievement Strategies." *Journal of Adolescence, 23*(2), 205–222.

Baker, B. L., & Heller, T. L. (1996). "Preschool Children with Externalizing Behaviors: Experience of Fathers and Mothers." *Journal of Abnormal Child Psychology, 24*(4), 513–532.

Barber, B. K., Stolz, H. E., & Olson, J. A. (2005). "Parental Support, Psychological Control, and Behavioral Control: Assessing Relevance Across Time, Culture, and Method." *Monographs of the Society for Research in Child Development, 70*, 1–137.

Baumrind, D. (1991). "The Influence of Parenting Style on Adolescent Competence and Substance Use." *Journal of Early Adolescence, 11*(1), 56–95.

Bednar, D. E., & Fisher, T. D. (2003). "Peer Referencing in Adolescent Decision Making as a Function of Perceived Parenting Style." *Adolescence, 38*(152), 607–621.

Cohen, D. A. & Rice, J. (1997). "Parenting Styles, Adolescent Substance Use, and Academic Achievement." *Journal of Drug Education, 27*(2), 199–211.

Day, D. M., Peterson-Badali, M., & Ruck, M. D. (2006). "The Relationship Between Maternal Attitudes and Young People's Attitudes Toward Children's Rights." *Journal of Adolescence, 29*(2), 193–207.

Dornbusch, S. M., Ritter, P. L., Leiderman, P. H., Roberts, D. F., & Fraleigh, M. J. (1987). "The Relation of Parenting Style to Adolescent School Performance." *Child Development, 58*(5), 1244–1257.

Ferrari, J. R., & Olivette, M. J. (1993). "Perceptions of Parental Control and the Development of Indecision Among Late Adolescent Females." *Adolescence, 28*(112), 963–970.

Maccoby, E. E., & Martin, J. A. (1983). "Socialization in the Context of the Family: Parent-Child Interaction." *Handbook of Child Psychology, 4*, 1–101, 119–138.

Patock-Peckham, J. A., & Morgan-Lopez, A. A. (2006). "College Drinking Behaviors: Mediational Links Between Parenting Styles, Impulse Control, and Alcohol-Related Outcomes." *Psychology of Addictive Behaviors, 20*, 117–125.

Querido, J. G., Warner, T. D., & Eyberg, S. M. (2002). "Parenting Styles and Child

Behavior In African American Families of Preschool Children." *Journal of Child and Adolescent Psychology, 31*(2), 272–277.

Smetana, J. G. (1995). "Parenting Styles and Conceptions of Parental Authority During Adolescence." *Child Development, 66*, 299–316.

Steinberg, L., Lamborn, S. D., Darling, N., Mounts, N. S., & Dornbusch, S. M. (1994). "Over-Time Changes in Adjustment and Competence Among Adolescents from Authoritative, Authoritarian, Indulgent and Neglectful Families." *Child Development, 65*(3), 754–770.

Steinberg, L., Mounts, N. S., Lamborn, S. D., & Dornbusch, S. M. (1991). "Authoritative Parenting and Adolescent Adjustment Across Varied Ecological Niches." *Journal of Research on Adolescence, 1*(1), 19–36.

Stice, E., Barrera, M., & Chassin, L. (1993). "Relation of Parental Support and Control To Adolescents' Externalizing Symptomatology and Substance Use: A Longitudinal Examination of Curvilinear Effects." *Journal of Abnormal Child Psychology 21*(6), 609–621.

Thompson, A., Hollis, C., & Richards, D. (2003). "Authoritarian Parenting Attitudes as a Risk for Conduct Problems: Results from a British National Cohort Study." *European Child and Adolescent Psychiatry, 12*, 84–91.

Parenting Teenagers (see other sections also)

Allen, J. P., Hauser, S. T., Bell, K. L., & O'Connor, T. G. (1994). "Longitudinal Assessment of Autonomy and Relatedness in Adolescent-Family Interactions as Predictors of Adolescent Ego Development and Self-Esteem." *Child Development, 65*, 179–194.

American Academy of Child and Adolescent Psychiatry. (2005). *Normal Adolescent Development: Middle and Early High School Years.* Retrieved from http://www.aacap.org/publications/factsfam/develop.htm

American Academy of Family Physicians. (2006). *Understanding your Teenager's Emotional Health.* Retrieved from http://familydoctor.org/590.xml

Berg-Nielsen, T. S., & Holen, A. (2003). "From Clinical Towards Research Interview: Parenting Problems with Troubled Adolescents." *Scandinavian Journal of Psychology, 44*(4), 319–329.

Beyers, W., & Goossens, L. (1999). "Emotional Autonomy, Psychosocial Adjustment and Parenting: Interactions, Moderation and Mediating Effects." *Journal of Adolescence, 22*(6), 753–769.

Blodgett Salafia, E. H., Gondoli, D. M., Corning, A. F. McEnery, A. M., & Grundy, A. M. (2007). "Psychological Distress as a Mediator of the Relation Between Perceived Maternal Parenting and Normative Maladaptive Eating Among Adolescent Girls." *Journal of Counseling Psychology, 54*(4), 434–446.

Borawski, E. A., Ievers-Landis, C. E., Lovegreen, L. D., & Trapl, E. S. (2003). "Parental Monitoring, Negotiated Unsupervised Time, and Parental Trust: The Role of Perceived Parenting Practices in Adolescent Health Risk Behaviors." *Journal of Adolescent Health, 33*, 60–70.

D'Angelo, S. L., & Omar, H. A. (2003). "Parenting Adolescents." *International Journal of Adolescent Medicine and Health, 15*(1), 11–19.

DeVore, E. R., & Ginsburg, K. R. (2005). "The Protective Effects of Good Parenting on Adolescents." *Current Opinion in Pediatrics, 17*(4), 460–465.

Fohr, S. A., Layde, P. M., & Guse, C. E. (2005). "Graduated Driver Licensing in Wisconsin: Does It Create Safer Drivers?" *Wisconsin Medical Journal*, 104(7), 31–36.

Galambos, N. L., Barker, E. T., & Almeida, D. M. (2003). "Parents Do Matter: Trajectories of Change in Externalizing and Internalizing Problems in Early Adolescence." *Child Development 74*(2), 578–594.

Giedd, J. N., Blumenthal, J., Jeffries, N. O., Castellanos, F. X., Liu, H., Zijdenbos, A., et al. (1999). "Brain Development During Childhood and Adolescence: A Longitudinal MRI Study." *Nature Neuroscience, 2*(10), 861–863.

Henricson, C. & Roker, D. (2000). "Support for the Parents of Adolescents: A Review." *Journal of Adolescence, 23*, 763–783.

National Institute of Mental Health. (2008). *Teenage Brain: A Work in Progress.* Retrieved from www.nimh.nih.gov/publicat/teenbrain.cfm

Parker, R. (2002). *Adolescence is Tough on the Brain.* Retrieved from www.futurepundit.com/archives/000603.html

Pedersen, W. (1994). "Parental Relations, Mental Health and Delinquency in Adolescents." *Adolescence, 29*(116), 975–991.

Sinha, J. W., Cnaan, R. A., & Gelles, R. J. (2007). "Adolescent Risk Behaviors and Religion: Findings from a National Study." *Journal of Adolescence, 30*(2), 231–249.

Sowell, E. R., Thompson, P. M., Holmes, C. J., Jernigan, T. L., & Toga, A. W. (1999). "In Vivo Evidence for Post–Adolescent Brain Maturation in Frontal and Striatal Regions." *Nature Neuroscience, 2*(10), 859–861.

Strasburger, V. C. (2000). "Getting Teenagers to Say No to Sex, Drugs and Violence in the New Millennium." *Medical Clinics of North America, 84*(4), 787–810.

Thompson, P. M., Giedd, J. N., Woods, R. P., MacDonald, D., Evans, A. C., & Toga, A. W. (2000). "Growth Patterns in the Developing Brain Detected by Using Continuum Mechanical Tensor Maps." *Nature, 404*(6774), 190–193.

Tiggemann, M. A. (2001). "The Impact of Adolescent Girls' Life Concerns and Leisure Activities on Body Dissatisfaction, Disordered Eating, and Self-Esteem." *The Journal of Genetic Psychology, 162*(2), 133–142.

Weiss, L. H., & Schwarz, J. C. (1996). "The Relationship Between Parenting Types and Older Adolescents' Personality, Academic Achievement, Adjustment, and Substance Use." *Child Development, 67*(5), 2101–2114.

Sexuality (see Media and Teenager sections also)

American Academy of Child & Adolescent Psychiatry. (2006, Jan 2). *Talking to Your Kids About Sex.* AACAP Facts for Families #62. Retrieved from http://www.aacap.org/publications/factsfam/62.htm

Brown, J. D., L'Engle, K. L., Pardun, C. J., Guo, G., Kenneavy, K., & Jackson, C. (2006). "Sexy Media Matter: Exposure to Sexual Content in Music, Movies, Television, and Magazines Predicts Black and White Adolescents' Sexual Behavior." *Pediatrics, 117*(4), 1018–1027.

Hacker, K. A., Amare, Y., Strunk, N., & Horst, L. (2000). "Listening to Youth: Teen Perspectives on Pregnancy Prevention." *Journal of Adolescent Health, 26*(4), 279–288.

Hornor, G. (2004). "Sexual Behavior in Children: Normal or Not?" *Journal of Pediatric Health Care, 18*(2), 57–64.

Moscicki, A. B. (2005). "Impact of HPV Infection in Adolescent Populations." *Journal of Adolescent Health, 37*(6 Supplement), S3–9.

Partridge, J. M., & Koutsky, L. A. (2006). "Genital Human Papillomavirus Infection in Men." *The Lancet Infectious Diseases, 6*(1), 21–31.

Rich, M. (2005). "Sex Screen: The Dilemma of Media Exposure and Sexual Behavior." *Pediatrics, 116*(1), 329–331.

Rose, A., Koo, H. P., Bhaskar, B., Anderson, K., White, G., & Jenkins, R. R. (2005). "The Influence of Primary Caregivers on the Sexual Behavior of Early Adolescents." *Journal of Adolescent Health, 37*(2), 135–144.

Rosenbaum, J. (2006). "Reborn a Virgin: Adolescents' Retracting of Virginity Pledges and Sexual Histories." *American Journal of Public Health, 96*(6), 1098–1103.

Santelli, J., Ott, M. A., Lyon, M., Rogers, J., Summers, D., & Schleifer, R. (2006). "Abstinence and Abstinence-Only Education: A Review of U.S. Policies and Programs." *Journal of Adolescent Health, 38*(1), 72–81.

Wilson, H. W., & Donenberg, G. (2004). "Quality of Parent Communication About Sex and its Relationship to Risky Sexual Behavior Among Youth in Psychiatric Care: A Pilot Study." *Journal of Child Psychology and Psychiatry, 45*(2), 387–395.

Temperament

Carey, W. (2005). *Understanding your Child's Temperament*. New York: Simon and Schuster Macmillan.

Keogh, B. K. (2005). *How Temperament Affects Parents, Children and Family Life*. Retrieved from http://www.greatschools.net/cgi-bin/showarticle/3060

Leve, L. D., Kim, H. K., & Pears, K. C. (2005). "Childhood Temperament and Family Environment as Predictors of Internalizing and Externalizing Trajectories from Age 5 To Age 17." *Journal of Abnormal Child Psychology, 33*(5), 505–520.

Thomas, A., & Chess, S. (1977). *Temperament and Development*. New York: Brunner/Mazel.

INDEX

Action limits, 120–32
  using with punishments, 121
  using with rewards, 131
  what they are, 121
Activities, 146
  over-scheduling, 153, 289
  relationship building. *See* chapter 2
Activity level
  temperament, 311, 315
Adaptability level
  temperament, 311, 316
Addiction, 82, 195, 200
  withdrawal symptoms, 195
Adoption, 287
Aggression, 53, 167, 174, 192
Alcohol, 10, 88, 175, 197, 204, 245, 258, 259
Allowance, 106
Anger
  affecting discipline, 125
  healthy expression, 54
  helping children control it, 288, 295
  helping parents control it, 53, 133
  in children, 17, 115, 189, 238, 261, 306
  in parents, 11, 13, 81, 114
  preventing, 7, 18
  unhealthy expression, 53
  ways to stay cool list, 55
Anxiety
  associated with drugs, 202, 259
  helping children with, 289

in children, 78, 137, 147, 152, 154, 157, 165, 193, 194, 214, 245, 309
  in parents, 11, 282
Arguing, 63, 68, 86, 93–100, 243
Assertive, 54, 190
Attention
  activities, 33
  children asking for, 50
  too little, 32
  too much, 31
Attention Deficit Hyperactivity Disorder (ADHD), 286
Attitude, 241–43
Bed wetting, 298
Bedrooms, 151, 198
Bedtime, 48, 300, 321
  infants, 231
Biting, 289
Body image, 157, 196, 246
Boredom, 152, 260, 262
Brain development, 194, 235–40
Bribing children, 105
Bullying, 85, 190
Capable versus able, 124
Cell phones, 169, 184, 258
Character
  building, 77, 84
Cheating, 150, 290
Child abuse, 175
  if you suspect it, 176
Children respecting parents, 14
Choices for kids, 63
Choosing your battles, 84, 137, 242, 318

Chores, 87, 150, 333
Cigarettes, 88, 197, 203, 259
Clubs, 146, 152
Colic, 231
Commands
    how to give, 58
Community service, 152
Complaining, 82, 93, 320
    attitude, 241
Compliments, 66, 156
Compromise, 90, 94, 242
Confidence, 87, 104, 149, 159,
    309, 317
Conflict resolution
    between parent and child, 94
    between siblings, 269
Consequences. *See*
    punishments, *See* rewards
    natural, 118–20
    what they are, 102
Consistency, 79, 92, 132, 134,
    136–42
    between caregivers, 140
    survey, 141
Controlling children, 145–152
    psychologically, 151
Correcting children, 70
Counseling help, 290
Crankiness, 15, *See* Mood
Criticism, 70, 157, 247
Crying
    at bedtime, 301
    colic, 231
    infants, 219, 220, 228, 231
    parents, 13, 54
    toddlers, 218, 220, 228
Curfew, 119, 244, 260
Dating
    parents, 284

teens, 203, 253
Day care, 292
Debate, 86, 95–98, 167, 243,
    257
    common debates kids use, 96
Defiance, 125, 244
Delaying gratification, 161
Denial, 9
Depression
    associated with drug use,
        202, 259
    in children, 137, 151, 154,
        156, 157, 165, 190, 193,
        197, 214, 245
    in parents, 11, 54, 217, 282
Disappointments, 159
Discipline. *See* chapter 5
    toddlers, 227–31
Disrespect
    children disrespecting
        parents, 81, 86, 187, 240,
        243
    parents disrespecting
        children, 68, 93
Distractibility level
    high versus low, 311, 317
Divorce or separation, 273–80
Domestic violence, 12, 176,
    276
Dressing style, 146, 183, 246,
    260
Driving, 80, 204, 258
Drugs. See substance use
Eating disorders, 151, 156, 197
Emotional intelligence, 40, 68,
    294, 336
Emotional reactions, 12–16, 81
    teenagers, 239
Empathy, 85, 266

teaching, 41, 299, 319
towards infants/toddlers, 221
Encopresis, 299
Enuresis, 298
Expectations
  for children, 6, 103, 323
  for parents, 7
  grades, 149
  neatness, 150
  other activities, 146
  sports, 148
Faith, 42, 43, 108, 147, 197,
  260
Family, 14, 42, 43, 80, 145,
  153, 186, 265
Family bed, 301
Family meetings, 49, 80
Fear, 11, 125, 193, 261, 292
  long lasting, 193, 208
  shy or cautious temperament,
    309, 317
Feeling words, 40, 69, 336–39
Feelings, 55
  sharing hurt, 69
  talking to kids about, 39
First reactions
  bold versus cautious, 311,
    316
Foster parenting, 293–94
Friends, 47, 185–189, 254–57
  bad influence, 188
  monitoring, 181
  rejection, 186
  using drugs, 202
  when they go too far, 255
Gambling, 201
Games. See video and computer
  games
Gangs, 105, 189, 190, 194, 204

Gifted and talented, 294
Giving up, 243
Good attention
  activities, 33
  ways to give it, 47
  what it means, 29
Good enough parent, 7
Grades, 82, 149, 153, 156, 172,
  187, 194, 260
  money and rewards for, 108
Grounding, 126
Guilt, 125, 139
Guns, 205
Happiness, 63, 109, 183, 197
  talking to kids about, 41
Helicopter parent, 168
Helplessness, 214
Hitting, 91, 115, 224, 288, 295
Homework, 48, 154, 244
Homosexuality, 253
House rules, 90, 123
Human papilloma virus (HPV),
  249
Hyperactivity, 260, 286, 316
I think/I feel statements, 68,
  110, 244, 252, 336
Illness, 156
Impulses, 237, 239
Impulsive behavior, 167, 286
Inconsistency, 79, 137
  definition, 92
Independence, 146, 163, See
  parenting styles
  teenagers, 240, 242, 244, 255
  toddlers, 229
Infants. See Chapter 8
  feeding, 219, 232
  helping them learn, 221–27
  holding, 220

Infatuation, 253
Intelligence, 40, 156, 237
Intensity level
    temperament, 312, 318
Internet, 196, 198, 200, 256
Intervention, 244
Intrusive parenting, 182
Irresponsibility, 78, 84, 135,
    170
Kicking, 295
Kindness
    teaching, 85
Laziness, 316, *See* Motivation
Learning, 149
    infants and toddlers, 221
Limits
    and temperament, 83
    compromising on, 92
    flexible, 92
    how to enforce, 121
    how to set, 88
    long-term, 89
    on character, 84
    P.S. I'M HELPING, 80
    personal choices, 84
    short-term, 89
    too hard, 78, 83
    too soft, 78
    what they are, 77
    wiggle room, 91
Listening
    to children, 39, 67
    to parents, 53, 71, *See* Talk to
        teach guidelines
Lying, 86, 296
Manners, 60, 80, 85, 138, 303
    toddlers, 227
Marijuana, 165, 167, 202, 258,
    259

addiction, 202
Masturbation, 206, 239
Materialistic values, 107
Media, 191–202
    body image, 196, 246
    decreasing risks of, 197
    influence of, 192
    internet, 200
    news, 194
    ratings, 198
    recommended limits, 197–
        198
        games, 199
    sexual content, 195–197
    substance use, 197
    television, 191, 192, 195, 198
    types of, 191
    violence, 192–195
Memory in teenagers, 238
Methamphetamines, 260
Mirror, mirror on the wall, 55
Money, 30, 31, 42
    for grades, 108
    materialistic values, 107
Monitoring, 189, *See* Chapter 7,
    See Parenting styles
    teenagers, 253, 260, 262
Mood, 15
    of children, 48
    of parents, 20, 55, 217
    of teenagers, 239
    temperament, 312, 319
Motivation, 64, 87, 104, 108,
    149, 172, 202, 238, 268
    toddlers, 221, 224
Music, 152, 199, 262
    videos, 193, 196
Natural consequences, 110,
    118–20

Neatness, 150
Neglect, 174
Nightmares and night terrors, 297
Obedience. *See* Chapters 4, 5, *See* Talk to teach guidelines
what to expect, 103
Obesity, 157
Open communication, 94, 172, 182, 262
Overreactions, 17, 318, 322
Over-scheduling, 153, 289
P.S. I'M HELPING, 79–84
How Emotional, 81
I'm Not Going there, 82
Important Morals and Manners, 80
Long-term Problem, 81
Personal Safety, 80
Pacifiers, 297
Parent playtime, 43–47
Parent time-out, 111, 217
Parenting style, 145, 163–176
balanced, 172–173
controlling, 164–166
helicopter parent, 168–172
neglecting, 174–175
permitting, 166–172
Parties, 257
Peer pressure, 184–185
Persistence level
high versus low, 313, 320
Personal choices, 84, 146
Playing doctor, 207
Pornography, 196
Potty training, 124, *See* toilet training
Practice sessions, 60, 138
Praise, 64–67, 87, 106, 131

danger of, 155
of toddlers, 229
Prayer, 9, 55
Prefrontal brain cortex, 237
Problem solving
teaching kids, 162
Psychological control, 151
Punishments, 110–18
defined, 102
five conditions for, 122
harsh, 114–18
mild, 110–14
using in action limits, 121
Pushing your buttons, 81
Reality testing, 83, 184
Regularity level
temperament, 313, 321
Relationship savings account, 30
Relationships. *See* Chapter 2
building activities, 33
good signs, 5
importance of, 4
strength survey, 21
Religion, 146, 152, 203
Requests
how to give, 58
Resilience, 159–163, 289
Respect
children respecting parents, 17, 19, 54, 80, 86, 93, 123, 125
parents respecting children, 67, 93
Respectful behavior
building in children. *See* Talk to teach guidelines
Responsibility, 63, 69, 87, 106, 135, 163, 169, 172, 258, 262

Rewards, 104–9
  defined, 102
  in action limits, 131
Rights of teenagers, 256
Routines, 90, 275
  infants, 225
Rule of 3's, 10
Safe personal choices, 84, 94,
  146
Screaming, 318
Self care for children, 327
Self defense, 208
Self-confidence, 64, *See*
  confidence
  infants, 223
Self-determination rights, 165,
  167
Self-esteem
  and punishment, 115
  building, 57, 72, 159, 246
  healthy, unhealthy levels, 71,
  161
  in children, 70, 147, 151,
  157, 172, 185, 189, 197,
  246
  of parents, 21, 147
Selfishness, 170, 299
Sensitive responding to infants,
  215–21
Sensitivity level
  temperament, 313, 322
Separation anxiety, 300
Sex. *See* sexuality, *See* media
  telling children about, 158
Sexual abuse
  prevention, 207–209
Sexual harassment, 205
Sexuality
  birth control, 250

brain center, 239
delaying activity, 251
pregnancy, 250
sex education, 250
STDs, 249
Sharing, 85, 226
Shyness, 317
Sibling rivalry, 264–71
  fighting, 268
Single parenting, 281–85
Sleeping problems, 300, *See*
  bedtime
Social skills, 61, 186, 330
Spanking, 114, 116, 175
Special time, 34–37
Special treatment, 161
Spoiling children, 30–32
  parenting style, 167
  with money, 107
Sports, 146, 148, 152
Stealing, 302
Stepfamilies, 278–80
Stinking thinking, 18, 66, 81
Stranger danger, 208
Stress, 6, 9, 13, 21, 53, 84, 176
  how to decrease, 9
Substance use, 10, 137, 174,
  175, 197, 259–61, 245, 259–
  61, *See* Meth, *See* Marijuana,
  See cigarettes, *See* Alcohol
  and money, 107
  decreasing risks, 203–204
  signs of, 260
Suicide, 245
Summer homework, 155
Supervision, 169, 181, 203, 253
Supporting children, 145, 152–
  159
  over-involvement, 153

too much, 166
Swearing, 302
Talk time, 37–43
Talk to teach guidelines, 57–71
Talking
  ages for, 324
Talking back, 86, *See* Arguing
Tatoos, 248
Tattling, 303
Teasing, 39, 73, 189
Teenagers. *See* Chapter 9, *See*
  your topic of interest
  brain development, 235–40
Television, 48, 191, 198, *See*
  media
  infants/toddlers, 226
  sexuality, 195
  violence, 192
Temper tantrums, 50, 82, 94,
  303
Temperament. *See* Chapter 14
  how to deal with, 307–22
  infants/toddlers, 232
  style, 307
    cautious, 309
    easy, 310
    spirited, 308
  traits, 310
    management, 314
Terrible twos, 229
Terrorism, 194
Texting, 184, 256, 258
Thoughts
  all-or-none, 18
  and emotional reactions, 14–
    20
  awfulizing, 18

challenging in kids, 68, 256
  stinking thinking, 18
Thumb sucking, 305
Time-out, 110–14
Toddlers. *See* Chapter 8
  discipline, 227–31
  helping them learn, 221–27
  holding, 218
Toilet training, 124, 297, 328
Tough love, 119
Toys
  for parent playtime, 44
  infants, 223
Trust
  children trusting parents, 14,
    17, 19, 123
  of teenagers, 237, 253
  parents trusting children, 18,
    135
  trust exercises, 135
Unsupervised teen time, 203,
  204, 253
Video and computer games, 32,
  80, 108, 194, 198, 199
Violence, 175, 192–195, 198,
  289
  in television, other media,
    192–195
Violent behavior, 124, 192,
  239, 269
Whining, 32, 41, 105, 241, 306,
  320
Worries, 15, 289, *See* Anxiety,
  See Fear
  of teenagers, 240, 255
Yelling, 11, 13, 55, 69, 70, 86,
  306

Printed in the United States
218896BV00002B/4/P